PRACTICAL
Boat Owner
BRITAIN'S BEST-SELLING SAILING MAGAZINE

SAILING AROUND THE
UK and
IRELAND

ROGER OLIVER

SECOND EDITION

ADLARD COLES NAUTICAL · LONDON

ADLARD COLES
Bloomsbury Publishing Plc
50 Bedford Square, London, WC1B 3DP, UK

First published 2009
Second edition published 2011
Reprinted in 2020

ISBN 978-1-4081-3713-0

Designed by Margaret Brain
Typeset in 10/16pt Glasgow

Printed and bound in India by Replika Press Pvt. Ltd.

Note: while all reasonable care has been taken in the publication of this edition, neither the publisher nor the author take responsibility for the use of the methods or products described in the book.

Acknowledgements

I would like to thank the staff of PBO, Dick Everitt, in particular, members of the RAYC, CSSA, the many harbour masters and lifeboat coxswains and crew for their support and encouragement during my circumnavigations. I would also like to thank the Coastguard for their help during these passages, and the many people who have assisted me in the RNLI fundraising presentations.

FSC
MIX
Paper from responsible sources
www.fsc.org   FSC® C016779

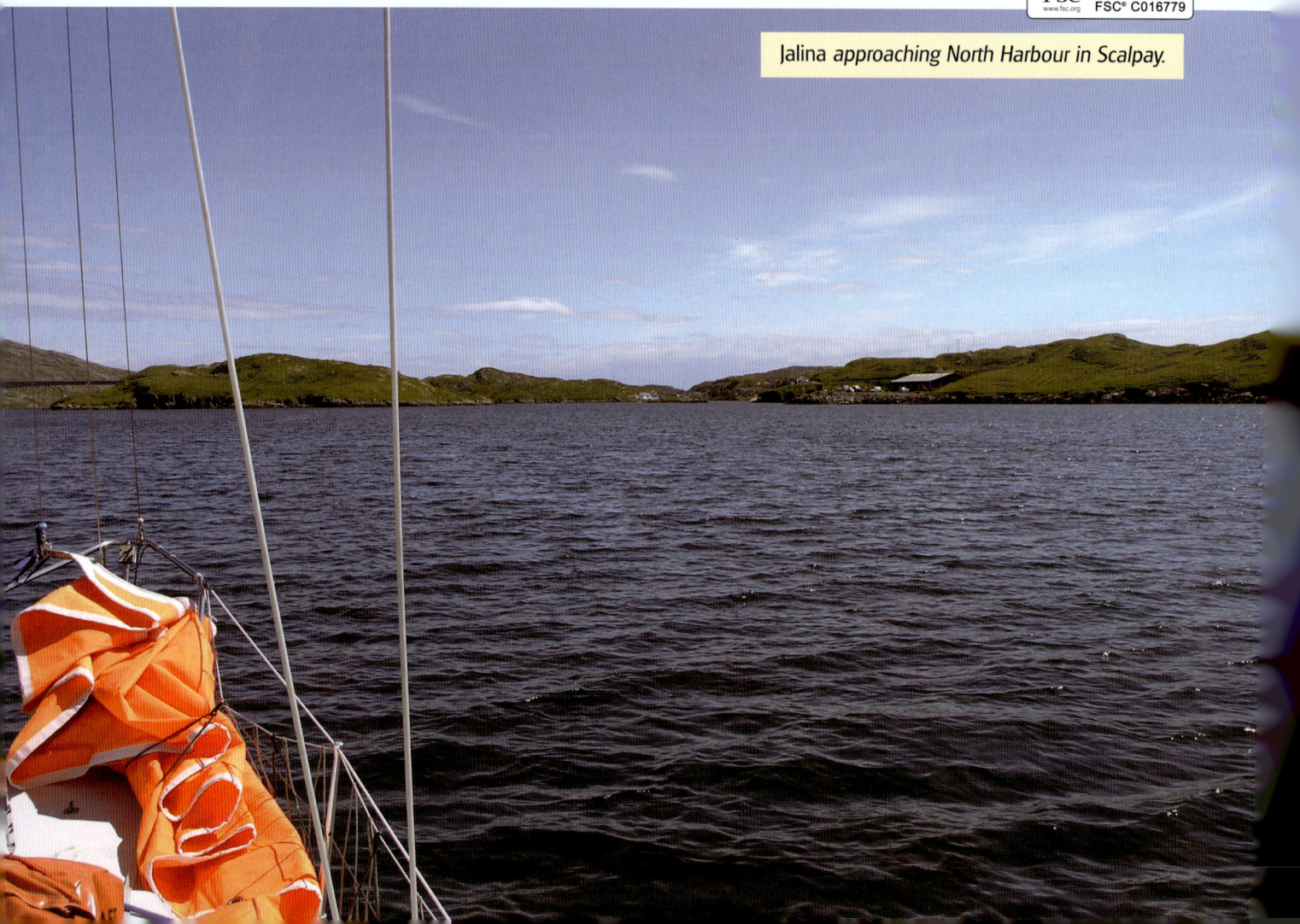

Jalina *approaching North Harbour in Scalpay.*

CONTENTS

INTRODUCTION

After taking early retirement at 60, and starting my own cabinet-making business, I decided that it was time to take some time out, and like my children, have a 'gap year'.

I had sailed a variety of boats over the years and cruised in many countries. But I had always wanted to sail round Britain by myself and so now seemed the ideal time to do it.

I decided that the right boat for my voyage would be a deep-finned Sadler 25. The only one I could find was built in 1978 and the mast, the original boom roller reefing, and the Lewmar aluminium winch tops were all badly corroded. The cabin sole had delaminated and all the electrical equipment apart from the depth sounder, needed replacing as well as the outboard and the two-ringed cooker. But all I was really looking for was a hull in good condition and after negotiating a price of £6000 for her, I was a happy man. I spent six months completely rebuilding her at a further cost of £6000.

Since her refit, *Jalina* and I have covered over 11,000 miles and have been through some quite heavy weather. She is a wet boat with low freeboard but drives to windward well, even when the decks are heavy with green water. I get quite a buzz from sailing alone in sea conditions that I would avoid if my wife was with me!

After I had done my first circumnavigation, I wrote a series of articles for *Practical Boat Owner* magazine about my voyage. The articles were so popular that I decided to put them together into a book. The aim of *PBO's Sailing around the UK and Ireland* is to inspire would-be circumnavigators and to be a detailed guide to assist skippers with planning and preparing the boat for the voyage, together with personal preparation for extended cruising.

The book is the most complete guide to circumnavigating the UK and Ireland that is available and includes in-depth passage planning, sample logbooks, VHF logs and lists of charts. I give detailed pilotage information, including chartlets, for each leg of my trip. I also have a section covering some of the pilotage problems that I encountered along the way and how I solved them; for example crossing the Pentland Firth and the Thames Estuary.

New to this edition is an appendix devoted to an alternative route north up the east coast of Ireland to the

Outer Hebrides; complete with advice on preparing for the trip, new chartlets for each leg and enticing photos – presenting the route as a tempting alternative.

I share many practical tips on seamanship including gathering weather information, reading synoptic charts for a passage, anchoring and mooring when gale-force winds are predicted and using a drogue in big seas. I offer practical tips on sail trim, the use of a high-visibility foresail to double as both cruising and storm jib, and using a cruising chute.

The information provided here applies to crewed yachts but it will be of special interest to other solo sailors.

I have now circumnavigated the UK single-handed twice, covering a total of 4,880 miles in six months and I am keen to pass on my experiences with all the highs and lows, and to impart some of my enthusiasm and joy at achieving my goals. Whether you want to do the entire circumnavigation or just a section of the route, there will be information in this book that will help you.

Safe sailing.

Roger Oliver

Facts and figures for one circumnavigation

- Total distance sailed in one circumnavigation: 2221 miles
- Total passage time: 569 hours
- Average sailing speed: 3.9 knots
- Total hours motoring: 138 using 168 litres (37 gallons) of diesel
- Ports visited: 48
- Longest passage: 126 miles (taking 26 hours)
- Strongest wind encountered: force 8
- Paraffin heater fuel used: 9 litres (2 gallons)
- Nights spent in a marina: 45
- Nights spent on a swinging mooring: 31
- Nights spent on a harbour wall: 27
- Nights spent at anchor: 12
- Full nights spent on passage: 2
- Cost: My budget was £3000 for the circumnavigation; in the event it cost about £2500, including mooring and marina fees which averaged £12 per night.

Holyhead Harbour, gales approaching.

PART I
PREPARING THE BOAT

FITTING OUT

'One thing that really tested me was fitting the new Yanmar 1GM10 engine from scratch. '

Rebuild

I really went to town with the rebuild. The cabin sole had delaminated; this was replaced with 18mm marine ply with access to all the stainless steel keel bolts – I carry a long extended socket wrench so I can reseat the keel should it move and need refitting. I also fitted new windows.

The refit included new heads, seacocks, pipes, electrical wiring, mast, boom, standing and running rigging, new stanchions plus guard wires. I also fitted plenty of new electrics, including a Simrad TP20 autopilot, Nasa SSB receiver and Simrad DSC VHF, together with spare aerial (see pages 5–6).

For cooking there was only a basic two-ring camping stove with the gas bottle fitted to its base – a dangerous

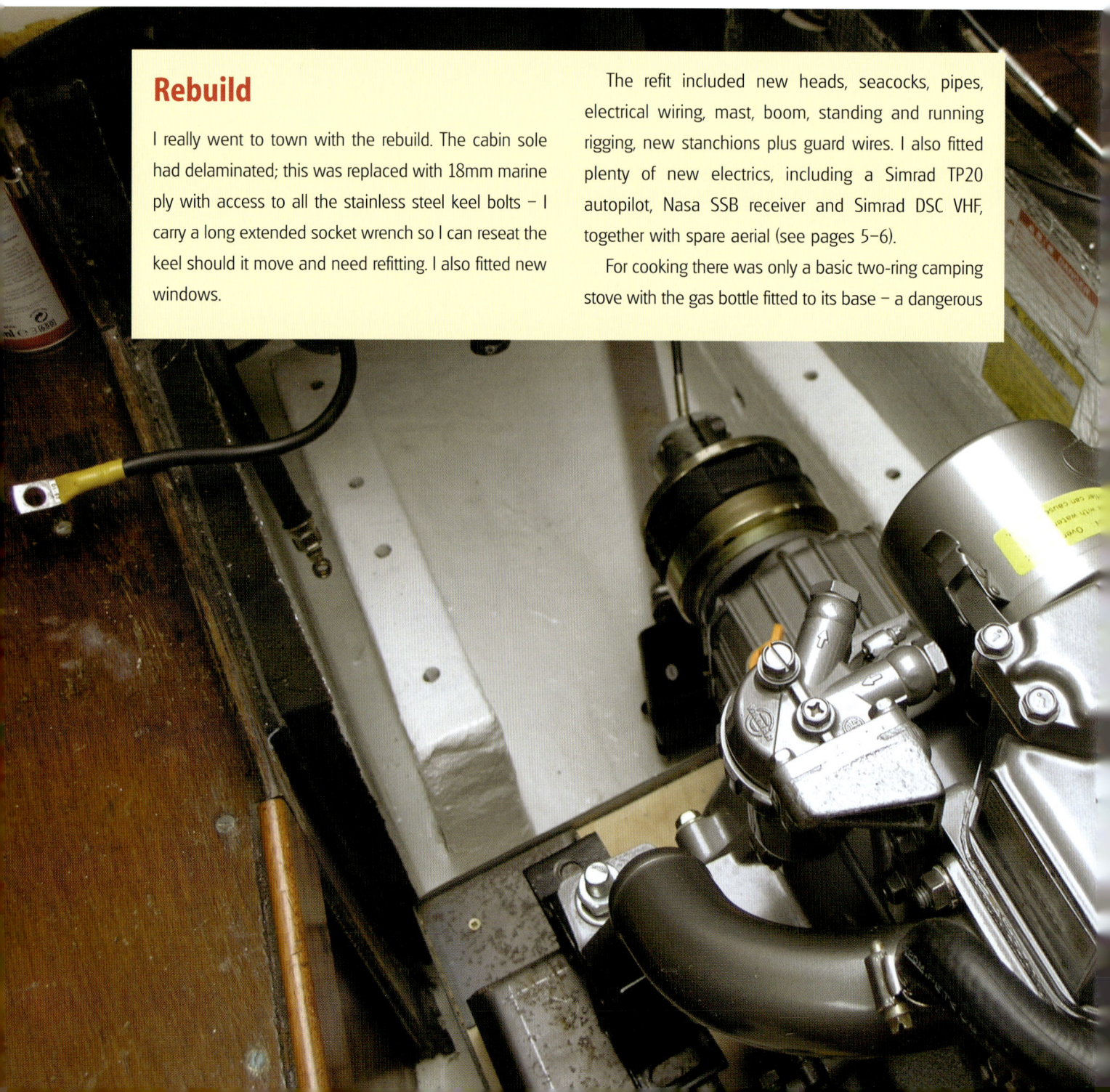

There was no chart table in the original layout, so I built a three-quarter sized one to starboard, just inside the companionway beside the galley.

arrangement. Because I love good hot meals, I fitted a Plastimo Atlantic oven which had an air-vented gas bottle in the aft locker with safety valves, so I can now cook casseroles, fresh, wholesome bread, and can also eat hot pies while under passage.

Being a cabinet-maker, my pride and joy was fitting out below with new bulkheads, lockers, a dining table, and a three-quarter chart table big enough to take a full size folio.

The one task that really tested me was fitting the new Yanmar 1GM10 engine from scratch. I thought it would be difficult, so I started by drawing a scale profile of the hull area for the engine, this gave me all the angles required to fit the bearers and stern tube. I then made up an engine template with reference points such as engine bearer positions and propeller shaft position and angle; this then gave me the drilling position and angle for the stern tube. Once all this was done, the engine was fitted to the bearers, the shaft was fitted through a loose stern tube (the

The new Yanmar 1GM10 engine being fitted in Jalina.

stern tube internal had a spacer through which the shaft ran) the 'P' bracket was fitted loose. Once all was lined up, the necessary glass fibre work was then carried out.

When fitting the fuel tank I made sure it was high enough so that it would not need the engine fuel pump should it fail. I fitted the prop shaft in such a way that it could be removed – being slightly to one side of the skeg.

The hull was also given the works. I replaced all the seacocks, fitted anodes, heavy-duty backing pads to the pintles and replaced all the keel plates with ones that were three times the size of the originals and twice the thickness; these were originally encapsulated so it was impossible to service the plates and bolts.

The external below-hull areas were stripped down to the gel-coat, dried and given five coats of epoxy, followed by one coat of hard racing antifouling, finished with two top coats of standard self-eroding anti-fouling.

Looking at Jalina in her cradle (it was now early April – less than one week to her launch) I was well pleased; it had been hard work, often carried out in bitterly cold winter weather. She was looking great and I was excited – two weeks and I would be casting off on my first circumnavigation!

A WINTER REFIT FOR JALINA'S SECOND CIRCUMNAVIGATION

Knowing the demands expected of Jalina for this circumnavigation, she was lifted out and everything was checked. The engine was given a thorough service, the fuel tank was drained and cleaned, all filters changed, a new Volvo sea seal fitted (the old one was kept as a spare).

I also decided to replace both batteries, and all the gas piping. The mainsail was sent to Banks for repairs and the other sails washed and bagged.

Once all the varnishing, painting, antifouling, and polishing had been done and all the checklists ticked and stores loaded, Jalina was ready.

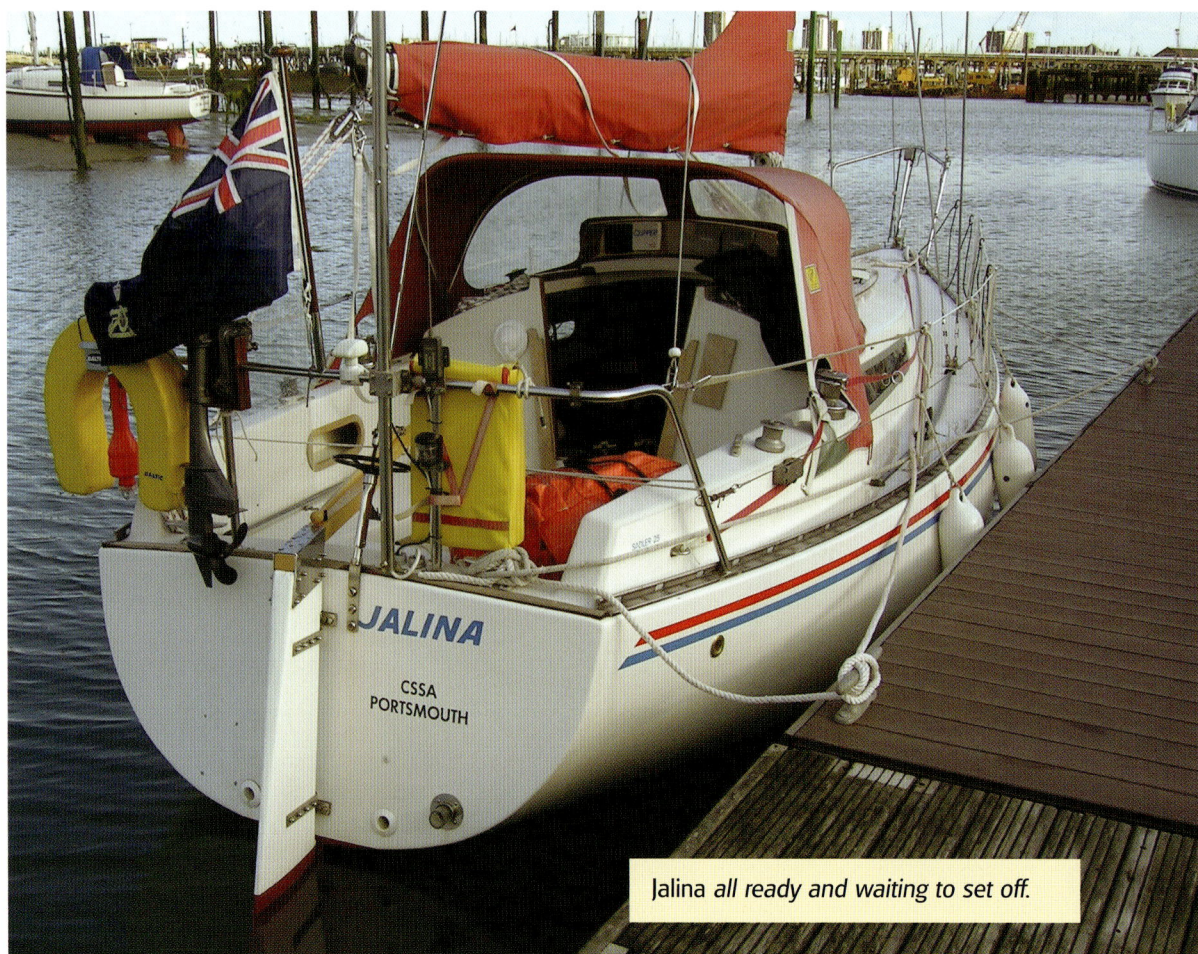

Jalina *all ready and waiting to set off.*

BOAT ELECTRICS AND ELECTRONICS

> 'I maintained a radio log and kept the Coastguard informed of my plans each day. It took a while to get used to being called by my MMSI number, but it pays to keep in contact.'

I'm often asked about my electrical kit; a voyage around Britain should be a good test of even the hardiest equipment. To illustrate my confidence in such things, I always carry a lead line, a manual trailing log and plenty of shock cord to jury rig sheet-to-tiller self-steering!

I have two 70Ah batteries wired so that both can be used for either engine – for starting or domestic use. I carry a portable 12V battery pack, which can be topped up from my 20W solar panel. The battery pack has jump leads, plus two 'cigar lighters', where the handheld VHF and mobile phone can be plugged in for charging.

The two main batteries are charged by running the engine for about an hour and half each day. The normal amount of in-and-out harbour motoring is usually sufficient, but my Rutland 503 wind generator can also top them up; this can be used in winds up to force 5, but above that I tie it off. During the entire 2,400-mile trip, I never had to use shore power to charge the batteries.

Autopilot

The Simrad TP20 autopilot, which is for yachts up to 42ft (12.8m), worked well. It steered a good course in most sea conditions and wind strengths, and coped well up to force 6 when beating and running, and up to force 7 when reaching. Autopilot performance is also subject to the sea state. For example, in the North Sea in depths of 6–8m, you would have sharp seas that might knock her off course

My Simrad TP20 autopilot steered a good course in most sea conditions and wind strengths.

when beating. But if you ease a few degrees off the wind and shorten sail (to avoid surfing) it will be fine. *Jalina* has virtually neutral helm, so there is very little battery drain. However, I did set the sails to simulate weather helm, and then fitted a bungee on the tiller to compensate for this. With a little tweaking, this worked well and the autopilot steered for about half of the trip.

VHF radio

I have a Simrad RD68 DSC and my VHF reception was very clear; the Coastguard confirmed that it was the same at their end. It's simple to use, and can store 16 MMSI numbers. The downside is the small screen, but you get

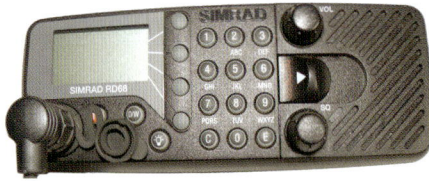

The VHF reception on the Simrad RD68 was very clear. It is easy to use and can store 16 MMSI numbers.

used to that. The main advantage is the GPS connection, so if ever I found myself in distress, a clear lat and long position would be broadcast automatically.

I maintained a radio log, and kept the Coastguard informed of my plans each day. It took a while to get used to being called by my MMSI number, but it pays to keep in contact. Once the Coastguard called to warn me of an imminent gale, which hadn't been forecast earlier. My nearest safe haven was 50 miles away and I was storm-bound for six days

Hand-held Simrad HT50

This lives in my bailing bucket in the cockpit, and the waterproof qualities were tested every so often, when everything was flooded with green water. Power is 1W/5W and the trans-mission and reception is very clear. Being single-handed, I found the radio invaluable when entering or leaving harbour and for calling nearby shipping. It can be charged by 240V and from the ship's supply.

SSB radio receiver

I fitted a NASA SSB for the long wave shipping forecast, which is on 198kHz, to act as a backup to the VHF and Navtex weather reports. In Scotland and Wales I was a bit concerned about the high mountains blocking out VHF broadcasts, but luckily, I only had to use the SSB in earnest on a couple of occasions. For my second circumnavigation I carried a laptop computer for synoptic weather charts. The aerial was fitted on the backstay and the reception was clear.

GPS repeater

My NASA repeater was easy to connect to the GPS, and was one of the most useful pieces of equipment on board. It displays all the GPS functions in large numerals, with a bright red back-light that can be easily read when the going gets rough.

NAVTEX

Except for the two occasions mentioned above, my NASA NAVTEX Pro received the weather report without fault, and was left on throughout my trips. My aerial is the whip-type, but there was a break in the centre core on the circuit board in the aerial box. I soldered it together without difficulty, and it has worked ever since.

GPS

Garmin 120XL fixed GPS

This unit is now six years old and has been superseded by the 128, which stores more waypoints. However, this one suits me, as I don't like to store any more waypoints than necessary for the next passage. This avoids picking the wrong one, and makes them easier to find. The software is easy to use without the manual, and I like the large letters and good back-light.

GPS Garmin 72 portable GPS

This unit replaced my old Magellan 2000xl for the second trip, the Garmin 72 software is easy to use without the manual. It can also be connected to the ship's supply.

SAILS

'I've yet to use the storm jib in anger, but in light airs I have rigged it under the main boom as a water sail to give an extra push.'

As *Jalina* is only 25ft (7.6m) long I decided that I could afford better sails for her. They are all Banks racing sails, as I find they work well and hold their shape. I also have wire halyards to reduce any stretch in stronger winds.

My main concern was to keep her well-balanced in all wind conditions, with as little weather helm as possible. This reduces the strain on *Jalina*'s rudder fixings (which I beefed up during her rebuild) and the battery drain under autopilot.

I use separate foresails, because I don't like the shape of roller-reefed ones. There seems to be a less disturbed airflow and the lift to windward is much improved. On both the trips round Britain I carried seven headsails:

Sailing with the No 2 genoa, I keep a jib hanked on and lashed down ready for a quick change.

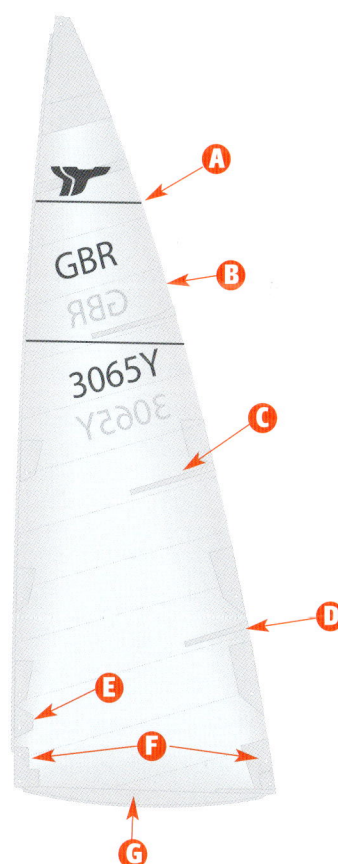

Mainsail
A Camber stripes. B Larger roach.
C Velcro closing batten pockets.
D Leech tell-tales. E Cunningham.
F Flattener cringles. G Soft foot.

- Two No 1 genoas (one heavy, one light)
- No 2 genoa
- No 1 jib
- No 2 jib heavy-duty coloured orange for safety (with slab reefing points). This I took on the second trip around Britain.
- Storm jib
- Cruising chute

Single-handed headsail changes under way are not a problem – you just bear off the wind a little and switch on the autopilot. I set the sail that suits the weather forecast and hank on the No 1 jib below it, lashed to the rail, just in case the wind should pipe up.

To save time on the foredeck, I am thinking of fitting a second forestay.

Mainsail

When I replaced the spars I asked Kemps (now Seldon) to fit a boom to take three reefing pennants, thus avoiding the dangerous task of putting in the third reefing pennant while under way. I asked Banks Sails to balance the second and third reefing points with the No 2 jib and its slab reefing point. This has now been tested, and *Jalina* is well-balanced, with very light weather helm, up to about force 7. There is also a good roach in the sail, so even when the third reef is pulled down, the sail is still a nice shape.

The sail is made of 6.5oz cloth to resist stretching, and is fitted with the following:

- Soft foot (for fuller shape off the wind)
- Flattener (to reduce camber on the wind at about force 3)
- Cunningham (to flatten the sail shape at about force 4, in conjunction with other rig controls)
- Larger roach as used on racing boats, for extra power and to help reefed sail shape
- Leech tell-tales (to check the wind flow over the sails)
- Camber stripes (to show shape of the sail)
- Velcro batten pockets for neatness.

These features give me the best of both worlds – a full footed main for off the wind and a flattened sail on the wind.

However, I encountered a problem off the Farne islands when the wind rose to over 30 knots. I was putting in the

The battens are held in their pockets with large tuck-in flaps, which are secured with Velcro. In one extremely strong gust, the sail whipped so hard that the battens were thrown out.

Bungee cord is a quick way of securing sails to hooks.

BOAT TRIM

One thing that does influence my helm balance is weight distribution in the hull. Where possible it should be low and to midships. For example, one anchor is stowed forward to the cockpit locker, and the other is fitted to the mid bulkhead over the keel. The liferaft, tools and heavy tins are also close to the keel, and I've found by doing this, her motion is much more comfortable in a seaway.

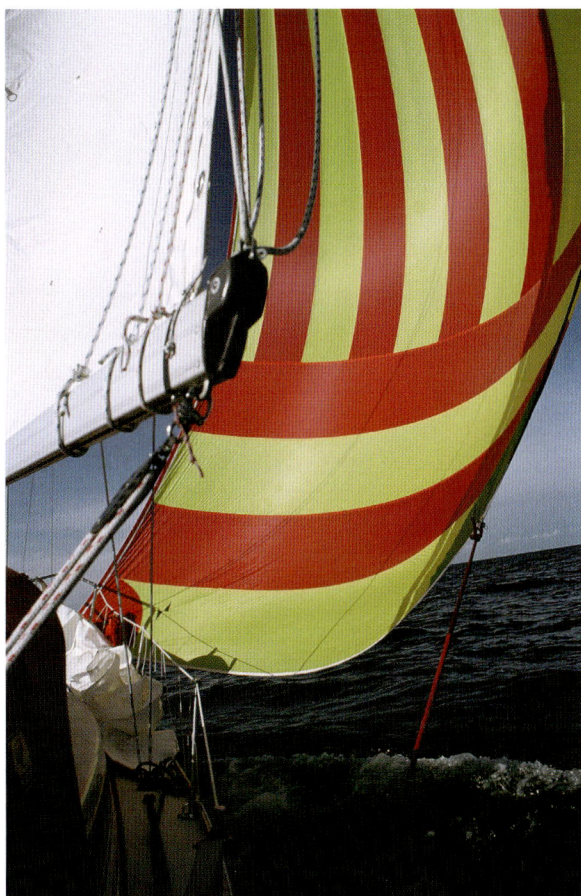

I fly my cruising chute whenever I can.

Long zip-up bags make sail stowing easy.

In light airs, to catch a bit more breeze, I copy the old square-riggers and rig the storm jib under the main or headsail, to form a water sail.

third reef when the sail whipped with such force that two sail battens shot out, ripping open the Velcro flaps as they passed! These flaps had been fine up until then, but I'm thinking of adding some lacing eyes as well. Incidentally, when the wind eased, I rang Banks sails on my mobile,

and they had two replacements waiting for me the next day at Whitby. I should have added sail battens to my spares list.

Extra sail area

I have yet to use the storm jib in anger, but in light airs I have rigged it under the main boom as a water sail to give

SAIL CHANGING SEQUENCE

With full main and No 2 genoa, as the wind strengthens I change down to No 2 jib and flatten the foot of the main. I then put the first slab in the main, then the second, then a slab in the foresail, followed by the third slab in the main. This last sail plan has worked well when reaching in winds up to force 7 and beating in force 6. I must add that when I put the slab in the foresail, I hank on the storm jib and lash it to the deck ready to hoist.

Here I am preparing Jalina's No 2 jib to hoist ready for an increase in the wind.

an extra push. Cruising chutes have become very popular in the past ten years, and I fly *Jalina*'s whenever I can. I do not use a snuffer as they just add more wind resistance aloft. To control the chute, I hoist it behind the genoa and often use the pole as you would with a normal spinnaker. Sometimes I fly the chute off the pole used as a bowsprit, with the genoa set behind it. I once sailed from Alderney to Yarmouth with full main and cruising chute, averaging 5.6 knots in a force 4 WSW wind.

Visibility to shipping

Several ships reported difficulty in seeing me in rough weather – even though I'd given them my position by radio. White sails and hull easily get lost in the spray, and even my radar reflector seems to blend in with the sea clutter. I now have a bright orange heavy duty No 2 foresail; this has slab-reefing points.

Even in heavy weather, shipping can see me for several miles now I have a bright orange foresail.

GROUND TACKLE

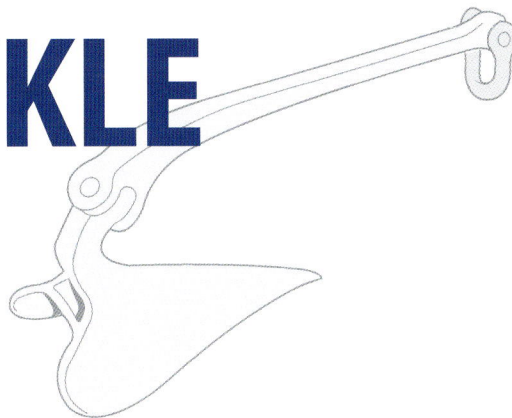

I carry two main anchors, a 25lb (11kg) CQR, an 18lb (8kg) Danforth, each with 60ft (18m) of 8mm (0.3in) chain, and 50ft (15m) of 14mm (0.5in) rhode, two extra 50 ft (15m) rhode in canvas valises as spares, plus an extra 60ft (18m) of chain. To support all this I keep on board a number of shackles and s/s seizing wire, and pliers. A Bruce kedge is kept in the aft locker, with chain and a light 10mm (0.4in), 50ft (15m) rhode.

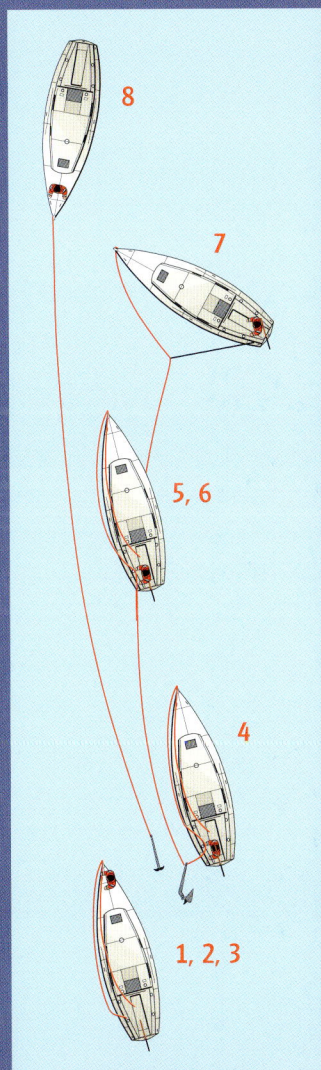

METHOD USED FOR ANCHORING

When I'm single-handing, I prefer to deploy my anchor from the cockpit, where I am in control of the tiller and engine. As always, describing it makes it sound more complicated than it is.

1 Lift the anchor chain and warp into the cockpit. (The warp is kept flaked in a canvas bag, and I have a permanent tripping line made up to the anchor and clipped to the end of the chain.)

2 Take the end of the warp forward over the bow roller and back outside everything. (I hook this end over the winch to prevent the stern swinging out when the warp comes under tension.)

3 Make sure you secure the other end to a strongpoint in the cockpit.

4 Attach the anchor and chain and gently motor forward as you lower them. You will feel when the anchor bites.

5 Once you have let out enough warp, make it fast (we are still stern to the anchor).

6 Tie a recovering line onto the warp at the cockpit position – this needs to be a little longer than twice the length of your boat.

7 Lift the anchor warp outboard away from the winch and with the engine in 'ahead' and the helm over, the stern will pull out away from the warp. As you do this, pay out the recovering line.

8 Once you are lying bows-to, the recovery line is led through the bow and secured.

Reverse the process to recover the anchor, but in big waves it might be best to do it from the bow.

PROVISIONING AND COOKING

You need plenty of carbohydrates to build up your energy levels to be strong enough to cope easily with the demands of long passage-making.

Proper food is vital for both mind and body – it is too easily skimped on when bad weather strikes. I enjoy cooking my own meals with as many fresh ingredients as I can include. There is nothing better than a piping hot hearty casserole to boost morale and make everything seem right with the world.

Before sailing north to the more remote parts of Scotland, I made sure that I had a very good supply of dry

A small oven lets you cook food slowly at sea, so you have a hearty meal ready on arrival.

and canned stores plus plenty of fresh fruit and vegetables. Also you may, like me, end up at anchor for five days, unable to land to buy stores.

Make sure you stow enough of your favourite treats on board to boost your morale on those long wet, windy nights on watch.

My larder

I use pasta, potatoes and rice as my energy fuel (the latter two being long-lasting and keep well once the packets are opened) and I always have salad and fruit to hand. You need plenty of carbohydrates to build up your energy levels to be strong enough to cope easily with the demands of long passage-making.

With limited space and battery power on board, I decided not to fit a 'fridge but to store perishable items such as eggs, cheese (farm cheeses kept the best) and cooked meats close to the hull where I found that, even in hot weather, it kept cool. Fresh pork was good for three days but I would use poultry the day after purchase. Milk was the easiest – I always kept 12 or so half-litre cartons of long-life in the forward locker; once opened, it kept for several days. Salad dressings kept well close to the hull.

Storing fresh food

I love cooking with fresh vegetables and enjoy eating plenty of fresh fruit and salads but storage of these foods had to be done with care. I store vegetables in open hanging nets, fruit in open containers in the top of my port locker – this makes them easy to access when under passage as well as venting the gases they give off which speeds ripening. I store salads in plastic containers in the cool food locker – lettuce keeps better if you peel off leaves rather than cutting it. I keep stocks of parsnips, carrots, swedes, potatoes and onions for stews. When in harbour or close to shops I buy fresh broccoli, cabbage, green beans and fresh fish – which I love poached and baked.

We all have our favourite foods but here is a list of my stores:

- Pasta and rice
- Bread mixes
- Half-baked French style baguettes

I had a good stock of cans:

- Baked beans (with pull-style openings); these I found useful emergency food as they are good cold as a quick snack

- Butter beans
- Red kidney beans in chilli sauce (used in my casseroles)
- Chopped tomatoes
- Fish – tuna, salmon, pilchards
- Meats – a good standby for making casseroles
- Vegetable soup
- Pasta sauces

I also kept a stock of:

- Pickles and sauces
- Salad dressings
- Garlic puree in a tube.
- Curry paste – I added this to many dishes, even to beans on toast
- Cup-a-soups
- Preserved meats such as salami which keeps well and is very useful to rustle up a quick hot meal (see below)
- Foil and clingfilm

SOME FAVOURITE MEAL IDEAS

Casseroles

I make two versions: one containing fresh meat and one without. I add other ingredients to the latter which could be fish or tinned meat.

Here is an example. I dice pork and fry on the hob in a little olive oil for about five minutes to brown and seal in the flavour. I then turn off the heat, turn on the oven (mine is a Plastimo Atlantic) to gas mark 5 (120°) and start to prepare the vegetables. I slice a large onion and spread the rings over the meat. I cut thickish slices (so it doesn't overcook) of peeled swede, and parsnip. I then add a tin each of vegetable soup and red kidney beans with chilli sauce and some sliced carrot and top with a layer of thinly sliced potato. Finally I grate a layer of cheese on top and bake in the oven for two hours turning the pot round every 30 minutes. This will provide me with dinners for two days.

Pork chops for two people

The following recipe works well for me and has met with the approval of many of my sailor friends.

Use a dish slightly larger than two decent-sized pork chops (I use Pyrex). Lay the chops in the dish and drizzle them with olive oil. Slice a large onion and spread the rings over the chops. Slice two Bramley cooking apples (do not peel) and scatter the slices over the onion and season. Put a lid on the dish or cover with foil and bake in the oven at 120° for two hours. The casserole is self-basting with the juices of the onion and apples.

Bread pizza – a quick, simple meal

Again this is a meal for two which uses half-baked French-style baguettes. I put two baguettes in the oven, following the packet instructions, to crisp bake. When the loaves are cooked, I slice them into four and place on an oven tray and spread each slice with either tomato purée or pesto. I then add grated or sliced cheese and follow with sliced chorizo, salami or pepperoni and a sliced sweet pepper. I put the tray in a low oven until the cheese has melted and serve, drizzled with olive oil, with a salad.

Utensils

I do not fry on board and cook on the hob only using saucepans. I also cook food in foil in the oven. To make cleaning the oven easier, I cover the base with foil.

I like modern plastic chopping boards; I find that for grating cheese, my small, straight-sided grater is ideal.

I keep several sharp knives for cutting and chopping and for the preparation of the fish that I catch myself. If the wind is light I use my fishing rod with a few spinners. I consider that a freshly caught mackerel is a very fine fish which requires very little cooking.

I enjoy catching my own fish which I cook with olive oil and garlic and serve with new potatoes and salad.

MAKING AND BAKING BREAD

I never want for fresh bread in remote anchorages, because I bake my own on a tray in the oven. Most supermarkets sell pre-prepared flour, with the yeast already added, for home baking and bread-making machines – and you just follow the instructions on the packet. I find it is best to prove the dough under the cabin heater and then transfer it into a pre-heated oven – it then does not get a chance to sink.

PERSONAL PREPARATION

Do lots of homework: gather information from the Coastguard, harbour master, pilot books, charts and other skippers before making your passage decisions.

Are you experienced?

The first question to ask yourself is: are you up to a circumnavigation? It goes without saying that you need to be a reasonably experienced sailor but it has been done by a canoeist and a Laser dinghy sailor. But you need to bear in mind that both these circumnavigators can, at short notice, land on a beach, which a yachtsman cannot; once you set sail you are committed to a certain passage. Also you may need to set off at night to catch a fair tide or need to enter a strange harbour at night. I have run into squalls and a force 8 gale. The squalls were not forecast and the gale was given as force 5 and I had no accessible harbour for ten hours.

If you have not had many years of good practical sailing experience than you should seek advice from the RYA. They are world class in the courses they offer: from Competent Crew through to Yachtmaster™ Ocean with bolt-on courses for diesel engine maintenance, radar, first aid and many others. The one course I would strongly recommend all would-be circumnavigators to attend is the Sea Survival course; here you will experience deploying a liferaft and righting it in a simulated sea environment.

Positive mental attitude

You need to be organised and self-motivated. Managing yourself is hard work; while on passage you will learn to maximise your time for essential tasks such as obtaining weather forecasts, passage planning, organising all the daily maintenance and domestic tasks; at the same time you have to motivate and organise your crew.

When a gale keeps you harbour bound; use the time to get in extra stores and fuel and to get some rest. I use my shore time for walking, painting and taking photographs. If you still feel tired when the weather forecast starts to look promising, stay another day or so until you feel fit to sail – a close friend of mine ran onto rocks due to tiredness.

Such an adventure will definitely change you. You may make mistakes and question your judgement; at times you will be anxious and at others be totally relaxed and at one with the sea – every day will be different. Your confidence will grow as you gain sea miles and your seamanship improves. This cruise will also give you a stronger respect for the sea as you will have to deal with it in all conditions. But it is an exciting challenge and all you need are competent sailing skills and experience and the keen desire to go.

Single-handed sailing

Single-handing is physically and mentally demanding. I am over 60 but don't see this as a barrier to extended cruising alone provided I stick to a nice steady routine.

My advice is not to rush – give yourself several days to get your sea legs and, most importantly, make time to prepare hot food and eat properly.

Sleep is also very important. Every year there are accidents caused by professional sailors falling asleep whilst on watch. Fortunately it has never happened to me but I carry an alarm clock so I can have 10-minute catnaps when I was well away from shipping. I planned all my passages to that I could have a proper sleep either at anchor or in harbour. If you get really tired, take a few days off so you can get some rest. Even at my age it is easy to think you are still 25 but you do need to be sensible. I have seen several skippers give up their UK circumnavigation because they over-extended themselves.

Being a single-hander means that managing yourself efficiently is paramount – you don't have anyone else to help or to blame. Do lots of homework: gather information from the Coastguard, harbour master, pilot books, charts and other skippers before making your passage decisions. You may have to postpone the passage for a day or two or change the route or distance. If the weather is a little demanding, but safe, then plan to do it in short hops.

If you are not comfortable with overnight sailing alone, build up to it. For example plan a passage to leave harbour early in the morning, say 0400 – this will increase your confidence.

Dressing for the part

Sweating in my non-breathable oilies aggravated dehy-dration. I was conscious of the problem and tried to drink plenty of orange juice and water. However, when I arrived in Whitby after a spell of bad weather it took me three days to rehydrate and feel better. So for my second circum-navigation, I invested in a set of Henri Lloyd Ocean Gore-Tex. I carry the old set as back up.

I wear a maximum of three layers under my water-proofs: the body layer is by Helly Hansen which I find keep their shape and do not sag; my second layer consists of salopettes and jacket by Gill which have given me good service. I find that thin multi-layers are easiest to wash and quicker to dry, especially if they are made of Polartec. I also wear a Polartec hat and scarf, and Thinsulate gloves. I have several pairs of these gloves which dry quickly but are not waterproof; I have waterproof Gill gloves too.

I took a wide-brimmed hat and a peaked cap to give protection against UV rays. Neck towels stop water from dripping down your neck.

For footwear I use Gill sailing boots with two pairs of socks (subject to the weather conditions). I also have a pair of Chatham oiled sailing deck shoes.

On passage good Gore-Tex waterproofs reduce dehydration. I'm taking no chances as I plot my course – fully kitted up for heavy weather. Notice that my harness is long enough to allow me to remain hooked on at the chart table.

With the exception of underwear and two shirts, all my clothing on board was drip-dry and non-iron. Much of it was of 'fleece' material as it is warm and easy to wash and dry. I kept spare sets of clothes wrapped in polythene.

My sleeping bag was of a medium weight with a liner and a waterproof outer bag. If it was cold I wore thermals at night. My essential luxuries were two pillows and earplugs (not used when at anchor).

One of my main problems was trying to dry damp clothing. For my second circumnavigation I fitted a Taylors paraffin heater which needed no battery power.

SHOWERING

After a good day's sailing I always like to relax under a hot shower. Because of the lack of space on *Jalina* I use a solar heated plastic bag hoisted in the rigging.

SAFETY

'It is important to inform the Coastguard of your passage plan, destination, ETA and number of persons on board. Don't forget to inform them of any changes, and sign off when you arrive. Never be too proud to ask for help, whether it be a person on the pontoon, harbour master, or the ever helpful Coastguard.'

During my first circumnavigation, there was a close encounter in the Thames Estuary with a ship not seeing *Jalina* in heavy seas. My white sails were lost in the clutter; for the second circumnavigation, as I previously mentioned, an orange-working jib that could be reefed with a slab was made up − now ships can spot *Jalina* easily.

Safety equipment

I have been asked whether I needed to carry a liferaft when I am coastal sailing. In a man overboard situation it can act as first-stage recovery until help arrives.

My liferaft was an Avon four-man type serviced up to RORC standard. While under way (to keep the weight as low as possible) I kept it in a valise on the cabin sole. In foggy conditions, I placed it in the cockpit; in heavy weather I put it below on the cabin sole to assist as ballast. I also made up a grab bag with flares, thermals, Kendal mint cake, GPS and water. I used the waterproof Simrad VHF while under way, but would obviously take that with me, too.

I was once washed overboard while single-handing in mid-Channel. Despite being clipped on to a jackstay, I had great difficulty getting back aboard. So on this boat I rigged a special long harness line that ran from the bow, but enabled me to remain clipped on when at the chart table. Fully extended it didn't reach past *Jalina*'s stern. I also had a second, shorter strop that clipped onto the jackstays for moving about on deck. It seemed awkward at first, but I got used to it, and it's better than the alternative of watching *Jalina* sail away by herself.

ESSENTIAL SAFETY EQUIPMENT

- Safety harness
- Lifejackets with hood and water-activated light (serviced)
- Spare gas bottles and firing devices
- EPIRB
- Hand-held VHF radio
- GMDSS/DSC VHF radio
- Buoyancy life ring with danbuoy, light and drogue
- Fire extinguishers and fire blanket
- Two bilge pumps, plus a portable one to pump out lockers
- First aid kit adapted to suit you. In the past, my hands have been cut badly, so I now include rolls of zinc tape and lint which lasts longer in seawater

One of the main problems I had once I had got back on board was getting into a change of dry clothing and getting warm quickly. I therefore advise any single-handers to wear a dry suit in heavy weather conditions.

I had white flares attached to the port cockpit bulkhead, ready to deploy as an anti-collision warning.

In Part III of this book you will read about the times that I have injured myself. So you have to be prepared for any incident. Can you administer basic first aid? When do you need to call for assistance? I have, fortunately, always been able to sort myself out without help but I did have to have surgery later. I would strongly advise that at least one crew member has attended an RYA First Aid course.

Dealing with injuries

Being a single-hander I needed to be able to deal with injuries myself so an RYA First Aid course was essential.

Whilst under passage in heavy seas I was thrown heavily against the winch and cockpit bulkhead. I suffered a groin haemorrhage, a broken nose, a broken bone in my hand and fractured ribs. Treating the nose was simple: a strong plaster across the bridge. I used a splint for the hand with Duck tape. The groin was very painful – I put on my wet suit (with difficulty) and put some packing inside and zipped it up. This also helped to ease the pain of my damaged ribs. I did not take pain killers as these would have made me drowsy.

Fog

This is my greatest worry when cruising. I have seen yachts coming into a fog-bound harbour with a young family on board without radar.

The first action I take when the visibility closes in is to avoid major shipping routes. I record my depth every 15 minutes so that I have data to assist me in determining my position if the GPS fails.

I am not one for setting off on a passage if fog is forecast – but let's face it, most of us have been caught out at some time. If it happens, I call 'all ships' on VHF Ch16 giving my position and ask for the position and heading of other shipping that may affect me. I know many ships don't have to monitor Ch16 now, but I find they mostly do, so at least they are aware of my presence and position.

FIRST AID KIT

- First aid manual
- Fabric and waterproof plasters
- Sterile dressings
- Sterile eye pads with headband
- Wound cleansing wipes
- Bandages in various sizes (self adhesive rolls, open weave elasticated rolls, tubular bandages plus a plastic tubular gauze applicator, waterproof bandages
- Disposable gloves
- Plastic face shield
- Safety pins
- Scissors
- Tweezers
- Waterproof Duck tape (some people are allergic to the adhesive, if so use hypoallergenic tape)
- Off-cuts of thin plywood for splints
- Aspirin
- Paracetemol

NB Even though my cruise took me to Scotland I never needed midge repellent – possibly due to the amount of garlic I used in cooking!

GRAB BAG

Ideally, this should be a waterproof bag that will float (a fender attached may solve the problem). Check what items are carried on your liferaft. My yacht *Jalina*'s liferaft conforms to RORC standards. The service agent will provide a list of what's included and what has been replaced for the service. Extras can then be added.

My grab bag contains:

- Three rockets, two flares (three flares in the liferaft) one orange smoke.
- Spare glasses, seasickness pills, small blanket, Thermal Protective Aid (TPA suit, spare sea anchor, marker dye, chocolate bars, glucose, torch, batteries and spare bulb, inflatable radar reflector, first layer thermal underwear, first aid kit, water (I litre), credit card, photocopy of my passport, sun block, personal medication.
- A hand-held GPS, VHF radio and EPIRB.

SKIPPER'S CHECKLIST

It's easy to forget vital bits of information and paperwork when setting off on a long passage. I find it helpful to make checklists.

Ship's papers and personal documents

As well as taking the ship's papers and your personal papers, list their numbers and dates. For example, if your boat insurance expires while you are away, your boat will not be covered. You could be open to public liability claims.

- ☐ Registration SSR number and expiry date
- ☐ Ship's radio licence/registration
- ☐ Insurance certificate number, expiry date and telephone contact
- ☐ VAT papers (Customs may want to see them)
- ☐ Sail number
- ☐ ICC certificate and expiry date
- ☐ RYA number
- ☐ RYA sailing certificate number
- ☐ First aid certificate expiry date
- ☐ MMSI number
- ☐ VHF/DSC certificate number, and call sign in phonetics
- ☐ Long range radio certificate number
- ☐ Yacht length and draught
- ☐ Mooring expiry dates
- ☐ MCA CG66 Coastguard details and expiry date

- ☐ Passport number, visas and expiry dates
- ☐ National Insurance number
- ☐ Credit card number, expiry date and home telephone number
- ☐ Telephone numbers and e-mail addresses
- ☐ Website addresses
- ☐ Mobile phone number

Engine details

It is useful to have these details to hand if you need advice from the manufacturer over the phone.

- ☐ Engine type and number, propeller diameter, pitch and shaft diameter
- ☐ Oil type and capacity for engine and gearbox
- ☐ Service dates
- ☐ Details of ancillary equipment
- ☐ Service department phone number

Victualling

This list could be endless, and is to personal taste (see Provisioning and cooking). But you might want to keep a list of your stores in lockers to avoid running out of essentials.

Liferaft, lifejackets, flares, and fire extinguishers

It could be awkward if a service date comes up while you are in a remote area. Out-of-date safety equipment may invalidate your insurance, so check all these before you start.

- ☐ Liferaft service date, and list of contents
- ☐ Lifejacket service dates
- ☐ Flare expiry dates
- ☐ Extinguisher expiry dates

Medical supplies

A list of onboard medication makes a docor's job easier if he is giving you medical advice over the radio. Many chemists will accept a faxed prescription from your doctor.

- ☐ Medication and expiry dates
- ☐ First aid kit contents and expiry dates
- ☐ Doctor's phone number

BOSUN'S LIST – SPARES AND REPAIRS

You should be able to do some basic servicing en route, so it might be a good idea to go on a course. It will help you to decide what spares and tools you need to carry. Make a plan of where everything can be found on board and keep several copies in prominent places.

Engine

- ❏ Engine service kit, oils and spare parts. Arrange for your local supplier to send parts to you if needed.
- ❏ Manual and tools for servicing. Colour code the spanners (with tape or paint) used for particular jobs, for example changing the impeller.
- ❏ Sets of filters and several impellers.
- ❏ A spare stern gland (I have had trouble with this in the past).

Plumbing

- ❏ Pipes and gas clips.
- ❏ Spare parts for heads and bilge pumps. Do you have a manual bilge pump that can be operated from the helm? If all else fails use a bucket.
- ❏ Spare gas regulator. (Mine failed in a remote area in Scotland.)

Electrical

- ❏ Fuses (including those for the engine) electrical wiring, spare spade terminals, crimping tool, portable gas soldering iron and other items. Label all fuses so you can see their rating in poor light.
- ❏ Batteries for torches, hand-held VHF radio, GPS, anchor and emergency navigation lights.
- ❏ Check the condition of main batteries. Carry a portable power pack that can be charged from a solar panel or the ship's alternator or generator; this can be used for charging your mobile phone, VHF radio, searchlight and for starting the engine.

Sails and rigging

- ❏ Repair tape, sailcloth, needles, thread, wax, sailmaker's palm.
- ❏ Enough line to replace halyards – the topping lift and spinnaker sheet could be used as spares.
- ❏ Rigging wire (the same length as the longest stay on board) with an end-fitting already in place, cutters, staylock terminals, bulldog grips.
- ❏ Endless small items such as blocks, sheaves, shackle mousing wire, spare shackles, swivels, special winch grease, whipping twine. Don't forget to include a decent fid and several sharp knives.
- ❏ Regularly check all sails and lines for damage. I carried a spare mainsail.

Other spares

- ❏ Gas and paraffin emergency nav light sealants, glues, tape.
- ❏ A spare extending boat hook with knife attachment. With this, you may be able to remove a rope caught around the prop without needing to go over the side.
- ❏ Fender boards: two short ones are easier to store.
- ❏ Tender spares: outboard service kit, spare plug, filter, shear pin, pump, repair kit with fresh glue for an inflatable.
- ❏ Water: a couple of gallons, just in case you forget to fill the tank or it becomes contaminated.
- ❏ Diesel: four one-gallon containers are easier to carry, store and transfer when under way.

Personal items

- ❏ Personal medication: make up a card to carry.
- ❏ Spare glasses – perhaps put these in the grab bag.
- ❏ Bank credit cards – put one in the grab bag.

- ❑ Keep ship's papers in a waterproof bag and have a means of attaching it to a float in case it's dropped during transfer to a rescue vessel.
- ❑ Camera. Don't forget batteries and/or film. Apart from normal use, a camera is handy to record any damage in the event of an insurance claim.

- ❑ Sunblock
- ❑ Ear plugs (harbour use)
- ❑ A wetsuit (in case you need to do hull repairs)

Emergency hull repairs

- ❑ Underwater-setting sealants, glues, tapered bungs, self-amalgamating rubber tape (hoses and seacocks).

BOSUN'S CHECKLIST

The following is a basic checklist that I use in my preparations for the season and for my long passages. I keep catalogues of several suppliers of chandlery on board.

1 Each season remove running rigging for checking and cleaning. I carry two spare halyards.
2 Check all standing rigging, I replace mine every eight years.
3 I replace webbing jackstays every three years (store during winter).
4 Check all sails for damage (see sails section for details of the sails I carry)
5 Check all electrical wiring and navigation lights (carry two bulbs of each light as spares including fuses). I label the rating on fuses for easy night recognition.
6 Emergency lighting.
7 Spare batteries. I carry many rechargeable batteries, charged through *Jalina*'s 12V system.
8 Engine oil fuel and oil filters (enough for one mid-season change and top up).
9 Main battery check (*Jalina* has two 70-amp batteries plus a spare).
10 Check lifejackets.
11 Check liferaft is within service date.
12 Check that fire extinguishers are in date.
13 Are the flares and rockets in date?
14 Check spares for bilge pumps and heads.
15 Emergency repairs: glass fibre kit, waterproof Duck tape.
16 Are bolt cutters for removing rigging on board?
17 Check the contents of tool boxes – I have three: one for metal tools (spanners are marked with coloured tape to identify them in poor light for specific jobs), another for spares, the third for whipping line, shackles, split pins, etc.

Like most boats, *Jalina* absorbed many spare parts and tools – the list is endless. However, you must have an inventory and know where everything is – make a recording system that works for you.

For a long passage like mine, you should carry enough parts for one engine service. I fitted a Volvo Seaseal stern gland because it requires no lubrication during the season. I also carried a spare. As a precaution, I had a large wrench to tighten keel bolts should the keel move, plus several tubes of underwater-setting sealant.

I carried three extra gallons of fuel and empty plastic one-gallon cans that could be filled if needed.

CHARTS AND PILOT BOOKS

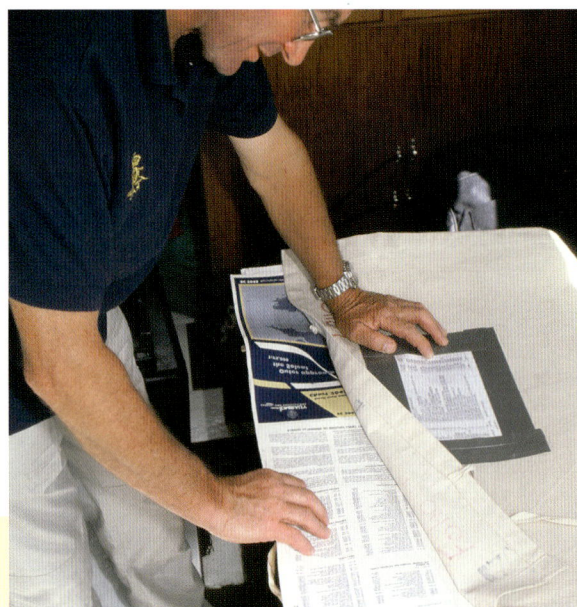

'All my charts were stored in canvas folios –
I had 120 second-hand Admiralty charts on
board, each under five years old. I updated
them by using *Notices to Mariners*.'

*The list of charts on the front of the canvas folio also notes
their chart datums.*

Folio No 1 North Foreland to Isles of Scilly			
Chart No	**Consec No**	**Description of the chart**	**Scale**
323	1	Dover Strait, eastern part	1:75000
1892	2	Dover Strait, western part	1:75000
536	3	Beachy Head to Dungeness	1:75000
1652	4	Selsey Bill to Beachy Head	1:75000
SC5600 1–10	5	The Solent and approaches	Various
2656	6	English Channel central part	1:325 000
3418	7	Langstone and Chichester Harbours	1:20 000
2045	8	Outer Approaches to the Solent	1:75 000
2175	9	Poole Bay	1:20 000
2615	10	Bill of Portland to the Needles	1:75 000
2610	11	Bill of Portland to Anvil Point	1:40 000
2255	12	Approaches to Portland and Weymouth	1:20 000
3315	13	Berry Head to Bill of Portland	1:75 000
2454	14	Start Point to the Needles	1:150 000
1613	15	Eddystone rocks to Berry Head	1:75 000
422	16	Lizard Point to Berry Head	1:150 000
777	17	Land's End to Falmouth	1:75 000
1178	18	Approaches to the Bristol Channel	1:200 000
1148	19	Isles of Scilly to Land's End	1:75 000
34	20	Isles of Scilly	1:25 000
883	21	Isles of Scilly. St Mary's and the principal off-islands	1:12 500

Folio No 2 Cornwall to Galloway

Chart No	Consec No	Description of the chart	Scale
1178	1	Approaches to the Bristol Channel	1:200 000
1168	2	Harbours on the north coast of Cornwall	Various
1156	3	Trevose Head to Hartland Point	1:75 000
1164	4	Hartland Point to Ilfracombe plus Lundy	1:75 000
1076	5	Linney Head to Oxwich Point	1:75 000
1478	6	Saint Govan's Head to St David's Head	1:75 000
1410	7	Saint George's Channel	1:200 000
1411	8	Irish Sea Western Part	1:200 000
1973	9	Cardigan Bay – southern part	1:75 000
1972	10	Cardigan Bay – central part	1:75 000
1971	11	Cardigan Bay – northern part	1:75 000
1970	12	Caernarfon Bay	1:75 000
1862	13	Irish Sea – eastern part	1:200 000
1977	14	Holyhead to Great Ormes Head	1:75 000
1978	15	Great Ormes Head to Liverpool	1:75 000
1981	16	Approaches to Preston	1:75 000
1320	17	Fleetwood to Douglas	1:100 000
1346	18	Solway Firth and Approaches	1:100 000
2094	19	Kirkcudbright to Mull of Galloway and Isle of Man	1:100 000

Folio No 3 West of Scotland

Chart No	Consec No	Description of the chart	Scale
2198	1	North Channel – southern part	1:75 000
2199	2	North Channel – northern part	1:75 000
2126	3	Approaches to the Firth of Clyde	1:75 000
2168	4	Approaches to the Sound of Jura	1:75 000
2724	5	North Channel to the Firth of Lorne	1:200 000
1907	6	Little Cumbrae Island to Cloch Point	1:25 000
2131	7	Firth of Clyde and Loch Fyne	1:75 000
2169	8	Approaches to Firth of Lorn	1:75 000
1778	9	Stanton Banks to Passage of Tree	1:100 000
1790	10	Oban and Approaches	1:10 000
2171	11	Sound of Mull and approaches	1:75 000
2378	12	Loch Linnhe – southern part	1:25 000
2379	13	Loch Linnhe – central part	1:25 000
2380	14	Loch Linnhe – northern part	1:25 000
1796	15	Barra Head to Point of Ardnamurchan	1:100 000
2207	16	Point of Ardnamurchan to Sound of Sleat	1:50 000
2208	17	Mallaig to Canna Harbour	1:50 000
2209	18	Inner Sound	1:50 000
2210	19	Approaches to Inner Sound	1:50 000
1795	20	The Little Minches	1:100 000
2721	21	Saint Kilda to Butt of Lewis	1:200 000
2722	22	Skerryvore to St Kilda	1:200 000
2769	23	Barra Head to Greian Head	1:30 000
2770	24	Sound of Barra	Various

2825	25	Lochs on the east coast of Uist	Various
2904	26	Usinish to Eigneig Mhor	1:25 000
2841	27	Loch Maddy to Loch Resort including Sound of Harris	1:50 000
2642	28	Sound of Harris	1:20 000
2905	29	Loch Tarbert	1:12 500
1794	30	North Minch – southern part	1:100 000
2529	31	Approaches to Stornoway	Various
1785	32	North Minch – northern part	1:100 000

Folio No 4 Cape Wrath to Orkney & Shetland

Chart No	Consec No	Description of the chart	Scale
1954	1	Cape Wrath to Pentland Firth inc the Orkney Islands	1:200 000
2162	2	Pentland Firth approaches	1:50 000
2249	3	Orkney Islands – western sheet	1:75 000
2250	4	Orkney Islands – eastern sheet	1:75 000
35	5	Scapa Flow and approaches	1:30 000
2568	6	Harbours in the Orkney Islands	1:12 500
2584	7	Approaches to Kirkwall	1:25 000
1119	8	Orkney and Shetland Islands, Fair Isle Channel	1:200 000
3283	9	Shetland Islands – south sheet	1:75 000
3281	10	Shetland Islands – north-west sheet	1:75 000
3298	11	Yell Sound	1:30 000
3282	12	Shetland Islands – north-east sheet	1:75 000
3291	13	Approaches to Lerwick	1:17 500
1233	14	North approaches to the Shetland Islands	1:200 000
115	15	Moray Firth	1:200 000
222	16	Buckie to Fraserburgh	1:75 000
1462	17	Harbours on the north coast of Scotland	Various
213	18	Fraserburgh to Newburgh	1:75 000
1438	19	Harbours of the east coast of Scotland	Various

Folio No 5 NE Scotland & E to SE England

Chart No	Consec No	Description of the chart	Scale
210	1	Newburgh to Montrose	1:75 000
190	2	Montrose to Fife Ness and the Isle of May	1:75 000
175	3	Fife Ness to Abb's Head	1:75 000
734	4	Firth of Forth – Isle of May to Inchkieth	1:50 000
160	5	Saint Abb's Head to Farne Islands	1:75 000
111	6	England east coast Berwick-upon-Tweed to the Farne Islands	1:35 000
156	7	Farne Islands to the River Tyne	1:75 000
152	8	River Tyne to River Tees	1:75 000
134	9	River Tees to Scarborough	1:75 000
129	10	Whitby to Flamborough Head	1:75 000
121	11	Flamborough Head to Withernsea	1:75 000
109	12	River Humber plus Rivers Ouse and Trent	Various
107	13	Approaches to River Humber	1:75 000
108	14	Approaches to The Wash	1:75 000
1200	15	The Wash Ports	Various

106	16	Cromer to Smiths Knoll	1:75 000
1536	17	Approaches to Great Yarmouth and Lowestoft	Various
1543	18	Winterton Ness to Orford Ness	1:75 000
2695	19	Plans on the east coast of England	Various
2052	20	Orford Ness to the Naze	1:50 000
1183	21	Thames Estuary	1:100 000

Folio No 6 Channel Islands & French Coast

Chart No	Consec No	Description of the chart	Scale	Datum
2656	1	English Channel central part	1:325 000	WGS84
SC1106	2	Approaches to Cherbourg	1:50 000	ED1980
2669	3	The Channel Islands and adjacent French coast	1:50 000	WGS84
3653	4	Guernsey to Alderney and adjacent French coast	1:50 000	WGS84
60	5	Alderney and the Casquets	1:25 000	WGS84
SC3654	6	Guernsey Herm and Sark	1:50 000	ED
808	7	East Guernsey Herm and Sark	1:25 000	WGS84
3655	8	Jersey and adjacent French coast	1:50 000	WGS84
1137	9	Approaches to St Helier	1:25 000	WGS84
3656	10	Plateau des Minquiers and adjacent French coast	1:50 000	WGS84
C33B	11	Channel Islands and northern French coast	1:122 600	ED1950
C34	12	Cap'd'Erquy to Ile de Batz	1:110 000	ED1950

Folio No 7 East & Southern Ireland

Chart No	Consec No	Description of the chart	Scale
2093	1	South approach to North Channel	1:100 000
44	2	Howth to Ardglass	1:100 000
1415	3	Dublin Bay	1:25 000
1468	4	Arklow to Skerries Islands	1:100 000
1787	5	Carnsore Point to Wicklow Head	1:100 000
1772	6	Rosslare and Wexford harbours with Approaches	1:30 000
2049	7	Old Head of Kinsale to Tuskar Rock	1:150 000
2046	8	Waterford harbour	1:25 000
2017	9	Dungarvan harbour	1:15 000
2071	10	Youghal	1:12 500
1765	11	Old Head of Kinsale to Power Head	1:50 000
2092	12	Toe Head to Old Head of Kinsale	1:50 000
2129	13	Long Island Bay to Castlehaven	1:30 000
2184	14	Mizen Head to Gascanane Sound	1:30 000
1838	15	Bantry Bay – Shot Head to Bantry	1:30 000
2552	16	Dunmanus Bay – Dunbeacon harbour – Kitchen Cove – Dunmanus harbour	Various

Folio No 8 West & Northern Ireland

Chart No	Consec No	Description of the chart	Scale
2495	1	Kenmare River – Dursey Sound – Sneem Harbour	Various
2125	2	Valentia Island and Harbour	Various
2254	3	Valentia Island to River Shannon	1:50 000
2789	4	Dingle Bay and Smerwick Harbour	1:60 000

2739	5	Brandon and Tralee Bays	1:37 500
1819	6	Approaches to River Shannon	1:50 000
1547	7	River Shannon – Kilcredaun Point to Ardnore Point	1:20 000
1548	8	River Shannon – Ardnore Point to Rinealon Point	1:20 000
1549	9	River Shannon – Rinealon Point to Shannon Airport inc Foynes Harbour	1:20 000
1540	10	River Shannon – Shannon Airport to Limerick	1:12 500
3338	11	Kilkee to Inisheer	1:50 000
2420	12	Aran Islands to Broadhaven	1:50 000
3339	13	Approaches to Galway Bay inc the Aran Islands	1:50 000
1984	14	Galway Bay	1:30 000
2096	15	Cashla Bay to Kilkieran Bay	1:30 000
2709	16	Roundstone and Approaches	1:30 000
2708	17	Ballyconeely Bay to Clifden Bay inc Slyne Head	1:25 000
2707	18	Kingstown Bay to Ceggan Bay – and Inishbofin to Inishturk	1:25 000
2706	19	Ballynakill and Killary Harbours and approaches	1:25 000
2667	20	Clew Bay and approaches	1:50 000
2704	21	Blacksod Bay and approaches	1:50 000
2703	22	Broadhaven and approaches	1:50 000
2767	23	Porturlin to Sligo Bay and Rathlin O'Birne Island	1:75 000
2715	24	Killala and Donegal	1:15 000
2852	25	Sligo Harbour and approaches	1:20 000
2702	26	Donegal Bay	1:60 000
1879	27	Rathin O'Birne Island to Aran Islands	1:75 000
2723	27	Western approaches to the North Channel	1:200 000
1883	29	Crohy Head to Bloody Foreland inc Aran Island	1:30 000
2752	30	Bloody Foreland to Horn Head inc Tory Island	1:30 000
2699	31	Horn Head to Fanad Head with Mulroy Bay	1:30 000
2697	32	Lough Swilly	1:37 000
2811	33	Sheep Haven to Lough Foyle inc Inishtrahull	1:75 000
2499	34	Approaches to Londonderry and Coleraine	1:40 000
2798	35	Lough Foyle to Sandra Island inc Rathlin Island	1:75 000

Pilots and almanacs

Reeds Nautical Almanac
Reeds PBO Small Craft Almanac – this one is a must for tidal gate information
The Shell Channel Pilot, Tom Cunliffe
West Country Cruising Companion, Mark Fishwick
Lundy and Irish Sea Pilot, David Taylor
South and West Coasts of Ireland Sailing Directions, Irish Cruising Club
East and North Coasts of Ireland – Sailing Directions, Irish Cuising Club
The Yachtsman's Pilot – Clyde to Colonsay, Martin Lawrence
The Yachtsman's Pilot – Isle of Mull and adjacent coasts, Martin Lawrence

The Yachtsman's Pilot – Skye and Northwest Scotland, Martin Lawrence
The Yachtsman's Pilot – The Western Isles, Martin Lawrence
The Yachtsman's Pilot – North and East Scotland – The Farne Islands to Cape Wrath, Martin Lawrence
Humber to Rattray Head Sailing Directions, Royal Northumberland Sailing Club
The East Coast – A pilot-guide from the Wash to Ramsgate, Derek Bowskill
Clyde Cruising Club – Outer Hebrides
Clyde Cruising Club – N and NE Scotland and Orkney Islands
Clyde Cruising Club – Shetland Islands

PART II
PASSAGE PLANNING AND PILOTAGE

Glenarm marina.

PLANNING STRATEGIES

So far I have explained how I prepared my Sadler 25, and myself, for a single-handed trip around Britain, so now I'll explain how I coped with the navigation, general passage planning and pilotage problems.

Like many people, I combine GPS with traditional navigation, but I also enjoy being methodical and as precise as possible. I've found that when single-handing or sailing with my wife Liz, it's all too easy to let your navigation become sloppy. To keep myself disciplined I make up my own logs as an aide memoire; the sample log pages here show the preparation I made for a passage from Penzance around Land's End towards Padstow. The figures might look a bit complicated, but it means I keep all the information I need to hand. Navigation is quite personal, so using this as a guide, you could perhaps make up a logbook to suit your own needs.

Rounding Ardnamurchan Lighthouse.

Using the log and chart

The tides dictated my departure time of 0430, but I first had to decide on a departure point from which to shape up the course required (or course to steer). I also used this point to check the GPS. Then I plotted three bearings: a back sight (308°M) to Penzance breakwater light (Fl WR 5s 9M), a fore sight (128°C) to steer to, and 243°M on the Newlyn breakwater light (Fl 5s 9M). The plan was to check my back sight as I progressed along 128°C to maintain an accurate course. When Newlyn breakwater light was at 243°M, I'd be at my departure point and could set a new course of 199° (steer 200°C) as shown on the diagram.

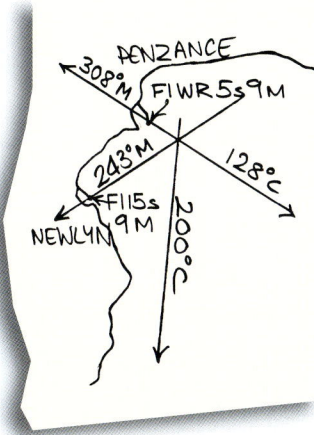

Establishing a departure point by plotting three bearings.

DECK LOG

When short-handed sailing it's all too easy to let your navigation become sloppy, so I make my own logs to act as an aide memoir and keep myself disciplined. For instance, on the back of my passage planner there is a reminder to work out and write down bearings (in case buoys have been moved), the distances of every leg, and an alternative port. My deck log includes a column to enter depths for every hour so that, if necessary, I can use these figures to plot my track.

I have my logs spiral-bound so they opened out flat, and combined both the navigator's and deck log in the same folder. I'll run through how I made passage preparations later.

Even though I was always sure of the predicted sea state and wind direction, I always sailed up-tide for a while. Then, if I wasn't happy I could easily abort and nip back into the harbour.

To shape a required course of 199°, I drew up a tidal vector using the navigator's part of the logbook. The details were entered in the stream section (set, rate and drift). The resultant wake course (water track) true bearing was entered as 191°. Working backwards to the left, accounting for leeway, true variation and deviation, I arrived at the compass course of 199°. This was then entered into the deck log section under course required (steer 200°C)

Plotting a course is carried out in reverse: the course steered is taken from the deck log and entered in the compass section of the navigator's log. Working from left to right, you apply deviation and variation to get true (T), then apply leeway to give you the wake course (water track), and apply tidal stream in its direction and distance to get your EP.

The deck log entries include date, time (Zulu+1), GPS latitude and longitude, log reading, course required, course steered, wind (strength and direction) and the barometer reading. The amount (and by what period the barometer falls and rises) will indicate the position of, say, a warm front – steady or falling as it approaches, rising suddenly as it goes through – along with a wind change.

Other entries include port (the point from where I'm sailing) and destination. Tidal information, such as constant port, and local port, is also used in working up my information in passage planning.

One of the most important sections in my log is for weather forecasts: time, sea area, and forecast. Finally, there is a section for logging engine hours/time.

Passage planning

All skippers are now required to have some form of passage plan aboard. The example I have given is that for my passage from Penzance to Padstow during my first circumnavigation. The weather was settled with light winds, and I had considered anchoring in St Ives Bay. I was not sure of my ETA; it was likely I would have to motor if the wind dropped. If I lost my engine for any reason, my only option would be to anchor. I therefore decided to work out tidal depths for each hour of the passage – for St Ives Bay and Padstow – thus allowing me to concentrate on other navigation tasks.

Navigators Log Book F:1Nav log

Date Z + 1 Time	Log		Course						Stream			Lat/Long or Waypoints
	Reading	Miles since Last plot	Compass	Dev	Var	True	Lee-way	Wake Co T	Set Deg	Rate Kn	Drift Miles	
MAY 9TH			A									
0420	1918		199	-2E	5W	196	⁵5°	191°	071°	0·2	0·2	
	1921	3	242	–	5W	237	–	237°	086°	0·6	0·4	WIND ASTERN - NO SWELL
	1925	4	NAVIGATION - BUOYS - CLEARING LINES - PILOTAGE									RUNNELSTONE ⚓ 3 MILES
			B									
									DATUM	WP NO		
			SEE PASSAGE PLAN ⟶						GB36	PENZ.		PENZANCE OUTER PASSAGE 50°06.75'N 05°31.15'W
			128°	BEARING DEPT. PENZANCE					WG84	442		RUNNELSTONE (S) 50°00.85'N 05°40.88'W
			(308°)	TO PENZANCE PIER FI W R 5s 17/12M					WG84	443		LONGSHIPS CLEARING (W) 50°04.00'N 05°45.89'W
			243°	TO NEWLYN PIER FI 5 s 9M					GB36	BIS		TO CLEAR BRISONS (W) 50°07.00'N 05°44.00'W
									GB36	K9		KETTLE BOTTOM (INNER) 50°04.00'N 05°40.50'W
									GB36	444		PENDEEN OVERFALLS - TO CLEAR 50°09.50'N 05°43.50'W
									GB36	TRE		TREVOSE HEAD - TO CLEAR 50°33.00'N 05°02.00'W
									GB36	STEP		STEPPER POINT - TO CLEAR 50°34.15'N 04°57.00'W
									GB36	BAR		PADSTOW BAR ⚓ 50°33.46'N 04°56.08'W

Weather Forecast: FALMOUTH/BRIXHAM C.G. WEATHER 0240, 0640, 1040, 1440, 1840
P97 ALMANAC   MILFORD HAVEN C.G. WEATHER 0435, 0835, 1235, 1635

Time	Sea Area	Forecast
	PORTLAND PLYMOUTH	NE 3-4-5 • ͻ M
	BISCAY	NE 4-5 occ 6 • ͻ M ⟶ P
	LUNDY FAST	NE 3-4 P

Note Dev E+ W- Var E+ W- Leeway P+ S-

PADSTOW H.M. CH 16 - 14 (0900 - 1700)

Sample log entries from Penzance around Land's End to Padstow.
In the navigator's part of the logbook, I put all the data needed to plan the departure point and work out a course.
I also make a note of all the waypoints that I might need, current weather forecast, future weather forecast times and any other information, such as the Padstow harbour master's radio channel, etc.

Deck Log Book   F: Decklog

Date	Time Z + 1	GPS Position Latitude	Longitude	Log Reading	Course Required	Course Steered	Wind	Baro	Remarks	
MAY				1918	A					Port: PENZANCE
THURS	0420				199	200			CLEARED PENZANCE SET	Destination: PADSTOW
9TH	0500	50°04·38'N	05°31·50W	1921	242	242			COARSE FOR PENZER PT	Tides: FOR ATLAS
	0535	50°02·46'N	05°34·94W	1924	B	242	NNE F1	1022	TIDE SWEEPING S. LIGHTS OFF	Constant Port: DOVER BST
	0544	50°01·96N	05°35·87W	1925		257	"		PILOTAGE	1st HW 1034 Ht 5·8
	0700	50°01·73'N	05°42·42W	1929		300	NNW F2	1021		2nd HW 2243 Ht 6·1
	0715	50°02·32N	05°43·63W	1930		310	"	1020	SIGHTED LONGSHIPS + ROCKS	Local Port:
	0724	50°02·58N	05°44·38'W	1931		295	"	"	CLOSING LONGSHIPS	1st HW Ht
	0900	50°05·22N	05°45·32W	1937		074	NNW F3	1018	TIDAL EDDY CLEARING LONGSHIPS	2nd HW Ht
	1018	50°08·02'N	05°45·07W	1942		324	"	1016	OFF ERISONS	Notes:
	1100	50°09·58N	05°42·75W	1945		334	"	1014		BE AT RUNNELSTONE > 0800
	1136	50°11·01'N	05°40·35W	1948		065	"		CLEARING 3 STONE OAR	DEPT PENZANCE 0400
	1210								CALM - ENGINE ON	PENZANCE LOCK + 1 HOUR
	1235	50°14·66'N	05°34·79'W	1953		040	NNE F·S	1011		
	1320	50°18·04N	05°30·96'W	1958		040	"	1010	CANNOT SEE COAST THICK MIST	

			Engine Hours / Time					
Start	0430	1210						
End	0535	1815						
Run	1·05	6·05						

The deck log is a running record that I try to keep up to date. Doing it regularly keeps my thinking methodical, and if the GPS goes down I can refer back to this and the plot on the chart. I log the time as British Summer Time (Zulu GMT + 1hr), GPS lat and long positions, the log reading of the miles run, the course required (course to steer) and the actual course steered. Weather information: wind and air pressure; engine running hours are also noted.

HARBOURS

| Port: PENZANCE | Destination: PADSTOW | Dep Time: 0430 | ETA 1800 | Charts Req'd: 777, 1149, 1168 |
| Pilot/pages: TAYLOR/PADSTOW 16—19 | | Almanac pages: PENZANCE 266 (WP214) PADSTOW 628 (WP601) | | |

Date:	Tide Cycle: B		LW	-6	-5	-4	-3	-2	-1	1st HW	+1	+2	+3	+4	+5	+6	LW
MAY THURS 9TH	Constant Port: DEVONPORT	Tide Times: UT								0340	0440	0540	0640	0740	0840		1006
		Height of Tide:								4·8	4·5	4·1	3·3	2·5	1·8		1·4
	Local Port: PENZANCE	Time Diff: BST								0342	0442	0542	0642	0742	0842		1034
		Height Diff: Total								4·8	4·5	4·1	3·3	2·5	1·8		1·3

Chart Datum + or -

Less Yacht Draft to give depth below keel

Date:	Tide Cycle: B		LW	-6	-5	-4	-3	-2	-1	2nd HW	+1	+2	+3	+4	+5	+6	LW
MAY THURS 9TH	Constant Port: MILFORD HAVEN	Tide Times: UT	1041		1145	1245	1345	1445	1545	1645							2259
		Height of Tide:	1·5		2·0	2·8	3·8	4·8	5·5	6·0							1·5
	Local Port: PADSTOW ST.IVES BAY	Time Diff: BST	1036		1140	1240	1340	1440	1540	1640 / 1653	1753	1853	1953	2053	2153		2316
		Height Diff: Total	1·5		1·8	2·0	3·7	4·5	5·4	5·7 / 6·4 6·0	5·1	3·8	2·7	2·0		1·6

Chart Datum + or - 3 PADSTOW   3·4 3·0 2·1 ·8

Less Yacht draft to give depth below keel — 1·5m   ·0   ·3 ·5 2·2 3·0 3·9 4·2 / 2·9 1·5   ·6   ← 1940 TOUCH BOTTOM

A	HW		LW		A	HW		LW		A	HW		LW		HEIGHT DIFF.
	Time	Ht	Time	Ht		Time	Ht	Time	Ht		Time	Ht	Time	Ht	PENZANCE H.W. 0·0 L.W. −0·1
Constant Port: DEVONPORT	0340	4·8	1006	1·4	Constant Port: MILFORD HAVEN	1645	6·0	2259	1·5	Constant Port: MILFORD HAVEN	1645	6·0	1041	1·5	ST.IVES BAY H.W. −0·3
Difference: — PENZANCE	0058	0·0	0032	−0·1	Difference: — PADSTOW	0052	0·4	0043	0·1	Differences: — ST. IVES BAY	0105	−0·3	0055	0·0	L.W. 0·0 PADSTOW H.W. −0·4
GMT	0242	4·8	0934	1·3	GMT	1553	6·4	22·16	1·4	GMT	1540	5·7	09.36	1·5	L.W + 0·1
BST	0342		1034		BST	1653		23.16		BST	1640		10.36		

File passageplan10.doc

My passage plan from Penzance to Padstow. I worked out all the depths for each hour of the trip in case I had to divert to St Ives.

This was my first UK circumnavigation, and not having rounded Land's End before, I had to plan a number of options. My main consideration was safety.

Even if all went to plan, I would be entering the Camel estuary on a falling tide. I needed to know by just how much it would have fallen, and if I could still get into the inner harbour. If not, I could anchor in the estuary, or delay my arrival by anchoring in St Ives Bay, and then catch the next tide. But if I made the estuary, the latest time to be there would be 1830.

When sailing short-handed I always prepare tidal depths for each hour for up to three harbours: the one I'm leaving, my destination and one other. The depths for each hour are used when approaching shallows using a navigation buoy as a check, such as the Camel Bar green can (as shown in my passage plan sketch chart on page 35).

If the visibility is poor, and the GPS packs up, you only need the depths and your echo sounder to safely navigate into waters free from shipping. And in many cases you can simply follow the contours with your echo sounder and find your way into harbour. This is an old technique, that was carried out using a lead line. Try practising, it's great fun and surprisingly accurate.

The other point of consideration is barometric pressure, not just for the weather but for its effect on the depth of water. Chart Datum is based upon 1011–1014mb which is the standard around the British Isles at sea level. Should the barometer rise to 1045mb, sea level will decrease by 30cm (12in). Conversely, if it falls by the same amount (low pressure) the height will rise by 30cm. Other considerations are wind duration and storm surges.

On passage

I slipped my lines from Penzance at 0420 and, on departing the harbour, I had enough sea room to hoist sail under engine. I then set a course of 128°C, to get into clear, safe water, checking my reciprocal bearing to Penzance Pier head (308°M) as I went. Once Newlyn Pier head bore 243°M I checked the GPS, and changed to 200°C. By now it was starting to get light and the shore was clear, although coastal mist was forecast. I had prepared a waypoint (442) for the Runnelstone south cardinal, but as the tide was likely to be fairly constant I decided to navigate by pilotage up to Merthen Point (my plot 0544/1925). About then the coastal mist started to come in, so I called up waypoint 442 for the Runnelstone.

I decided to go a little north of the track to take advantage of the stronger tide further offshore

These plots are close together to check the set of the tide

I needed to be here by roughly 1730, as the tide started ebbing then. But this would also help to keep me off Gulland Rock

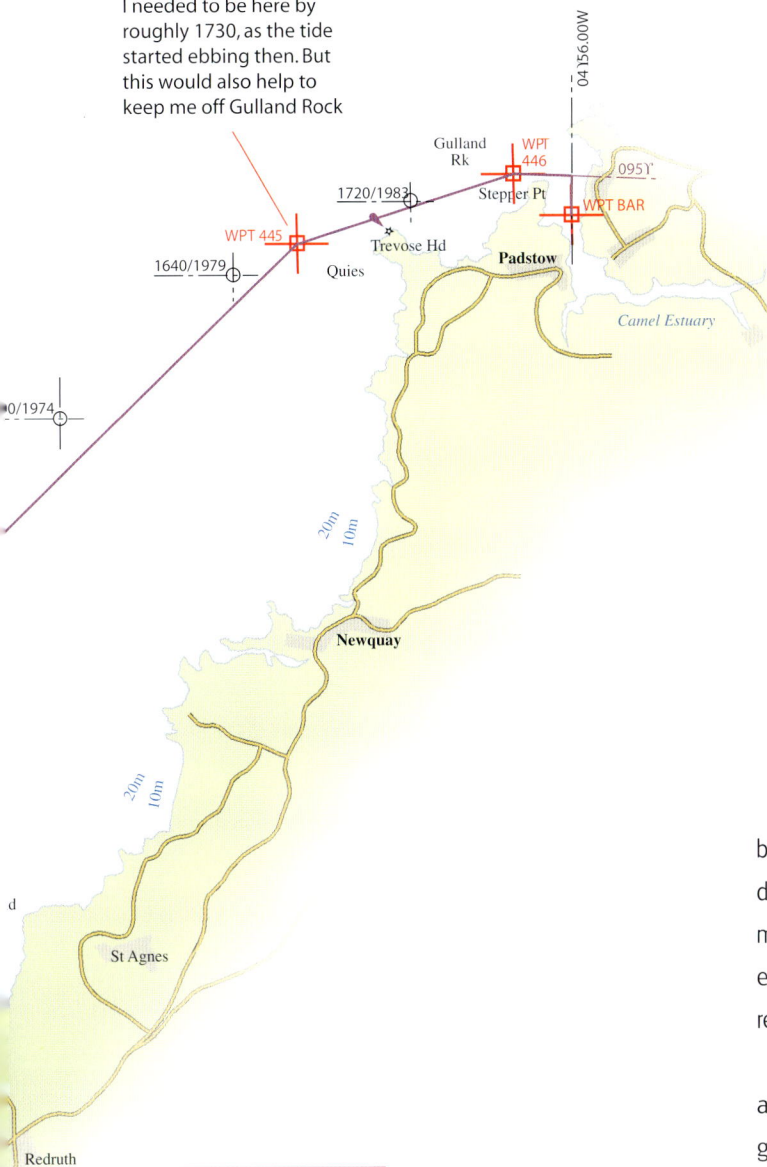

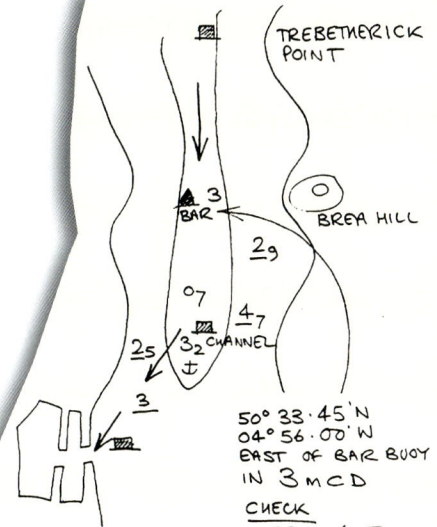

Gulland Rk

WPT 446

0951'

WPT BAR

Stepper Pt

1720/1983

WPT 445

Trevose Hd

1640/1979

Quies

Padstow

Camel Estuary

20m 10m

0/1974

Newquay

20m 10m

St Agnes

d

Redruth

TREBETHERICK POINT

BAR 3

BREA HILL

2₉

0₇

4₇

2₅ 3₂ CHANNEL

3

50° 33.45'N
04° 56.00'W
EAST OF BAR BUOY
IN 3 m CD

CHECK
1753   6.00 M
     + 3.00 CD
     - 1.50 KEEL
     _____
        7.5 M
     AT BAR BUOY

I did a little sketch of Padstow that I could keep in the cockpit. It also let me check the depth at the bar buoy, to see if there was enough water to get into the harbour.

Where I am able to, I plot a waypoint well clear of a buoy. Then, I can use the buoy to double check the direction and rate of the tide, as well as the GPS track and my compass heading. I am always mindful that I may have entered the incorrect waypoint into the GPS. I therefore regularly plot my position and assume nothing.

I have fitted a NASA GPS repeater to the bridge panel and I have found this a great help, with its large letters and good red back-light, when night sailing. When sailing to a waypoint in tricky tidal waters, particularly when short-handed, I use the GPS to work out clearing lines – the highway screen will indicate which side, and by how much, you are off the intended track. This was particularly useful as a heavy mist set in on the shore. I needed to be safe, and yet close enough inshore to take advantage of the fair tidal streams that assisted me to arrive at Pendeen Point for the start of the new flood tide. This would give me a full fair tide to Padstow. I have shown a couple of plots close together on the chart, between waypoint 442 and waypoint 443, to check the set of the tide.

At 0724 I was being set too close to the waypoint track, so I tacked to give the Longships a good offing, yet to keep

I needed to start going around Land's End by HW Dover −3 to make the most of the inshore currents.

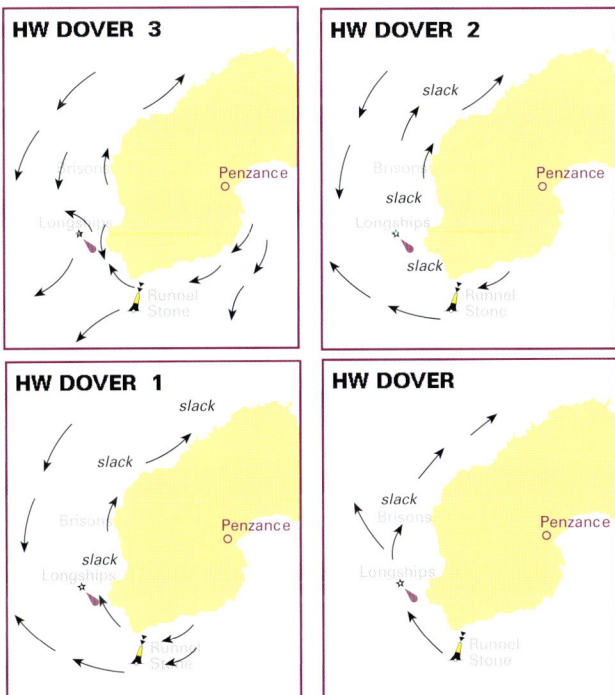

HW DOVER 3
Brisons
Penzance
Longships
Runnel Stone

HW DOVER 2
slack
Brisons
Penzance
slack
Longships
slack
Runnel Stone

HW DOVER 1
slack
slack
Brisons
Penzance
slack
Longships
Runnel Stone

HW DOVER
slack
slack
Brisons
Penzance
Longships
Runnel Stone

out of the foul offshore tide running further to the west. Visibility was still poor, so it was difficult to plot an accurate visual fix.

The planned track between waypoint 443 and 444 would be safe, and on reaching waypoint 444 I would clear the Three Stone Oar off Pendeen Point. But I was still close enough inshore to take advantage of the inshore tide running north, when the offshore tide was still foul.

It was HW Dover when I reached Pendeen Point and the flood had just started, so I had a full six hours of flood to take me up to Padstow. I decided to press on, and not to call in at St Ives. My next waypoint was 445, but I decided to go a little north of the new track to take advantage of the stronger tide further offshore. Visibility was still poor.

Waypoint 445 would keep me clear of Quies rocks, off Trevose Head, and 446 would take me south of Gulland Rock, NW of Stepper Point. I knew the tide may be slack or have started its ebb at 1730, so it would help me to keep me clear of Gulland Rock.

I reached waypoint 446 at 1740. From this point it would be a mixture of pilotage and pre-planned waypoint to the bar buoy. From waypoint 446 I sailed on 095°C until I reached longitude 04deg56'00W, at which point I handed the sails and prepared my shorelines.

I had a pilotage sketch chart ready (see above) and motored south on 04°56'00W until I reached the green can buoy. Visibility was now good, but had the mist worsened, this preparation would have helped me reach the bar buoy. It was now 1800, and on checking the depth at this point I had enough water to get over the drying 3.0m approach to the harbour.

As I approached the shallows, near the harbour, my depth alarm went off saying I had 0.6 to 0.8m under the keel. I must add I had a little pre-arranged help from the harbour master. I called him on my hand-held VHF and he talked me in saying 'a bit to port then a bit to starboard'. It pays to call ahead! Had my arrival been any later, I was already prepared to anchor in the pool off the harbour entrance.

Longships Lighthouse.

PILOTAGE PROBLEMS

Sailing around Britain taught me to take nothing for granted. So far I have described how I made methodical preparations, in the form of checklists and pre-calculated tidal information. Otherwise, I find it is all too easy to let your navigation become sloppy when sailing single-handed, especially when you are tired. However, I still made a few errors and had to think twice about what I was seeing around me. Here are examples of difficult pilotage situations that might act as memory joggers when you are entering unfamiliar waters.

Problem one: Loch Shuna to Ardantrive Bay, Kerrera, Oban, Scotland

My sail through the Kerrera Sound to Oban was magnificent, but I was a bit concerned when I saw what appeared to be red and green buoys the wrong way around. Checking with the pilot book and telephoning the local marina confirmed that they were in fact marking the channels either side of Ferry Rocks, situated mid-Sound.

Evidently, many sailors mistake these buoys for channel markers, head between them, and come to grief on the rocks. Even so, I had to make quite a dog-leg to clear the danger, and go very close to the shore to follow the channel round. When entering new places it pays to be wary of the position of buoys and how they are arranged – and a mobile phone allows you to get local advice.

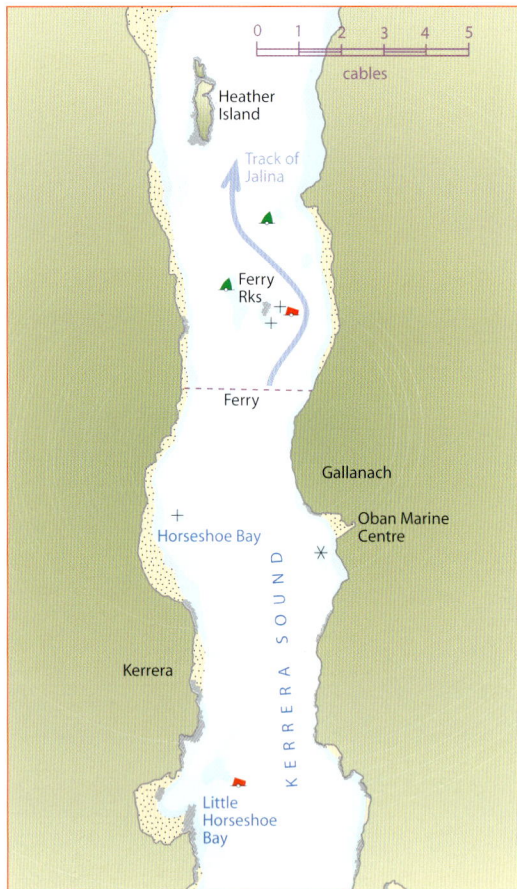

A chartlet showing Kerrera Sound.

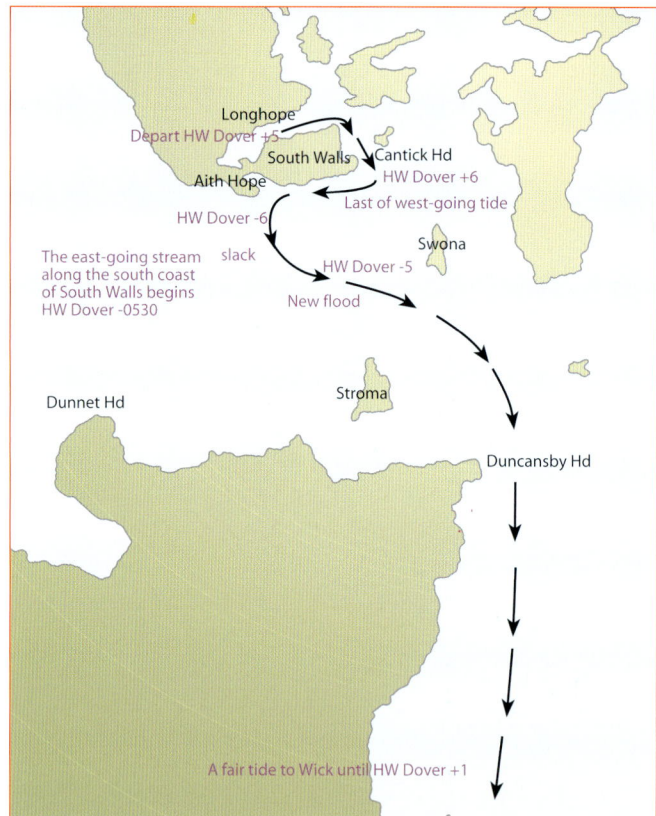

Passage beween Longhope round Cantick Head, between Swona and Stroma Island down to Wick.

Problem two: Longhope Scapa Flow – Pentland Firth – Wick

This is an area of very strong tides, which can run up to 12 knots at times! Because of this I needed to get uptide to pass between Swona and Stroma. My passage plan was to round Cantick Head lighthouse and head west, close to the shore, to let me ride the last of the west-going tide to Aith Hope, a small loch which faces the Pentland Firth. Then I could sail due south at slack water, and turn south-east to begin my sleigh ride between the islands of Swona and Stroma. Here, the plan was to catch the new east-going flood to take me down to Duncansby Head. The tides were between springs and neaps, so I was possibly being over-cautious to go so far west – but with spring tides I would certainly go that far west. All went well with the plan, but it is always wise to have something in hand in such hostile waters.

The weather was good, and it was an exciting ride as far as Duncansby Head, when I had to put a second reef in. The wind then went round to the SE and it rained like I had never seen it before, dramatically reducing the visibility. I was quietly relieved to safely enter Wick harbour.

Problem three: Stonehaven – Eyemouth Harbour

As I approached Eyemouth, it was murky and the sea was still with 4 knots of wind SW by W. I had left Stonehaven at 0040; it was now 1300. Having sailed 68 miles, I was tired. I thought Eyemouth would be a straightforward approach, so I put in a waypoint just north of the cardinal mark that's around 100m to the east of the 174° leading line. Had I been less tired, I would have followed my usual procedure and worked out clearing lines with the GPS.

After reaching my waypoint, I motored along on 174°, trying to pick out the north cardinal mark against the land, but all I saw was a raft of large red buoys close by. Slowing down to less than a knot to take a bearing, I happened to look over my starboard quarter – and there it was! The mark was now clearly visible against the sea, in the midst of the red buoys, which I later learned had been attached to it to prevent it from sinking. I realised I had drifted east due to the tide. I should have put in a waypoint for a clearing line to guard me from being carried onto the rocks. My heart missed a beat, I felt I was on thin ice that was

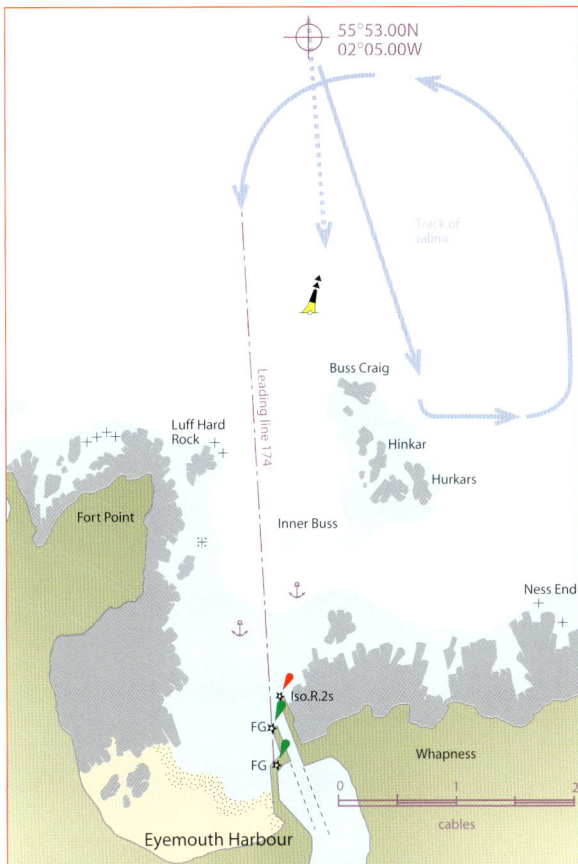

55°53.00N
02°05.00W

Track of
Jalina

Buss Craig

Luff Hard
Rock

Hinkar

Hurkars

Fort Point

Inner Buss

Ness End

Leading line 174

Iso.R.2s

FG

FG

Whapness

Eyemouth Harbour

cables

The approaches to Eyemouth harbour.

breaking. Realising what I'd done, I stopped *Jalina*, took a bearing, and altered course to clear the rocks and make a fresh, and safe approach.

Lesson learned

Never assume the marker is there, it may not be what you expect, and don't get complacent with your navigation; I placed my waypoint too far north of the mark given the murky conditions, and it would have been an easy matter to put in a waypoint to clear the rocks.

Problem four: Felixstowe (Shotley) to Ramsgate

My passage plan was to clear Harwich at Sheerness HW+5 and be at North Foreland at HW+3. I would sail south via the Medusa Channel, to keep clear of as much shipping as possible, and after that SE to Sunk Head Tower, SSW down Black Deep, then SE through Fishermans Gat and south to Margate red can, arriving at North Foreland.

Another option, and possibly safer with more room in the channel, was to clear north of Long Sand shallows and go south, down Knock Deep. Had there been a swell

running when departing Harwich, I would have avoided the Medusa Channel and gone east via Cork Sand yacht beacon, NE Gunfleet E cardinal, Sunk Head Tower N cardinal or Long Sand Head N cardinal.

As things turned out, I had strong reaching winds of force 6/7 from Sunk Head Fort to Ramsgate, so I could have set off two hours later. That would have saved me an hour's foul tide off North Foreland and I would have still had four hours of fair tide into Ramsgate – plus I would have had an extra metre of depth in the Medusa Channel. If the winds had been forecast force 3/4 then I would have set off at the earlier time. One thing I have learned in sailing down the east coast of the UK is to treat the depths and sandbanks with caution. I have encountered changing depths not shown on the chart, no doubt influenced by storms. I check depths using buoys and check their position against a waypoint from the GPS. In the Thames, storms can cause sandbanks and buoys to move. A new chart can quickly be out of date, so check it against the *Notices to Mariners* and *BA NP74 Lights and Fog Signals*.

For this passage I made up my 'passage plan logbook' to include depths for each hour. These details would be necessary to clear the Medusa Channel and to safely cut across the Long Sand. But I ruled this out, because when I got to Black Deep the wind had risen to force 6/7 and the

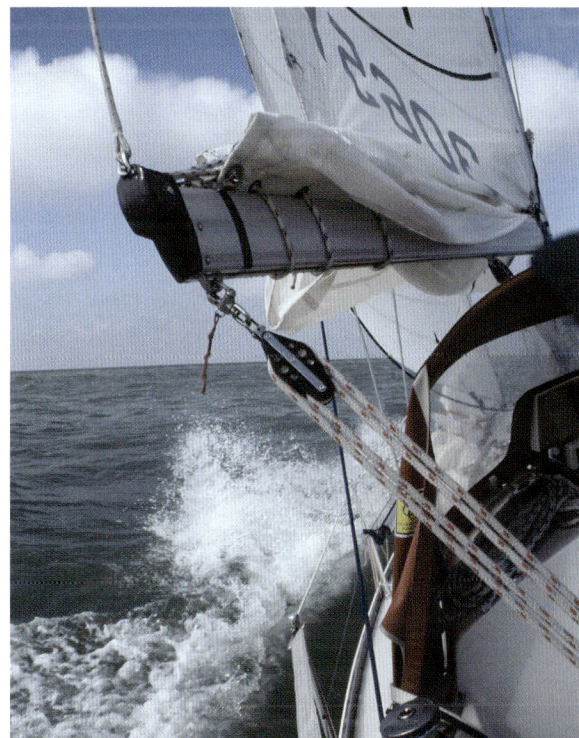

Three reefs in as the wind builds in the Thames Estuary.

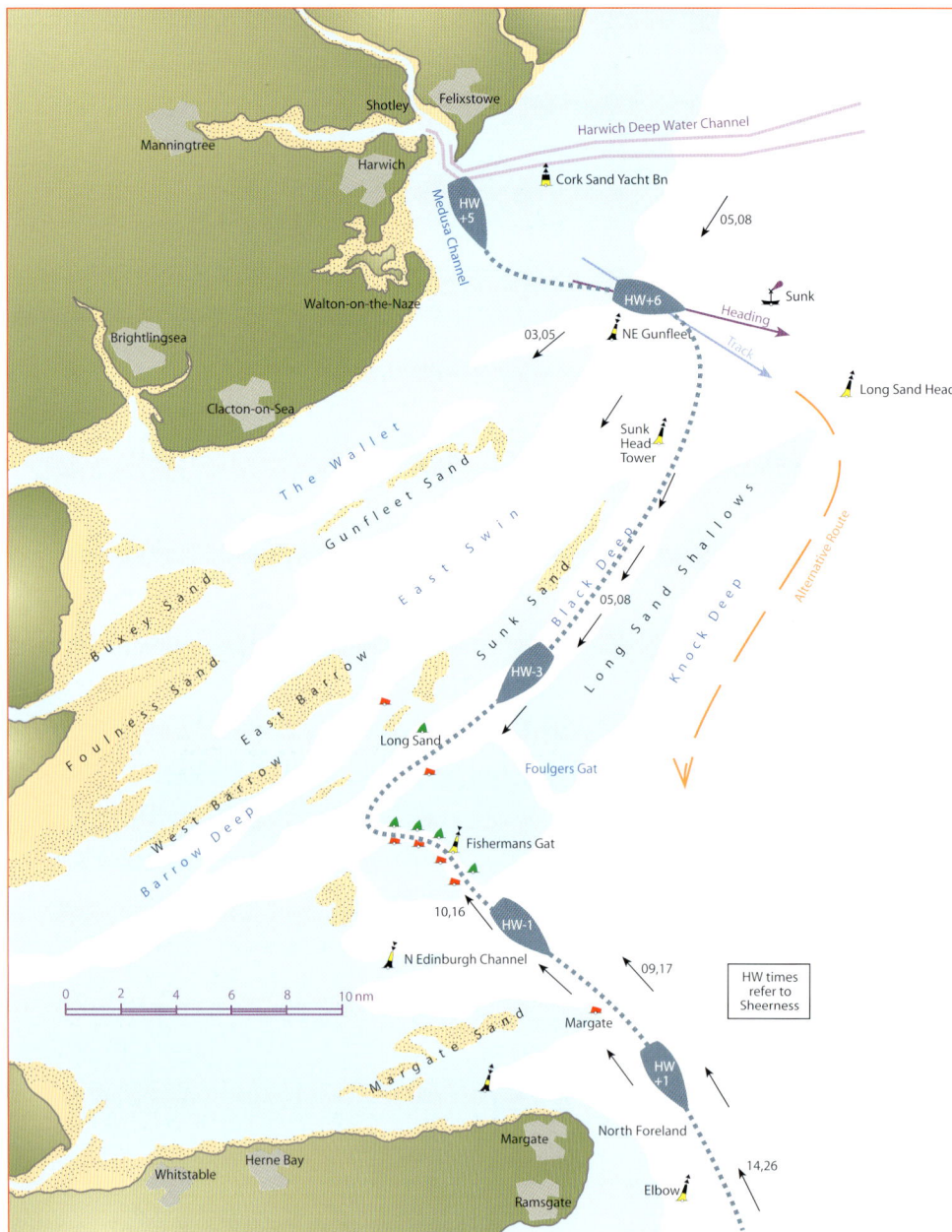

Passage plan from Felixstowe to North Foreland.

Map labels:
Shotley · Felixstowe · Manningtree · Harwich · Harwich Deep Water Channel · Cork Sand Yacht Bn · Medusa Channel · HW +5 · 05,08 · Sunk · HW+6 · Heading · NE Gunfleet · Track · Walton-on-the-Naze · Brightlingsea · 03,05 · Long Sand Head · Clacton-on-Sea · The Wallet · Gunfleet Sand · Sunk Head Tower · East Swin · Buxey Sand · Sunk Sand · Black Deep · Long Sand Shallows · Knock Deep · Alternative Route · 05,08 · Foulness Sand · East Barrow · HW-3 · Long Sand · West Barrow · Foulgers Gat · Barrow Deep · Fishermans Gat · 10,16 · HW-1 · N Edinburgh Channel · 09,17 · HW times refer to Sheerness · 0 2 4 6 8 10 nm · Margate · Margate Sand · HW +1 · Herne Bay · Margate · North Foreland · Whitstable · 14,26 · Elbow · Ramsgate

troughs were enough to make it a dangerous proposition. The depth sounder was now showing a good 2m swell and troughs got even deeper over the shallows. I stayed in Black Deep and Fishermans Gat, but if it was calmer I could have cut across Long Sand, at the 2m channel just north of Fishermans Gat.

As the level changes near the sandbanks, the directions of the tidal streams alter dramatically. At HW they flow over the sand, but as the water drops they follow the channels more. There are cross tides over the channels particularly HW −1 to HW+1 and even more so at springs, so a constant check on the GPS highway is needed to maintain an accurate course. It's also a good idea to have your standby GPS up and running to treble-check your waypoints.

I had also worked out my tidal depths for when I reached North Foreland, so if I was early I could sail close inshore, along the 2m contour, to avoid the worst of a foul tide. This is a simple technique − I just match the depth shown on the echo-sounder to the pre-calculated depths, and sail along that contour. My depth sounder is set to water depth and the alarm is set to depth under the keel.

Shipping and local knowledge

Be watchful for ships in the Thames, as they have very little room to manoeuvre in many of the channels. I once had a ship astern, on the same track, when there was a lot of breaking white water around. I managed to raise him on my handheld VHF and he advised me which side he was going to pass. But, he had not seen me visually, and my radar image was lost in the clutter on his radar screen.

PART III
CIRCUMNAVIGATING UK AND IRELAND

STARTING OUT: Portsmouth to Padstow
Total distance: 289nm
Passage time: 9 days

Stromness
Longhope
Scrabster
Kinlochbervie
Wick
Lochinver
Gairloch
Whitehills
Peterhead
Kyleakin
Mallaig
Stonehaven
Tobermory
Arbroath
Oban
Craobh Haven
Loch Suna
Edinburgh
Gigha
Eyemouth
Ardiminish Bay
Sheep Haven
Downe's Bay
Aran Island
Blyth
Portrush
Belfast
Hartlepool
Broadhaven
Whitby
Bridlington
Inishbofin
Kilronay
Inishmore
Dublin
Waterford
Lowestoft
Dingle
Fenit
Valentia
Shotley
Harwich
Dungarven
Milfordhaven
Cardiff
Crosshaven
London
Glandore
Baltimore
Croohaven
Ramsgate
Dover
Portsmouth
Weymouth
Padstow
Yarmouth
Newlyn
Falmouth
Dartmouth

Previous page:
A view over Oban looking towards the south of Mull.

Portsmouth to Yarmouth

Distance: 24nm

Passage time: 4.15hr

Yarmouth to Weymouth

Distance: 39nm

Passage time: 9.40hr

My first passage, 24nm west down the Solent to Yarmouth was a shake-down trip to check that everything worked. The adventure had started!

I was late getting started which meant I couldn't round southern Ireland before the salmon fishing season which starts on 1 June. This is quite an important date, as under certain conditions the nets, which extend from the head-lands, can create a hazard as far as two miles offshore.

As I departed from Portsmouth I was given a great 'bon voyage' by the RAYC flagship *St Barbara* with all her flags up and a farewell signal blast – what a send off!

The weather forecast was good, so I could sail short day-hops to build up my energy levels, get plenty of sleep, and go through my check lists to settle me into a routine. I tied up at 1500.

A little more care was needed as it was spring tides. The main points for this passage:

- Clearing the Needles
- Clearing St Albans Ledge
- Clearing Lulworth firing range

A mobile phone call to the MOD Range Control Officer reported no firing for my trip. As the forecast was NW force 2–3, this good news meant I could keep my heading as north as possible, so avoiding having to tack against the spring tide from the southern part of the range to Weymouth.

I cleared Yarmouth at 0420 so I would have a fair tide until 0630 and foul until 1300. Progress was good – I was early as I approached St Albans Ledge, and the wind was light W force 2. I was not happy to take the inner passage, close to St Albans Head, because if the wind went lighter and SW it would put me on a lee shore. I decided to tack out and cross the Ledge between the DZ buoys then tack onto port for Warbarrow Bay. Here I picked up a favourable tidal back eddy. Further south, the tide would be foul for another two hours at least.

St Albans Ledge to Weymouth. With no firing at Lulworth, I was able to make a better course; closer to shore taking advantage of a favourable tidal back eddy.

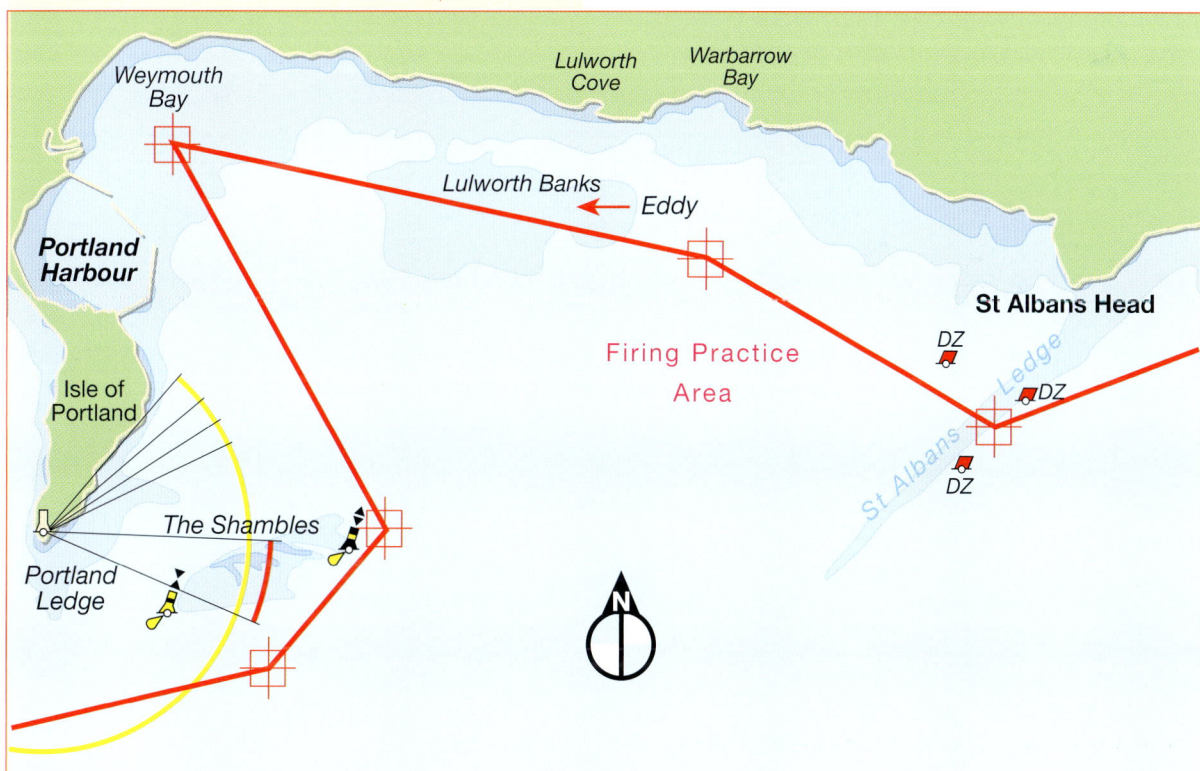

Things to do

sandwiches ✓
hot flask of tea ✓
bottled water ✓
WPs checked ✓
two reefs put in the main ✓
hi-visibility orange foresail
hanked on ✓
signed on with Portland CG with
my passage plan ✓
search light checked ✓
white flares in place ✓

Jalina in Weymouth harbour.

The wind went back to NW, so I could make the Weymouth entrance in one tack. I called on VHF Ch12 for clearance to enter, because the IPTS (International Port Traffic Signals) must be obeyed to avoid the ferries.

Being early into Weymouth gave me the opportunity for an early start the next day. But the forecast was not good – winds WNW force 5–6. The following day it would be NW force 3–4 – much better. I didn't need an on-the-nose passage of 65 miles as it would be too wearing; so I decided to stay an extra night.

Weymouth to Dartmouth – I tacked above the rhumb line so the later tide would keep us on track.

Weymouth to Dartmouth
Distance: 65nm
Passage time: 13.45hr

The pre-passage thinking for my sail to Dartmouth was that if the wind was NW, the fair ebb tide would drop me below my required course, but the flood sweeping slightly north would push me back towards Dartmouth.

My main concern was the many crab pot markers I had noticed just off the entrance to the harbour. The best time to slip was 0015 (HW Dover −2.5hr) so I would not be able to spot the pot markers.

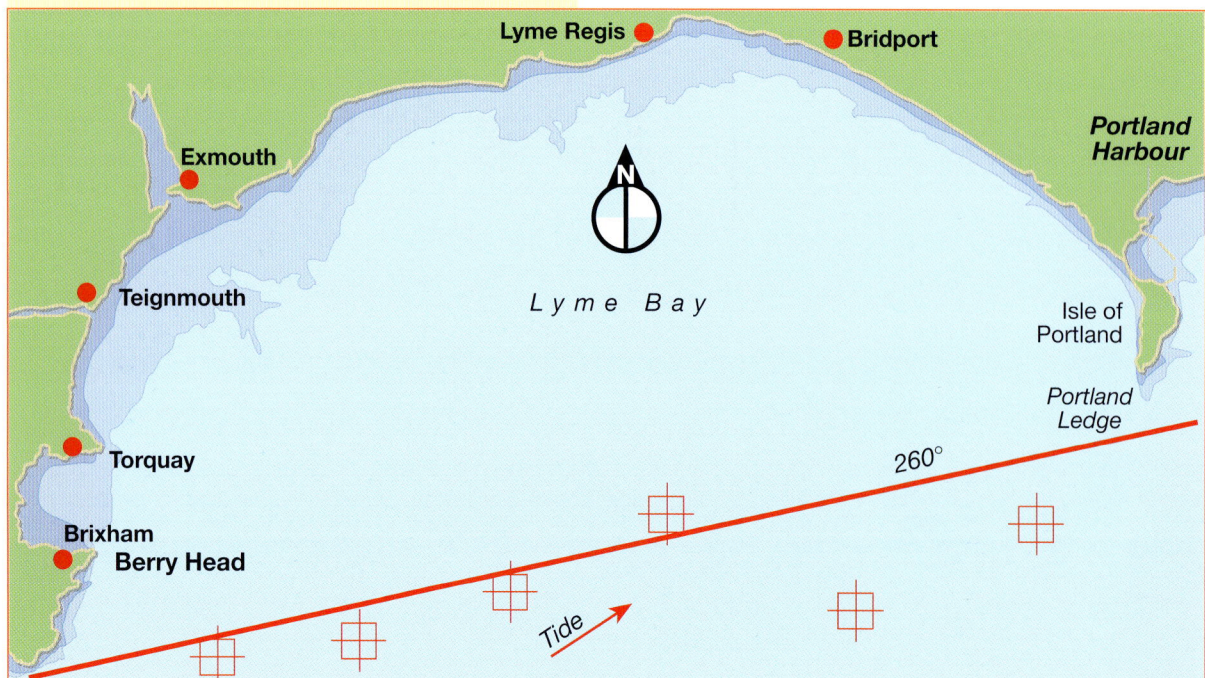

Lyme Regis
Bridport
Exmouth
Portland Harbour
Teignmouth
L y m e   B a y
Isle of Portland
Portland Ledge
Torquay
260°
Brixham
Berry Head
Tide

Looking down on the moorings in the River Dart.

My passage plan was to a fixed point, using two harbour lights and a WP to confirm my position. From here I set a course to another WP east of the Shambles, and then set a course south of Portland Bill for Dartmouth. You may say 'Why go so far east, and not go between west Shambles and the Bill?' Well, as a single-hander, I would prefer to be in the lee of the rough Shambles shallows, and clear of all the crab pots. Even with a reefed main I could reach at 5 knots, so the extra three miles didn't matter and gave me an extra safety margin.

I left under engine and main and, as I approached the entrance, I put the engine into neutral to reduce the chance of being fouled with the crab pot lines. Once clear, I hoisted the jib and the harbour lights soon slipped away. By 0300 I had cleared the Shambles and set a course for Dartmouth, with the wind gathering in strength. I put in a third reef, however, since the tide was now setting west, my speed over the ground was 7.4 knots!

The wind did not have enough northing to fetch Dartmouth and I would be set below the course. This would be corrected in part by the new flood that would push *Jalina* north. As I closed Dartmouth, I tacked to correct the course. I reached the Mew Stone, and the two cardinal markers guarding it showed up just like the chart corrections I had made earlier in the year.

I made very good progress – working the tide had gone well – and I was tied up in Dartmouth Yacht Club pontoon by 1400. After signing off with the coastguard, I decided to rest up for two nights and visit the sights of Dartmouth – and try the local pasties.

Dartmouth to Falmouth
Distance: 66nm
Passage time: 12.15hr

Throughout my day off I checked the CG weather forecast, NAVTEX, and shipping forecast. The forecast for Lyme Regis to Land's End was N force 2–3 variable force 1–3, locally force 4; sea state slight; good visibility. The tides for this passage were not so important, except to clear Start Point and Bolt Head and get as close to the Eddystone lighthouse as possible before the flood.

Slack water was 0300. Departure time was not critical but leaving with a little light would help me spot any crab pot markers.

Intended Route
Actual Route

Torquay
Plymouth
Dartmouth
Start Point
Eddystone Rocks
Falmouth
Firing Zone
Lizard Point

N

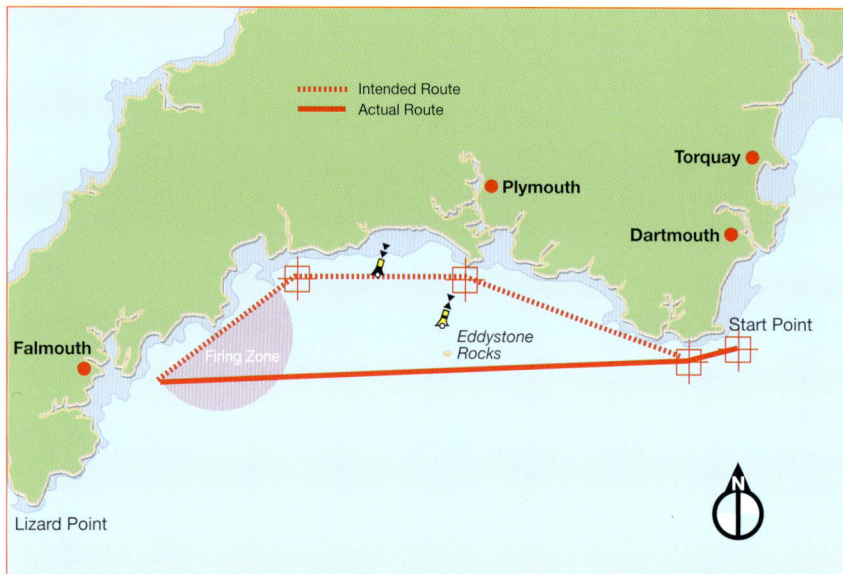

FIRING RANGES

There are over 32 live firing ranges around the UK coastline. Live firing notices are issued to the coastguard, local police and tourist information centres.

I called the Coastguard with my passage plan, slipped at 0430, hoisted the sail in the harbour and sailed out with the engine in neutral. The ebb had just started in the harbour and with a little moon I could make out the well-flagged pot markers.

I reached Start Point doing 6.8 knots – a good start to the passage. My plan was to pass north of Eddystone lighthouse close to the coastline, but on arriving at Prawle Point, the wind was WNW not N, so I changed to a more direct course heading south of the lighthouse.

Live firing!

At 0930 an all-vessel warning went out from HMS *Manchester* that there would be live firing within an area 12 miles off Dodman Point until 1200. I had to slow down as at 1130 *Jalina* was only 1 mile off the limit. I hove-to and put the kettle on, letting the tide take me to the limit. The rest of the passage went well. We rounded St Anthony's Head by 1600 and were tied up on a swinging mooring by 1645.

St Anthony's Head, Falmouth – I found flat calm conditions here.
Insert: Crab pots were well flagged off the Eddystone lighthouse.

In Falmouth

I was not happy with the weather forecast for the passage to Newlyn – it gave N backing NW force 2–3 with mist and fog. It might burn off with the sun, but I wanted to slip early. The last time I cleared the Lizard, the sea was wild and misty with driving rain. However, while the weather was good I wanted to keep on the move, but had to guard against tiredness – and all the dangers that go with it. When I am underway on a long passage I don't sleep, but get some rest by cutting down my activity levels a notch or two and setting my alarm just in case I doze off. Cooking good, hot, wholesome food on a regular basis is also vital for a successful and safe voyage.

Falmouth to Newlyn

Distance: 34nm
Passage time: 7.15hr

I rose at 0400, and again at 0800, to find thick fog, so went back to my bunk. I eventually slipped my mooring at 1100 but the tide had turned against me at 1015. It was slow going along the rocky coastline – too hazardous to get close to stem the foul tide.

After clearing St Anthony's Head, the wind fell to zero so I put the engine on and set a course to clear the Manacles and Lizard Point. With a flat, calm passage I decided to prepare a meal – potatoes, salad and tinned salmon. By the time I had made a fresh fruit salad, I had cleared Lizard Point and set a course into Newlyn. I was tied up by 1830, and as Newlyn is accessible 24hrs, I could depart when I chose.

Newlyn to Padstow

Distance: 61nm
Passage time: 14.15hr

Days earlier I had worked out a passage plan to round the Longships at Lands End. I had arrived at Newlyn on the earliest date, so now had up to five days to time my departure between 0300 and 0700 to arrive in Padstow between 1500 and 1900. I find that by pre-planning like this you can bracket the best weather window for your passage. It also meant I would arrive at the Runnel Stone south cardinal, the Longships and Padstow in daylight with the best tides to make the inner harbour (see detailed passage plan for this passage on pages 32–4).

Weather forecasts gathered the previous day gave winds NW force 2–3, locally force 4, going N force 2–3; mist and fog patches with showers; sea state slight.

Like the last time I had rounded the Longships, I was hoping to go through the inner passage (the Kettle) but because of the threat of fog I decided on the safer option.

In passage planning there can be critical arrival points. In this passage it was to be at Pendeen point at HW Dover or before, Longships by HW Dover −2hr or before, and Padstow by HW Dover −5hr or before.

At 0345 I set off for Penzer Point, the Runnel Stone, and the Longships. I had a little tide against me until 0600, but with a good beam breeze I made progress and by 0530 I had cleared the Runnel Stone. It was still quite dark and I could see the flashing light of Longships. A WP west of the Longships let me plot my progress, so that I was not swept inside the Longships with the north-going eddy, or too far west so that I was swept south by the foul ebb tide.

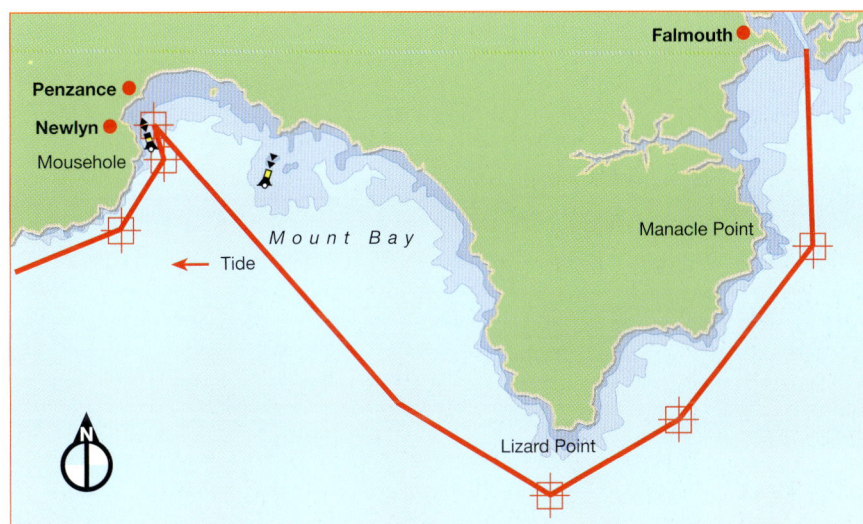

Falmouth to Newlyn – the rocky shore and foul tide can spell danger on this section of the coast.

Jalina in Newlyn harbour. Photo: Dick Everitt

Padstow's delightful inner harbour – one of my favourites.

By 0620 we had cleared the Longships and I was beginning to feel the warmth of the sun through my waterproofs. The mist kept coming and going, but the visibility and progress were good. By 0800 we had cleared Pendeen Head – one hour ahead of schedule.

The wind dropped, so I motored in order to meet my tide window at Padstow. I went a little offshore to pick up the stronger flood tide, where visibility reduced a little. On entering the River Camel the sun shone brightly and it was good to see so many tan sails enjoying themselves. By 1530 we were tied up in one of my favourite harbours.

In Padstow

I had two days and three nights good rest and took the opportunity to sort out my domestic chores. During this period there had been fog at sea, and no wind but in harbour I enjoyed hot sunshine.

During this rest period, I had prepared my next passage to Milford Haven, plus a rough plan for the passage to cross over to the coast of Ireland. This felt like a big step – I was going foreign.

Subject to weather forecasts and visibility, I decided to leave Padstow the next day and cross to Ireland on the following day.

Doom Bar, Padstow, north Cornwall – the critical arrival point is HW Dover −5hr.

Padstow to Milford Haven and across to Ireland

Originally I had considered crossing directly to Ireland from Land's End – a distance of around 160NM. But this is a very busy shipping area and, being single-handed, I decided it was safer to cross the Irish Sea from Milford Haven in Wales. From there the two traffic separation schemes (TSS) would channel the shipping into more predictable positions – which would at least give me a good idea of which direction they would be coming from.

Before that though, I needed to cross the strong tides of the Bristol Channel from Padstow to Milford Haven, just as I had done on my previous round-Britain trip.

Padstow to Milford Haven
Distance: 63nm
Passage time: 15hr

For this passage I had to calculate my course to allow for the tide changing direction. Assuming a boat speed of 5 knots, I made up a plastic guide with lines spaced at 10NM. I placed this over the relevant tidal hour page and noted the corresponding tidal rate and directions in my tidal log. This is not precise as tidal streams don't always run at right angles to a given course.

I had considered crossing directly to Ireland from Land's End, but this is a very busy shipping area.

My plastic guide shows me which arrow to look at on each tidal atlas page. I estimate its effect and add it to my tidal log.

For the first hour out of Padstow (hour 1 – 0439) for example, the tidal rate was 0.5 knots. I estimated that the current's oblique direction would influence my heading by about 0.25 knots. By adding up each column I could see how much to aim off. However, the ebb tide was due to turn at about 1800, so to be sure, I aimed up-tide by another two miles. Then, closer to the coast, I would be able to make adjustments, keeping a little tide in hand to set me down nicely to the entrance to Milford Haven. In a similar way, the amount of leeway would depend upon the strength and direction of the wind and swell. This can vary between 5° and 10°. On a fine reach in a force 6 with a heavy swell, for example, I would allow up to 10°.

The weather forecast was WNW force 2–3 with mist patches, sea state slight, with more of the same for the following 24 hours. It was looking very much like a motoring passage.

Padstow lock opened at 0300 and I could see the lights right across the Camel Estuary – so it was clear visibility! At 0410 I left, with only the odd fishing boat for company. I love the peace of leaving in the dark. It fills me with excitement. Within half an hour the sky and sea were shades of grey and there was still a slight chill in the air. After clearing Doom Bar I was soon out into the open sea.

The Longship's lighthouse is a mile to the west of Land's End and warns sailors of the dangerous rocks off the headland.

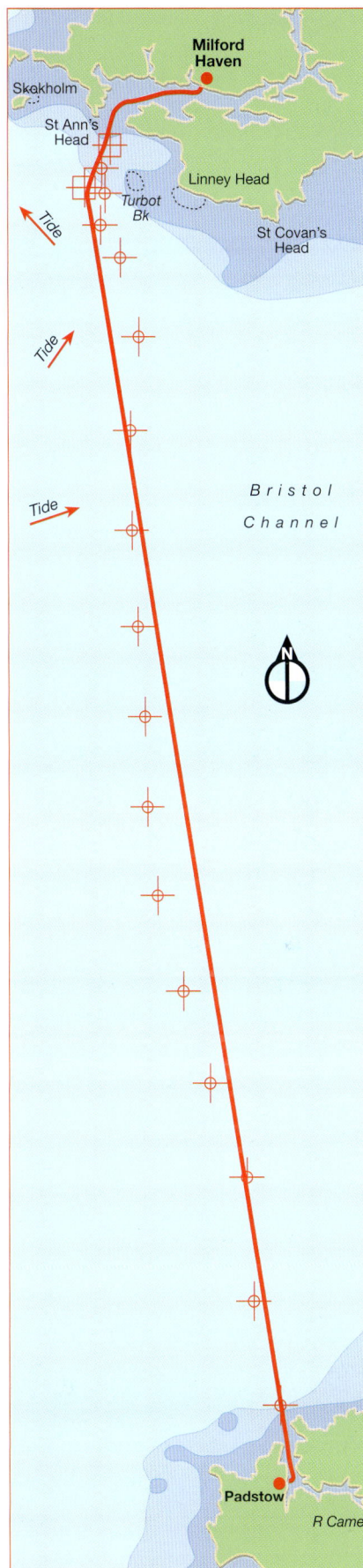

The nav worked well – the total tidal effect was allowed for and I was swept in a flat 'S' curve.

There was very little wind during the morning and the sea was like glass. The engine purred away until 1300, when wind piped up to a gentle force 2 from the WNW. What a relief to switch off the engine! By 1740 I was abeam off Turbot Bank heading towards Milford Haven entrance and marina, which has diesel, a supermarket, chandlers, showers and a laundrette. *Jalina* was tied up by 1900.

Even though it had been a quiet day with little wind and a slight sea state, I was pleased that the course had worked out as planned.

Milford Haven to Waterford Harbour

Distance: 98nm

Passage time: 22hr

My broad plan was to use the flood running north which would turn in my favour at approximately 1800. This would assist my passage and set me to clear to the north of the easterly TSS (Traffic Separation Scheme). I wanted to be at Skokholm Island by 1800 to make the most of the flood tide. I had planned my tidal vector into three parts:

1 Skokholm Island to NE of the north-going shipping lane.
2 Shipping lane to Coningbeg light vessel (situated approx 10nm SE of Waterford Harbour).
3 Lightvessel to Dunmore East (situated west of the entrance to Waterford Harbour)

Taking into account the tide rates and directions from the vector sheets, my course would be up-tide of my rhumb line. The highway on my GPS to the WP would show me off course and up-tide until I made full use of the ebb. By doing this I would make the quickest and shortest passage to the WP. When working out the compass course, the other major consideration is leeway. When possible I lee-bow the tide, but as mentioned earlier the amount of swell influences the amount of leeway to allow.

The weather forecast had mentioned mist and fog patches, visibility moderate to good, and having two sets of shipping lanes to cross I would have to keep alert – no dozing with the alarm set.

If visibility did deteriorate I had a number of options:

1 Abort the passage.
2 Call the shipping on my VHF, give my position and ask for the position and heading of other shipping that may affect me. There is a problem with some ships not monitoring Ch16 but I find they mostly do – and at least they would be aware of my presence.
3 Call the Milford Haven Coastguard and ask what shipping they could identify using their AIS (Automatic Identification System), again being aware that not all ships have to comply.

Preparing for the passage

During the day I checked my torches, searchlight and navigation lights, leaving plenty of daylight to deal with any failures. I learned a valuable lesson during my previous circumnavigation – always carry four empty jerry cans to hold extra diesel for those long periods when there is no wind. I decided to get them filled up, so I would have 41 litres (9 gallons) in the tank, plus 32 litres (7 gallons) spare. I was also unsure of the availability of diesel in Ireland.

A night crossing of the Irish Sea seemed to make sense for two reasons: firstly to make the most of the tides, and secondly because I find ships are easier to see at night.

I had gradually got used to sailing in the dark by slipping early in the mornings, but this would be the first full night passage of my voyage – I was excited about the challenge but apprehensive at the same time.

Proper food is vital for the mind and body and it is easily neglected in bad weather. In my preparation before casting off I had made a double portion of a hot casserole. I ate half before slipping; the other could be heated up either on passage, or on arrival. I had also bought some fresh meat pies to heat up while underway.

I slipped my lines at 1610 the day before spring tides. While in the lock I called Milford Haven coastguard on Ch16 then went to Ch67, a working channel, to sign on and give them my passage plan.

- Milford Haven to Waterford
- ETA 1200 tomorrow
- One person on board

Within the Haven you must keep a listening watch on Ch12 (Milford Haven Port Control). For the marina call Pierhead

ChM. Lock hours: earliest entry is HW −4, last exit is HW −3.5. The earliest I could slip from the marina would be 1530.

The tide was in full flood as I sailed west to the entrance of the Haven, but it would turn in my favour off Skokholm Island at 1800. I was quite exited but the presence of a little haze did not please me, as the weather forecast had mentioned mist and fog patches – not good for crossing two sets of shipping lanes.

As I cleared the Haven, what little wind there was fell away to nothing, so I had to use the engine to meet my tidal gate. We arrived SE of Skokholm Island at 1830, a little later than planned, and using the tidal vector prepared earlier, I set my course to get the full benefit of the current's flow.

Two shipping lanes

As I approached WP Bishop, NE of the first shipping lane, the sun started to go down. Visibility was good with a little haze and I could feel a chill in the air. All was prepared for the night passage.

The searchlight was ready to shine onto the mainsail, together with spare torches and white anti-collision flares.

On departing I kept well over towards St Ann's Head to keep clear of the busy shipping entrance.

ECONOMIC CHART FOLIOS

The only way I can afford to navigate safely on extended passages is to buy secondhand charts from the shipping lines. Then I update them from the Hydrographic Office website www.ukho.gov.uk. I'm not happy with electronic charts, as plotters carry a disclaimer 'Not to be used for navigation'. The bottom line is that Admiralty paper charts will take a lot of sea water before they pack in!

To buy 173 new charts for my circumnavigation would have cost me £2,975. I only bought four new and the rest came from www.marinechartservices .com The total cost for my charts was £562.

I also lowered my masthead pennant to avoid covering the masthead tricolour light. The weather forecast for the Irish Sea was for wind SW force 3–5, rain showers, visibility moderate to good, with some fog patches in the south.

By midnight I had cleared the first set of shipping lanes and had seen only four ships. Visibility was about two miles, but all the sails were running with condensed mist giving a cold chill to the night. Then a little wind picked up

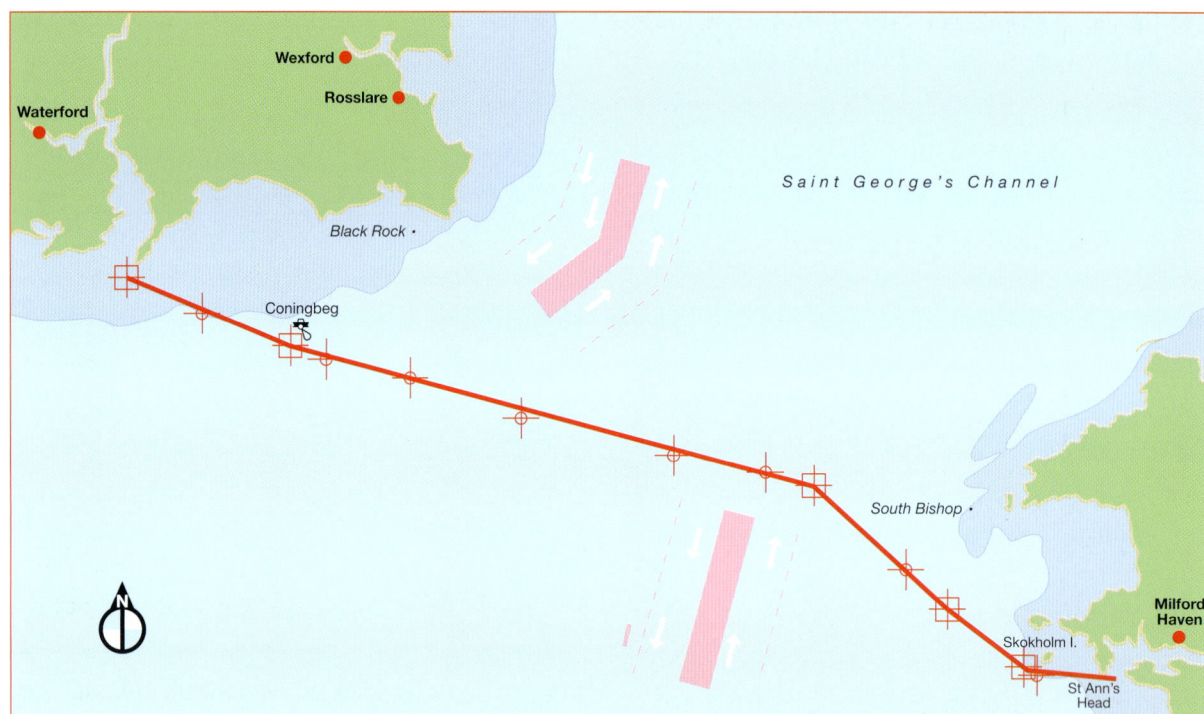

I avoided crossing the separation zone but still knew where to expect shipping. My total tidal calculations meant I was swept either side of the rhumb line, and the Coningbeg light gave me an ideal aiming point in case the GPS went down.

from the south-west force 2–3, just enough to give me 5 knots. At 0200, visibility got a little better and I spotted the first ships heading for the second set of shipping lanes north of our course. At 0300 I could make out the loom from the Coningbeg light vessel, my next WP. At 0400 I spotted the light from the Black Rock south cardinal, 5NM to the north on a bearing of 010° (this was an update I had recently added to this chart).

On went the kettle for a hot cup of tea, and as I ate the other half of the casserole I felt all was good with the world – here I was closing on Ireland and free for the whole of the summer! The sun was slowly coming up from the east and by 0500 I was clearing the Coningbeg light vessel. Everything was very grey – the sea had merged into the sky. As the wind picked up, the rippled sea set a line on the horizon and I began to feel the weak morning sun heating my damp waterproofs.

By 0900 I entered Waterford Harbour – *Jalina* and I were in Ireland. Under full sail I reached up the wide entrance, taking care to keep out of the shallows. I was tired and progress was slow as the tide was ebbing. I tied up at the marina by 1400. A magnetic gate card is available at the Tower Hotel opposite the marina for the use of their showers. You can take on water and the shops are a short

walk away. The shower at the Tower Hotel was very welcome – they even provide a hot towel! I was soon back on board planning my passage to Helvick Harbour.

Reginald's 10th century tower at Waterford.

Sailing westwards: Waterford to Glandore

Waterford Harbour in Ireland provided shelter and a good rest after leaving Milford Haven in Wales and crossing the busy shipping lanes of St George's Channel. But after a brief stay, the time came to continue my journey west along the southern coast of the Emerald Isle. There was adventure and plenty of legendary Irish hospitality in store as I planned my passage to Helvick Head and my next port of call, Dungarvan Harbour.

Waterford to Dungarvan

Distance: 36nm

Passage time: 7hr

The weather forecast was good, NNW force 3-4 with scattered showers and good visibility. The following 24 hours were forecast NNE to take me down to Crosshaven, just inside Cork Harbour. Would my luck hold I wondered?

I decided to take the tide down the river at 1000 to Dunmore East and on to Helvick Head and Dungarvan Harbour. The tide runs fast at Waterford marina so I slipped at slack water to avoid having to spring off. I soon cleared the river on a quick beam reach and was on the open sea with a full main and working jib. This coastline is so beautiful with soft green and brown rolling hills – a land for poets and artists and, of course, sailors!

For a safe approach to the Dungarvan Harbour moorings, you have to avoid Carrickapane Rocks, The Gainer Rocks and Helvick Rock. My approach was to sail between Helvick Head and Helvick east cardinal to a point east of them, then on toward the moorings off Crow's Point and its flag staff (see chart).

The moorings are a little open to northerly winds, and as we approached, the wind was coming in from the NW. This soon settled down as the evening wore on.

Crow's Point moorings

The eight moorings which will take up to 15 tonnes each, look well-maintained but have a line prepared to pick up the buoy as there are no strops fitted. The area is a sanctuary for wild birds so you won't need an alarm clock and the surrounding hills are covered with yellow gorse.

Once safely moored, I settled down to eat a meal I had prepared on passage, then began working out the pilotage to Crosshaven.

I would have liked to have gone ashore but I needed to get to bed early. The weather forecast put out by Mine Head Coastguard on Ch83 was good for the passage to Cork; wind NNE force 2–3 aft of the beam sounded too good to be true and I would also have the tide with me.

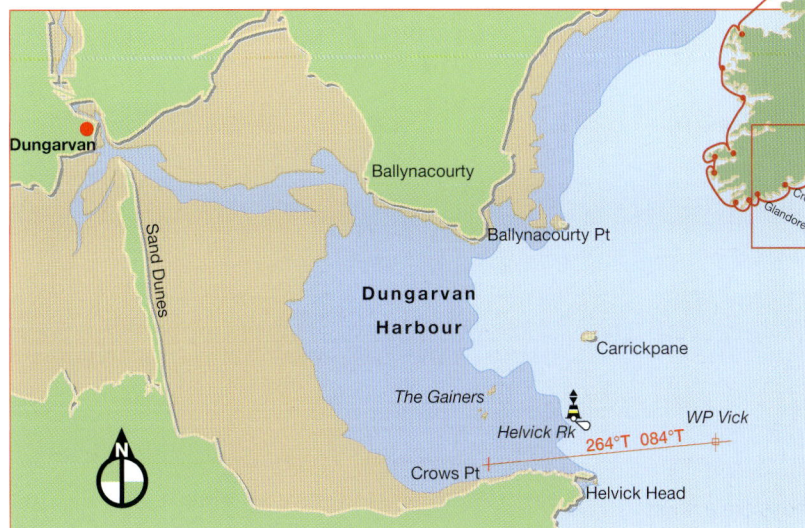

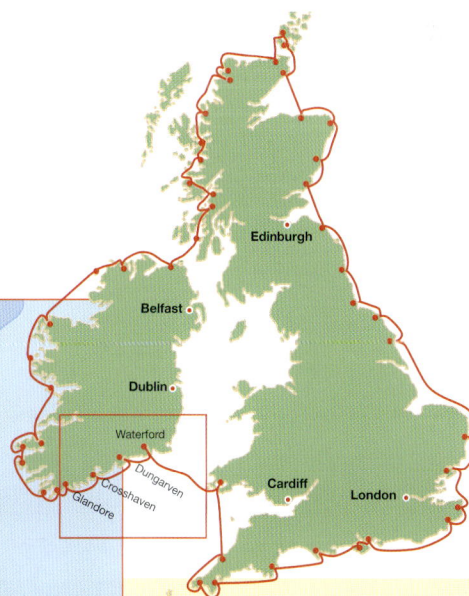

I set a waypoint and course to the moorings off the flag pole at Crow's Point. This was because the east cardinal can sometimes be hard to see, and people have been swept onto The Gainers rocks.

One thing I've yet to get used to are the Irish weather forecasts and, in particular, the sea areas. I made an encapsulated copy of the sea areas, plus stations taken from the *Reeds PBO Almanac* and placed it in front of me whenever I took down the forecasts.

Dungarvan to Crosshaven
Distance: 35nm
Passage time: 8hr

I woke at 0630 to the glow of a bright orange sun – nearly as bright as my foresail! *Jalina's* bow was nodding gently to the oncoming swell and the wind was now force 2–3 coming from the NW. It was looking like a fetch to Cork Harbour.

I prepared a good bowl of porridge mixed with museli and dried fruit plus a hot cup of tea. I had a sandwich prepared for lunch and some ham salad packed in a plastic box. With only a gentle breeze forecast, I planned to cook and make hot drinks underway.

It was time to leave. I hoisted the main and, as I was the only boat using the moorings, decided to sail off. With the autopilot set for WP 'Vick' (off Helvick Head and outlying rocks), I hoisted the orange foresail and we were underway. The weather forecast was good with winds NW to WNW force 4–5, veering N to NE force 3–4, with showers and good visibility – so it would be a beam reach. As the tide direction was more or less along the rhumb line for this passage, I made no allowance for my course bearing.

My plan to clear the moorings and Dungarvan Harbour was in reverse to my approach the previous day. Once at WP 'Vick' we changed course SW for Mine Head light, which is over 150 years old and stands 87m (285ft) tall.

Even though the tides were at springs +2 days there would be approximately one knot of foul tide until 0930, followed by slack water until approximately 1230. This is a strange phenomenon along this part of the Irish coast – three or four hours of slack water! With LW Cork at 1400, I aimed to be off Roche's Point by 1500 for the flood to take me into Crosshaven.

I was aware that there can be salmon nets stretching two to three miles out to sea from the headlands. The season should start on 1 June but I was told to keep an eye open for the nets anyway. They have small floats to keep them at the surface, with a marker on the seaward end. You can raise the fishermen on Ch6 (provided that they have a radio!) and if they're there and spot you they rush out to guide you around the nets.

The wind picked up to force 3 from the NW, which meant I was on a weather shore. With very little swell, I went in closer to look at the coastline and at Mine Head with its distinctive, black-girdled white lighthouse which is visible for miles. As I cleared the Head I was careful to look out for salmon buoys and nets.

Helvick Head: the yellow gorse shone brightly in the morning sun.

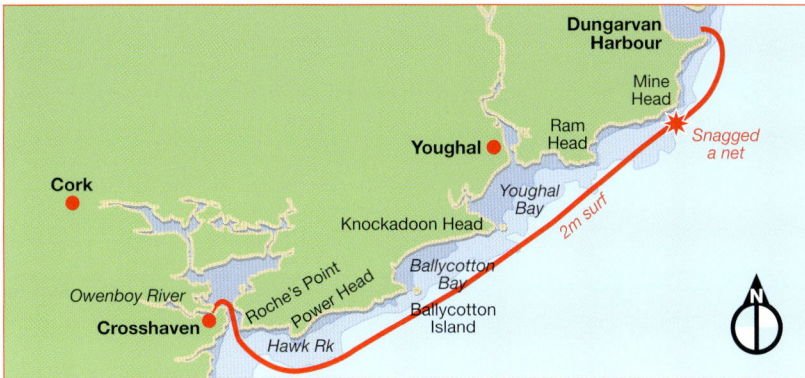

Along this part of the Irish coastline I snagged a two-mile long net, had the strange experience of sailing through several hours of slack water and surfed along at 6 knots through 2m swells.

Some nets are two or three miles long and marked at the outer end with a tall dan buoy.

Snagged on a net

As the winds were light, I was under engine when we came to an abrupt halt. I have been caught up on a crail line before and because the buoy was under the water and not flagged, I had difficulty in getting to the line to cut myself free.

This time I was better prepared and was able to get at the line using a long tree-pruning pole with a hook screwed onto the end. I was able to pull up the line and secure it onto both port and starboard stern cleats. I then cut it free, and added a short length of line to reach to my engine shaft in the locker – after first removing half a ton of locker contents. I turned the shaft, letting the tension on the line direct me as to which way to turn the shaft to free it. Finally, I released the secured lines from the cleats. I was fortunate to be on a weather shore in light winds so freeing myself was not too difficult. I always carry a wet suit in case I do have to go over the side but I may fit a rope cutter.

I was relieved to be underway again. The sky was clear blue and it was so warm that I shed my waterproofs. I kept getting welcoming waves from the fishermen, and being a weather shore the agricultural waft made it seem as if I was actually on someone's farm! Keeping a steady 5 knots, I gazed at the fields covered for miles with bright yellow gorse. What a contrast with the rocky shore!

As I cleared Ram Head, the long fetch of Youghal Bay opened up and with it a 2m swell aft of the beam. *Jalina* and I were now surfing at over 6 knots and I felt good with the world. I looked up at the puffs of well-rounded cloud and the sun shining through them cast shades of contrasting white and grey. I couldn't help noticing vapour

The net I hit was not marked, and the 'rugby ball' floats were running just under the water.

trails high up in the atmosphere – all those people going about their hurried lives.

Ahead I noticed the sea building up so I put a reef in the main. Now we were surfing at 8 knots. This is what I call sailing! As the wind picked up I eased the main to reduce the weather helm.

We cleared Knockadoon Head by 1030. I had kept fairly close to the shore on the 20m contour and I could now make out the distinctive shape of Ballycotton Island ahead in Ballycotton Bay. I was soon off Power Head taking care to clear Hawk Rock. It was now low water. The fair tide after slack was less than a knot. I would be at Roche's Point and its fine lighthouse very soon.

Crosshaven, Cork Harbour

It was good, for once, to have plenty of room to tack into a harbour. After clearing Roche's Point with a fair flood tide

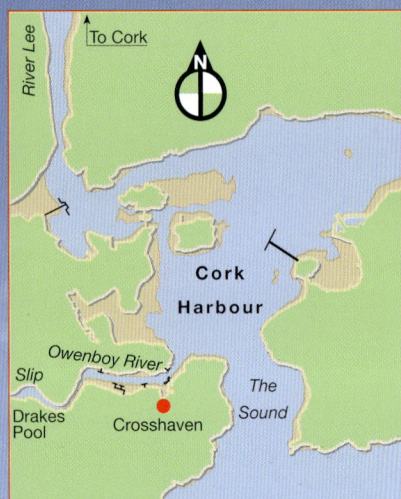

Peaceful moorings at Drake's Pool on the Owenboy River at Crosshaven.

Insert: Once through the Sound I turned to port to find a quiet spot up the River Owenboy.

I was soon sailing towards the Owenboy River and Crosshaven. I decided to hand my sails. According to the chart, care would be needed at low water to keep to the centre of the river to avoid going aground.

It had been the best sail so far with some really beautiful coastline and it had been hot and sunny. This was a good omen for my circumnavigation!

Arriving at Crosshaven

By 1500 I had picked up a swinging mooring in the river. These are let by Salva Marine and cost €10 per night including showers. There are several marinas, boatyards and chandlers nearby. The well-lit town quay pontoon is a great help if arriving at night.

Crosshaven is famous for its pubs, which all serve good food; you are spoilt for choice. There is also a good hardware store, a supermarket and a post office. There are no banking facilities – the nearest are in Cork. Next door to Salva Marine is the oldest yacht club in the world – the Royal Cork Yacht Club (RCYC), founded in 1720 – where visitors are made very welcome. If you want the extra peace and quiet, they have a number of moorings available to visitors up-river from the club.

I was invited by a friend, Dave Cush, to stay on his mooring at Drake's Pool in the Owenboy River. It is reputed that Sir Frances Drake, being pursued by a larger Spanish fleet, hid his ships in the Owenboy River to evade the enemy. Fearing they could go aground, the Spanish gave up the pursuit. It was so peaceful, although so many

All dressed up, Jalina *is blessed by a priest at Crosshaven public pontoon.*

moorings have now been put down there, there is little room left to anchor. Even when anchoring some distance from the laid moorings, on two occasions I have fouled old ground tackle and had to use my trip line to get free.

Fisherman friends

I was made very welcome by the local people during my stay at Crosshaven. I got to know many of the fisherman who all gave me a great deal of friendship. Due to bad weather I decided to pack my rucksack and take a walk to some of the recommended local beaches. I found Church

Pretty Crosshaven village with its brightly painted waterfront houses.

Bay and Weavers Point, which are popular with visitors for their sand and pebble beaches.

On the Sunday I was invited to tie up on the public pontoon next to the RNLI Station to have *Jalina* blessed with all the other local small craft. The priest shook his bottle of water twice on *Jalina*. He must have thought she would need that extra blessing – or did he know something I didn't!

Crosshaven to Glandore
Distance: 46nm
Passage time: 9hr

For several days there had been gale-force winds along the south coast of Ireland coming in from the SW so I was expecting to meet the Atlantic swell running along the coast as I departed. Offshore Atlantic gales produce a swell that adds another dimension to passage planning around Ireland. The Coastguard weather forecasts put out 'Small Craft Warnings' if the wind exceeds force 5. This amount of wind on top of the swell and the post-storm surges – plus a spring tide – can give you a good bruising.

MET EIREANN

Most harbour masters can give you a print-out of a four-day report giving wave height, direction and wind speed. These are prepared by MET Eireann. I also visited their internet site with my second-hand laptop plugged in at various pubs, cafes, and harbour offices. Usually, I just offered them a few euros for a few minutes use. This then gave me the bigger weather picture, including satellite photos, that could be added to my synoptic charts that I received via laptop and SSB radio, more of which will be detailed later.

The weather forecast was NNE backing NW force 3–5, gusting 6 at first, then 2–4 later with showers and mist patches clearing from the west. This would be the first official day for salmon fishing so a sharp lookout would be needed.

With a good wind forecast I planned to slip at 0700 as it would be slack water until 0800 with a fair tide until 1400. I wanted to be at Galley Head by 1400 for the new flood to help me into Glandore Harbour. I would be crossing two large bays – Courtmacsherry Bay and Clonakilty Bay – both of which would give a little cross tide, say, 0.3 knots pushing me to port. So to play safe I allowed only half a mile knowing it would take me below my WP off Galley Head.

For my approach to the Old Head of Kinsale, I was concerned there could be salmon nets out. With the River Bandon on the east side and the River Argideen to the west there could be salmon swimming in the area, so I decided to set a course two miles offshore to be safe.

I was early to bed and slipped out at 0715 the next morning into the thin mist. The tide would be with me until 1130. It was a sad moment leaving Crosshaven, as I was leaving many good friends whose company and humour I had enjoyed. Still, the mist soon cleared and the first notable landmark was the white lighthouse with black girdles on the Old Head of Kinsale. Throughout the day I was constantly reefing with the wind going from force 2 to force 6.

Perfect sailing waters

I saw no other yachts all day and the only voice on the VHF was the Coastguard reading weather forecasts. As I

The photo shows Adam's Island in the distance and Eve is to its right. On the chart, a bifurcation buoy (green cone with red stripe) shows that the preferred channel is to port.

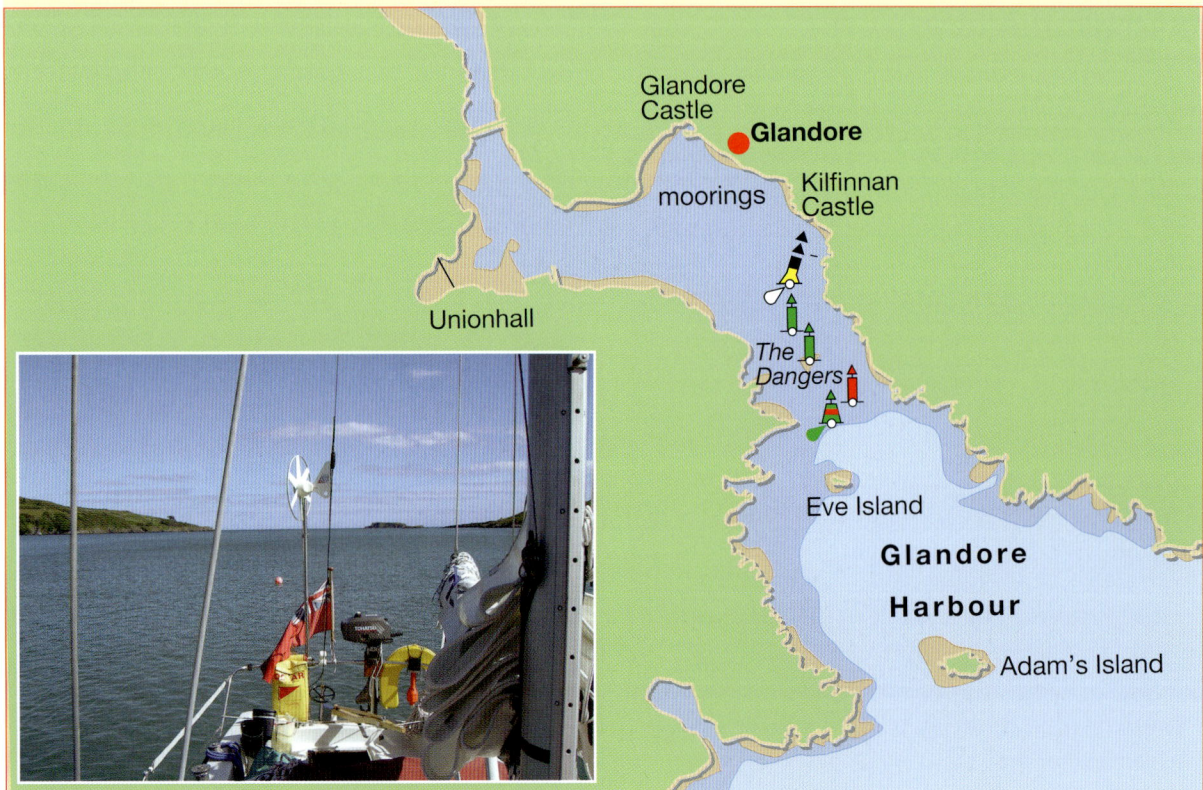

Adam's Island – Entering Glandore Harbour.

watched the flocks of wild birds, it seemed to me that these were perfect waters for sailing.

On entering Glandore Harbour, great care is needed to avoid the many rocks. The first, at the entrance, is Adam's Island standing 27m high, which divides the entrance into two channels. It's foul for one cable off its northern and eastern sides. There is a rock to the west of Eve's Island, which does not show at LW. The local saying is 'avoid Adam, hug Eve.' From here on there are a number of rocks in the centre marked with perches, a green can and a north cardinal. The Irish *Sailing Directions* has a good pilotage chart of this harbour. The scenery surrounding the bay is magnificent with vivid colours and tree-clad banks. As the sun set in the evening, the colours of the cottages reminded me of Crosshaven.

You can anchor off the cluster of visitors' moorings at Glandore. Water is available at the slip, plus showers and food at the hotel. If there is a swell coming in from the south or south-east, you can anchor in the more sheltered anchorage that is close to Union Hall. Admiralty chart 2092 shows the harbour channel to Union Hall and Glandore Harbour.

The Glandore Inn dates back to 1835 and was built by James Redmond, a local landlord who also built the present pier. Nearby there are two castles built by the Normans in 1215, which are still inhabited today. During my walk ashore I noticed the diverse flora – evidence of the Gulf Stream warming these shores.

Cruising south-west Ireland: Glandore to Dingle

On this part of the trip around the UK and Ireland *Jalina* and I started to experience the big Atlantic swells that roll in towards Eire, and we disappeared into the occasional fog bank before rolling up at the harbour of the colourful and pleasant town of Dingle which boasts 52 bars.

Glandore to Baltimore
Distance: 6nm
Passage time: 4hr

The weather forecast from Mizen Head to Roche's Point was NW variable force 2–3 going SW force 2–4 by mid-morning. The variable bit sounded more like a motoring job to me, with the wind backing first, and then picking up. I planned to slip at slack water, 0800 (HW Dover −3), knowing the fair tide would run from 0900–1300. With LW Baltimore at 1110 (springs +2 days), the new flood would then take me into Baltimore Harbour.

I rose at 0700 to be met by bright sunshine but no wind and had a pleasant breakfast of porridge with mixed dried fruit, and a glass of orange juice. With the full main and No 2 genoa prepared, I hanked on and lashed down the high-visibility orange working jib to the guard wires. Then I did my routine engine checks: oil, fuel and filters, oil level and the seawater inlet filter, alternator belt and a general

Lotti's Wife – a tall white obelisk appears on my starboard side as I approach Baltimore Harbour.

Looking towards Glandore.

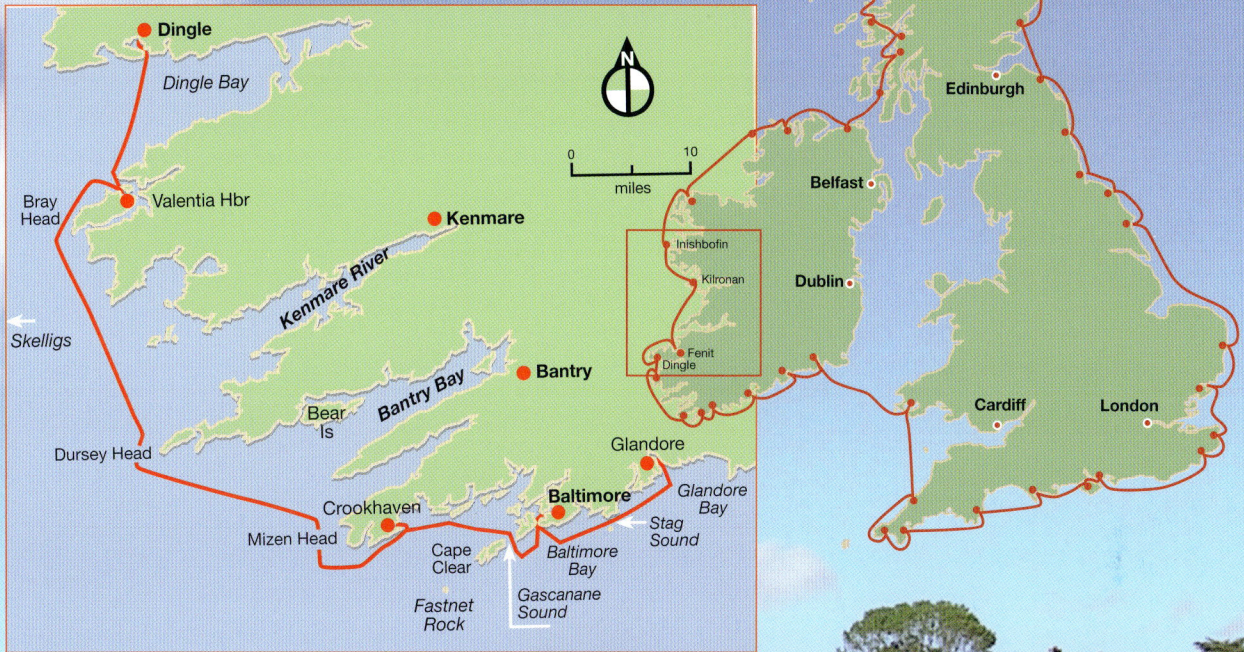

Baltimore Harbour has good shelter; it is one of my favourite harbours and has many good places to eat and drink.

check for anything loose. Also, after picking up the crab pot line on my prop off Mine Head, I regularly check the Allen bolts clamping the shaft to the universal joint.

By 0830 I had cleared the entrance and set a course to clear Low and High Island to go through Stag Sound. The sea was like deep blue glass, and the noise of the sea birds drowned out *Jalina*'s quietly purring engine.

By 1100 the wind piped up to force 2, so I hoisted the No 2 genoa. With the engine off, it was peaceful clearing Spain Point and Kedge Island, and with two miles to go I hardened up to close on the entrance to Baltimore harbour. Lotti's Wife, a tall white obelisk, stands high on Beacon Point to starboard. This coastline looked magnificent with warm sunshine to heighten the colours – the bright blue of the sea joins shades of brown and green on the land, with

wisps of white caps against a bold blue sky – truly a painter's paradise.

Pilotage

Enter the harbour between Barrack and Beacon Points keeping fairly close to the first green can, off Loo Rock, to avoid Quarry Rock. Steer N towards Lousy Rocks south cardinal, until Baltimore quays come into sight. Chart BA3725 identifies the many other rocks in the harbour.

At Baltimore there is a trot of eight visitors' moorings NE of Coney Island. Showers are available at the one hotel and at the Baltimore Sailing Club (when open). Water is available at the north pier and there's chandlery, gas, diesel and petrol. There's also a post office, a small supermarket, restaurants and pubs.

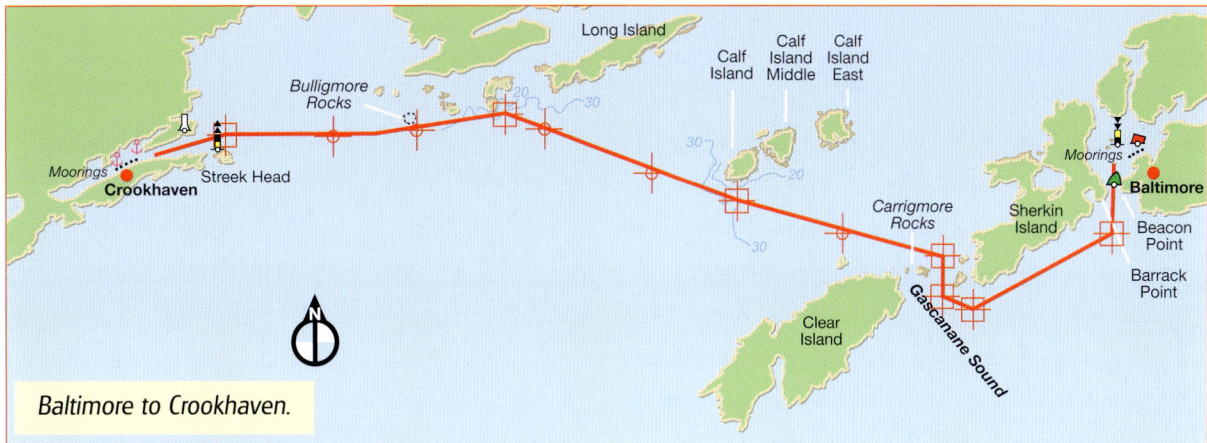

Baltimore to Crookhaven.

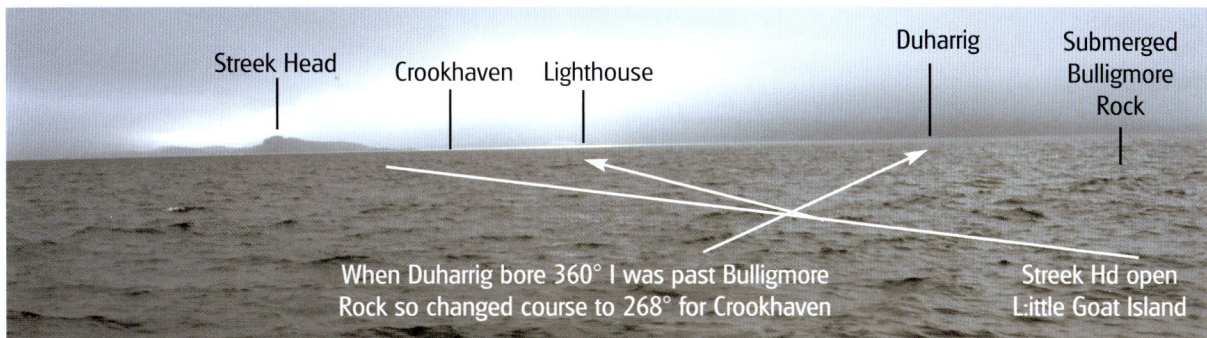

The visibility was good enough to use traditional navigation on the approach.

Baltimore to Crookhaven
Distance 16nm
Passage time: 3.5hr

This passage would involve either the longer route to go round Cape Clear, or the shorter route through the narrow Gascanane Sound – although salmon nets had been reported in the area. With a warm and cold front approaching, the weather forecast gave winds SSW force 4–5 veering W force 3–5, showers and fog patches. That meant I would make my final route decision when close to the sound – my immediate concern was the possibility of fog. I rose at 0500 but there was thick fog in the harbour. At 0845 it would be slack water and then a fair two-knot tide would take me through the sound – but now the precipitation from the fog was so heavy it felt more like rain. With all the charts and WPs prepared, clearing lines plotted onto the charts, sandwiches and flask of hot soup made – I had to sit and wait.

As a precaution I also loaded the WPs into my spare Garmin 72 handheld GPS. At 0930 there was still thick fog, so I checked the Navtex weather reports, called the Coastguard for an update and at 1201 I took down the shipping forecast from my NASA SSB receiver to get an accurate position of any approaching fronts. I also worked out the depths of tide for each hour of my intended passage in case I needed another means of confirming my position en route. The fog started to lift at 1500, so I hoisted the main and sailed off the mooring, leaving Barrack Point to starboard. It was one day off springs; slack water was 1445, after which the tide would turn foul.

Navigation test
As I approached Gascanane Sound, I must admit to taking a perverse pleasure in deciding to go that way to test myself, and my navigation.

I was under sail – in order to avoid the prop snagging nets – with two knots of foul tide and visibility of one mile. But pilot books had not warned me that the overfalls would be rough! Safely through, I set a course to cross Long Island Bay to Crookhaven. Here the tide seemed to go slack and the visibility went down to less than 200m. As I did not want to rely entirely on my GPS I set a course to clear west of Calf Island to pick up the 30m and 20m depth contour. I often position waypoints on charted contours as a double check.

Within the hour, visibility was down, and by 1730 I had

picked out Calf Island and my depth sounder confirmed my approximate position. The fog was lifting, but I couldn't get complacent, as it can come down with a vengeance when the sun sets and the day cools off. The coming and going of fog plays tricks with your sense of distance, as you see rocks and headlands that are not there, and my glasses were a pain as I had to keep wiping off the heavy dew.

A contour line (and waypoint) off Little Goat Island gave me a position to shape a course to avoid the submerged Bulligmore Rock. Keeping Streek Head 'open' south of Little Goat Island, I would clear Bulligmore Rock, and once Duharrig bore due north I knew I was well past the danger.

My next mark, Crookhaven lighthouse, showed up well with its white tower looking quite magnificent. By 1945 I had picked up one of the many vacant moorings in this beautiful harbour and the fog had cleared.

I was pleased with the day's passage, and although I had used the GPS to confirm my EPs (estimated positions), the practice of using both helped me avoid making too many mistakes.

Once inside the harbour at Crookhaven there are eight yellow visitors' moorings and ten bright red ones. If anchoring, beware of weed and shellfish beds to the north and east of Granny Island. O'Sullivan's Bar serves good meals, diesel is available and there is a bank in Schull.

Crookhaven to Valentia

Distance 54nm

Passage time: 11hr

This passage would take me out into the Atlantic swell so I needed to play safe and go when there was reasonable visibility. It would be foolhardy to make for either Bear Island at 11 miles, or Valentia Harbour at 54 miles in thick fog. Again I would work up my plans to go either way and make a decision when I rounded Mizen Head. I had a number of navigation and safety points to consider. The

ABANDONED YACHT

At 0810 Valentia coastguard broadcast a message about an abandoned yacht found with its engine running! I radioed to give my position, and was asked to keep a listening watch. At 0830 The Baltimore Lifeboat was launched to search for the mystery boat's skipper – this west coast with its Atlantic swell suddenly seemed a lonely place. I looked down at my two point safety harness and gave it a quick tug just to confirm I was clipped on. I always wear my lifejacket when underway, and also carry a spare, but I did reach down and put my portable VHF into my pocket – 'what if' I thought!

entrance to Valentia is only 300m (1.5 cables) wide, with rocks gradually sloping on either side of the channel. I had experienced similar entrances, where the swell ran up against the rocks and created so much mist that the leading marks were hidden. So, as usual, I prepared pre-plotted bearings to lead me down each leg into the harbour. I also plotted a WP where the bearings cross, so as I approached, I could compare the GPS highway to the ship's heading, to show up any tidal influences.

The weather forecast for the passage was for winds WSW force 4–5, with rain, drizzle, fog and poor visibility – and the following 24 hrs were forecast the same. I decided to catch up with my washing, clean *Jalina* and get an early night. The 1901 forecast was WSW force 3–4 becoming variable force 2–3, with fog patches and an approaching anticyclone. With that wind I could just fetch Durnsey Head and bear away for Bray Head on Valentia Island – any further west and I would be beating up to Durnsey Head.

Next day, at 0430, there was no wind, but the fog had

Crookhaven – O'Sullivan's bar is the second building from the left.

Crookhaven at sunrise.

Pilot lookout

Fort Pt
Lighthouse

Rocks
breaking sea

WP Fort

167°C

148°C   097°C

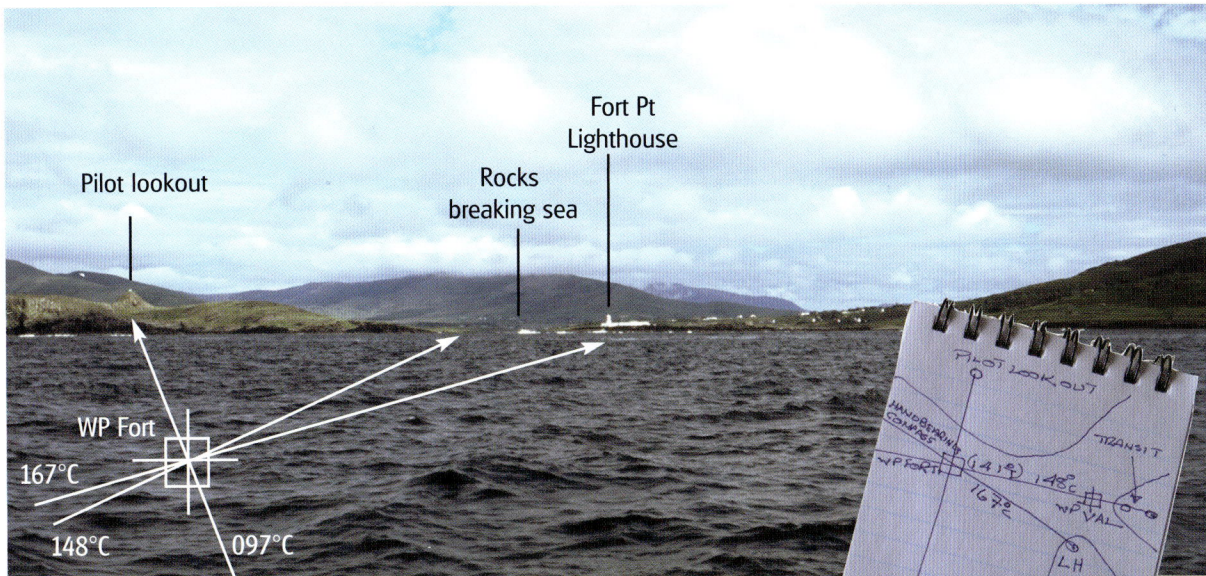

VALENTIA PILOTAGE APPROACH PLAN
From WP 'Guard' I sailed on 097°C towards Pilot lookout until the lighthouse bore 167°C. These two bearings met at WP 'Fort' to confirm the position, and the GPS highway assisted my approach. Once the lighthouse bearing and the WP positions were confirmed, I changed to the leading bearing of 148°C. To help locate the transit leading marks I put a WP 'Val' on the leading line. Again I was able to check my heading against the GPS highway for any tidal eddies that may have been pushing me off course. And if the visibility had deteriorated I would still have got in safely.

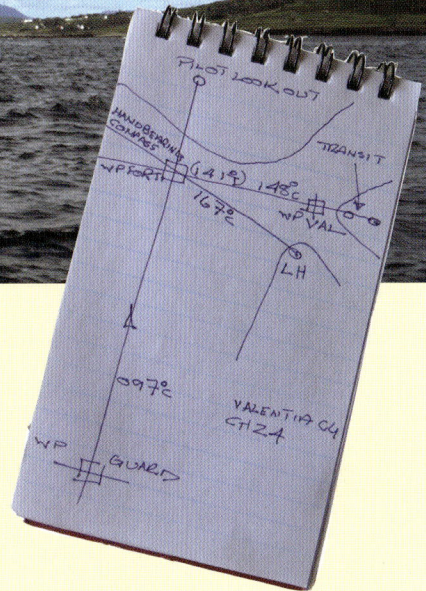

This is my pilotage plan that I keep in the cockpit.

lifted to the hilltops. I slipped at 0600, and as the visibility at Mizen Head was over two miles, I decided to go for Valentia. I called the coastguard and after all the usual questions, they asked 'have you entered Valentia before?' and then kindly gave me entry instructions and where to pick up a mooring – what a service!

The sky was grey, and the lack of ripples on the water made it difficult to pick out the horizon. *Jalina* purred away under engine and autopilot, so I decided to cook breakfast underway: boiled egg, marmalade on toast with a hot mug of tea – mmm! By 1200 the high rocks of the Skelligs could be seen to the NW with many hundreds of puffins diving below the surface to catch fish.

As I approached Valentia there was a deep Atlantic swell running and the wind had picked up. I was sailing under full main and jib with the engine ticking over just in case the wind dropped as I rounded the headland.

Once in, I picked up a visitor's moorings to the north of Knight's Town, close to the lifeboat. I signed off with the Coastguard and settled down to enjoy the evening sun,

with sea birds calling all around. The clouds looked menacingly dark but the sun shone, highlighting this magnificent harbour's breathtaking views. Even a long-abandoned Russian ship looked attractive with its red rusting hull. There are six visitors' moorings at Knight's Town where there is also a boatyard, a mechanic, petrol and diesel, gas, a bar, some shops and a laundrette. The nearest bank is at Chersiveen, three miles away.

Valentia to Dingle
Distance: 14nm
Passage time: 3.5hr

This would be a short passage to clear Doulus Head and cross Dingle Bay. Once clear of Valentia Harbour, the problem was Crow Rock just south of Reenbeg Point to the west of the entrance to Dingle harbour. With my chart prepared and WPs loaded, I signed on with Valentia Coastguard. OK, I know it's only a short distance, but I feel

Dingle's colourful mainstreet.

that keeping in touch with the Coastguard maintains continuity, reassures them about a small boat on passage, and they do impart a wealth of local knowledge.

At 0915 I was clear of the entrance, using bearings from the previous day. As I cleared Doulus Head I could make out the notorious Great Blaskets Islands and Blasket Sound, where I would be going after Dingle.

We soon closed Dingle harbour with its brightly coloured houses and well-maintained fishing fleet. In the marina I was met by the harbour master, who kindly took my lines, and invited me to a barbecue at the local yacht club.

For yachtsmen, Dingle has water, diesel (cans), gas, pubs, supermarkets, banks, laundrette, mechanical engineering facilities, rail and bus connections. The town is a 'must' to visit with no less than 52 licenced pubs and colourful shops, all surrounded by magnificent green hills and mountains.

The fishing fleet in Dingle harbour.

Cruising the Irish west coast: Dingle to Inishbofin

The white windmill near Tralee is well worth a vist.

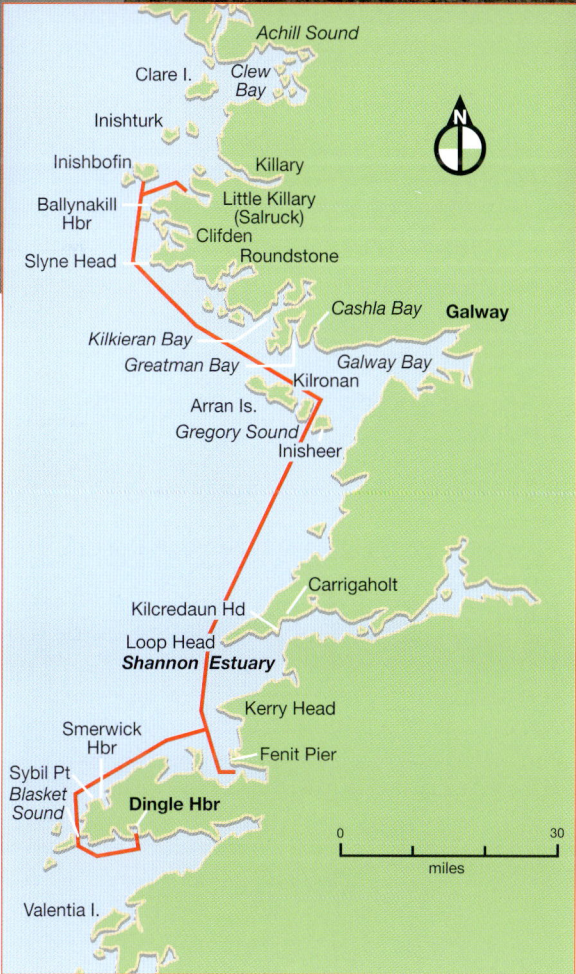

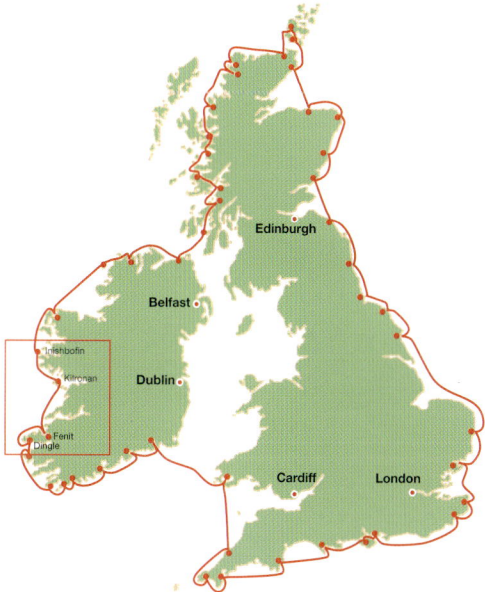

Buoyed by the success of my previous few legs from Glandore to Dingle, I was full of confidence and impatient for the next couple of passages. I love the challenge of sailing *Jalina* in rough weather, however I also take pride in being safe and practicing good seamanship – which occasionally leaves me facing a dilemma. The west Coast of Ireland is one of the most exposed sailing areas bearing the brunt of a full fetch of the Atlantic swell mixed with the unpredictable flow of the Shannon, Irelands biggest river.

Dingle to Fenit via the Blasket Sound

Distance: 41nm

Passage time: 8hr

This passage can be quite tricky, as you have to go through the Blasket Sound and clear the Marrharees to get to Fenit in the Shannon Estuary. The tides here can be dangerous, there are masses of rocks to focus the mind, and bearings become difficult if the mist obscures the tops of the mountains. I planned an eight-hour daylight passage, going through the sound on the last of the flood. The tide turned south at the Blaskets at 0840 (HW Dover +5), so I slipped lines at 0420 and crept along the dredged channel guided by the two leading lights (Oc 3s bearing 182°). Once clear of Dingle Harbour I took care to avoid Crow Rock, half a mile off Reenbeg Point.

The weather was grey and overcast with fog patches; winds SSW force 2–3. Once clear of Crow Rock, I set a course for Slea Head, then to WP 'Carr' off Great Blasket

Early morning sunrise over Little Sampshire Island and the sheltered waters of Tralee Bay.

Island. From there I sailed along a transit of the summit of Sybil Point in line with Clogher Rock (bearing 015°T), until I reached WP 'Dunn' at 0700. I then set a course to clear Sybil Point arriving there at 0720, an hour ahead of the tide turning south.

A number of ships from the Spanish Armada of 1588 came to grief among these dangerous rocks, but this dogleg keeps you clear of the ones north of Great Blasket Island. I also kept well clear of Brandon Point to avoid any salmon nets. The final obstacle was a group of rocks called the Marrharees. In good visibility, you can sail through them, but with the mist coming and going I decided to keep well clear to the north.

There was very little tide in Tralee Bay and I arrived in Fenit at 1215. The harbour master, local RNLI secretary and the local sailing club gave me a warm welcome. More visitors' pontoon berths were being fitted while I was there and the harbour master provided five-day weather and

I had to keep an eye on the rocks, as the tide was crabbing us sideways through Blasket Sound

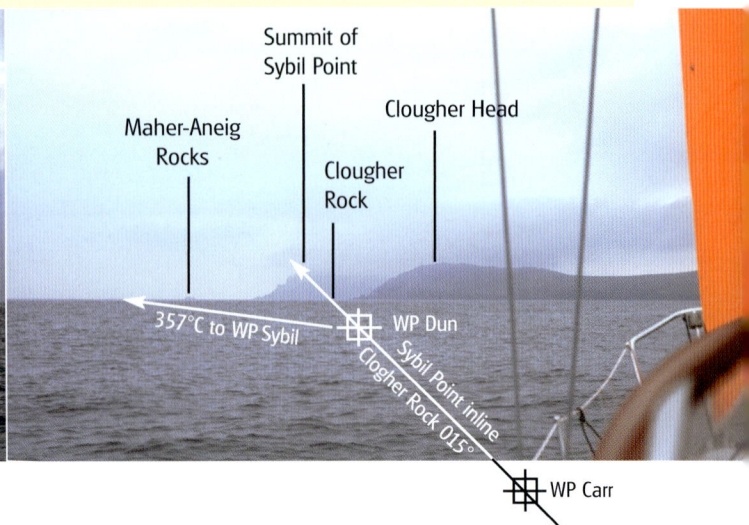

wave height reports. Other first class facilities at the marina include showers, washing machines, dryers, fresh water, power and diesel.

The food at the West End restaurant is excellent, going down well with a good pint of Murphy's. Fenit has a fine golf course, and the white windmill at Blennerville near Tralee is well worth a visit. It is here that the replica of the *Jeanie Johnston*, a 19th century sailing ship that took potato famine immigrants to America, was built and launched.

Fenit to Kilronan Inishmore
Distance: 22nm
Passage tine: 4hr

The weather had deteriorated so I stayed in Fenit Harbour for several days. The forecast then was WSW force 4–6 coupled with a small craft warning, as the wind was in excess of force 5.

I slipped at 0430, a little concerned about the earlier SW gales that had been blowing into the Shannon. This would mean there would be some tidal surge coming back out of the river, giving bumpy wind against tide conditions. The harbour master suggested I wait another day, but as it was only going to be force 4–6. I decided to give it a try. The wave and swell height print-outs from MET Eireann also showed a reduction, But I had not allowed for the large surge coming out from the Shannon.

I soon realised the 4m Atlantic swell running at an angle to the waves created such confused seas that it was almost as dangerous to abort as to go on. The swell up ahead was something to behold. The sails were flapping uselessly in the troughs and overpowering her on the crests. I needed to tack around, rather than gybe, to prevent possible damage to the rig, so I had the engine ticking over just in case her head would not come round fast enough. I turned through the wind, but before *Jalina* could pick up speed, several waves came breaking over her. The force smashed me into the cockpit bulkhead. My hands buckled as I attempted to break my fall, letting my face hit something solid. There was blood everywhere!

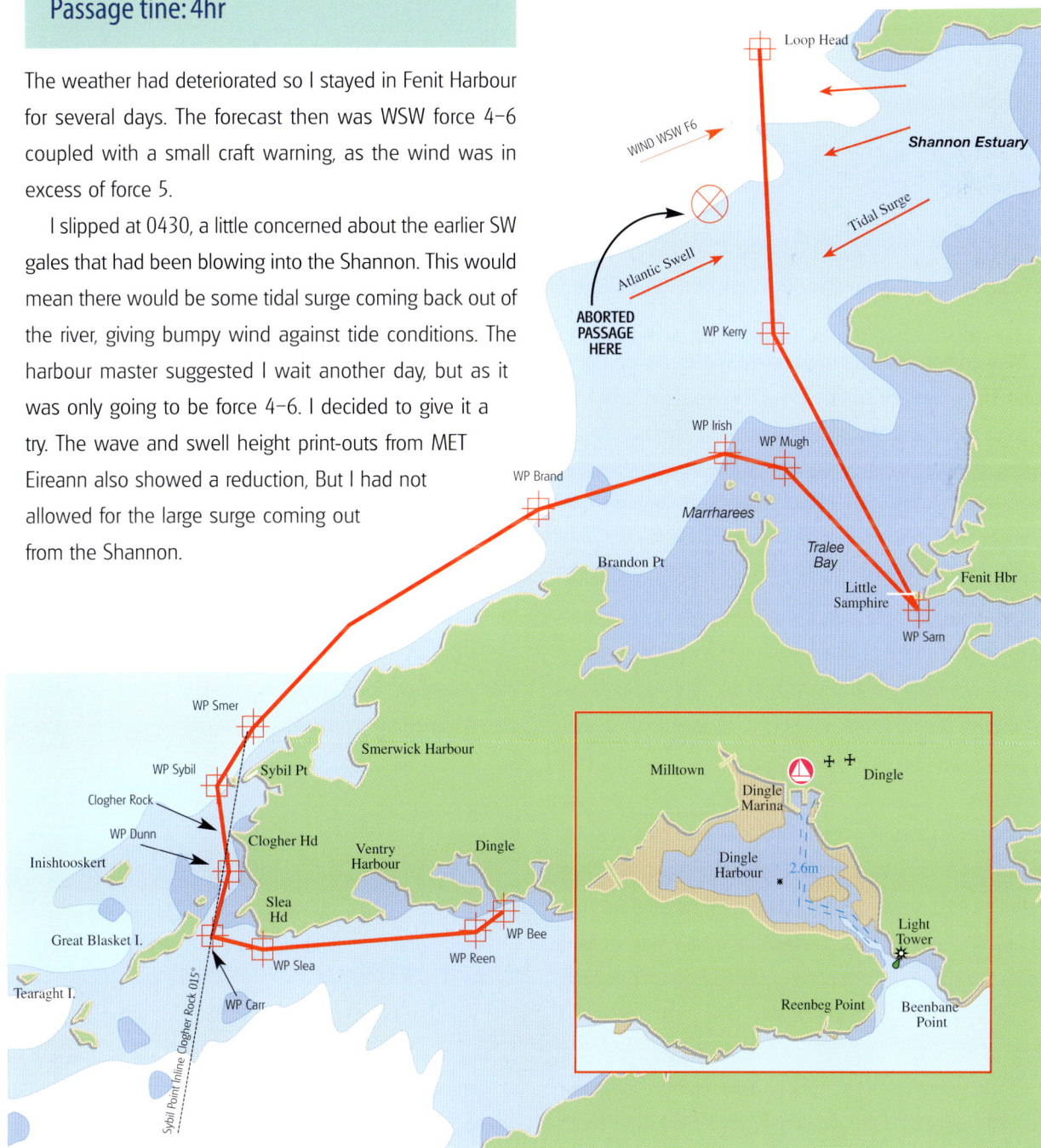

Fenit Harbour marine office and showers are in the left-hand grey-roofed building.

With no-one at the helm *Jalina* slowed and came up to wind. Then I was thrown to port where my groin smashed into the winch with the force of a hammer. I am convinced that without my harness I would have gone over the side. I was now in some pain. My hands felt as if someone had cut them off, my face was running with blood and my groin felt as if it had been kicked by a mule! I quickly slammed the engine into gear, pulled the helm over and ducked down below the cockpit coaming just as another heavy wave broke over me, I was now in full control, riding the swell at over nine knots, a very exciting speed! *Jalina* was in good order and once again she was pulling me out of a deep hole.

One thing for sure – adrenaline does not come with an off switch! Soon I was within Marrharees again, heading back to a safe, sheltered Fenit Harbour. My mistake was not to use the engine before I tacked because I was worried about straining her. With power I would have got through the crest more easily and been able to run with the swells. Once alongside, I soaked my wrists in ice cold water but they had gone several shades of black and the left hand was hurting badly. The pain in my groin eased, but I could

feel a lump and the area was bruising rapidly. I put on my wet suit, packed with a pad of cotton wool, to act as a truss. The tight support felt much better, so I wrapped all the areas with bandages and Duck tape.

I should really have seen a doctor, but as I could deal with the pain and I thought nothing was broken, I decided to leave it a few days. Some weeks later, however, a doctor found I had actually fractured a couple of bones in my hand. But at least I had learned some good lessons – always listen to local knowledge and never underestimate the combined power of wind, tidal surge and Atlantic swell.

Fenit to Kilronan Inishmore
(second attempt)
Distance: 60nm
Passage time: 12hr

The weather forecast was WNW force 3–4 backing SW force 5–6 with showers and a small craft warning (winds exceeding force 5). For a full flood tide to take me north I would have to depart about midnight or midday. But I

Kilrohan Harbour taken from the wool market.

wanted to sail the passage in daylight – so as it was neaps, I decided to slip at 0530 to clear Loop Head between HW Dover –1 and HW Dover +1. At Dover HW, the stronger foul tide would set in off Loop Head, but once round, I could close the coast to find slacker water. The fair tide would start at HW Dover +4.

This time all went well. The tide was later at the mouth of the Shannon, the build up and outflow of water had eased and the Atlantic swell had died down a little. I cleared the Shannon Estuary at Loop Head by 0830, and with winds WSW force 2–3 throughout the day the remainder of the passage went well. As we closed on Gregory Sound between Inishmore and Inishman I noticed three wind generators close to the shore – but had not seen a Notice to Mariners' update on the UKHO website. I arrived at Kilronan Harbour at 1740 feeling very bruised indeed.

There are a number of visitors' moorings just south of the piers, and anchoring is not advisable in winds NW, N or E. You can fill up with water from a tap on the main pier, but you will need a pliers to get the tap to turn. Fog and high winds forced me to stay a whole week, and made the mooring a bit lumpy. I still wore my wet suit taped up with Duck tape and my ribs were very painful. I found I could not grip properly with my left hand where the bruising was now black and yellow!

Kilronan Harbour is well sheltered in all but strong north-west to easterly winds, so I had prepared a passage plan to shelter in Cashla Bay seven miles to the north if the wind was forecast from that direction. The Arran Islanders are really friendly and true men of the sea. Here you can go back in time with pony-and-trap rides, eat at good restaurants, walk golden beaches, or just sit outside a pub with a nice pint of Murphy's. The local supermarket has all the stores you may need, there is diesel at the local garage and even an internet café located in the local gift shop and museum.

Kilronan (Killeany Bay) to Inishbofin
Distance: 52nm
Passage time: 14hr

The weather report was NW force 4–5; gusty with showers. After reporting to the Coastguard with my passage plan, I slipped my lines at 0440. The first danger on clearing Killeany Bay is Bar Rock, to the west of the entrance. I then set a course for Slyne Head 30 miles to the NW. The flood

Weather planning

Offshore Atlantic gales produce a swell that adds another dimension to passage planning around Ireland. The Coastguard weather forecasts will put out 'Small Craft Warnings' if the wind exceeds force 5. This much wind on top of the swell and the post-storm surges – plus a spring tide – can give you a good bruising. Most harbour masters can give you a print-out of a four-day report giving wave height, direction and wind speed. These are prepared by MET Eireann via their 'Weatherdial' fax service on tel: 1570 131 838 charged at €1.27 per minute.

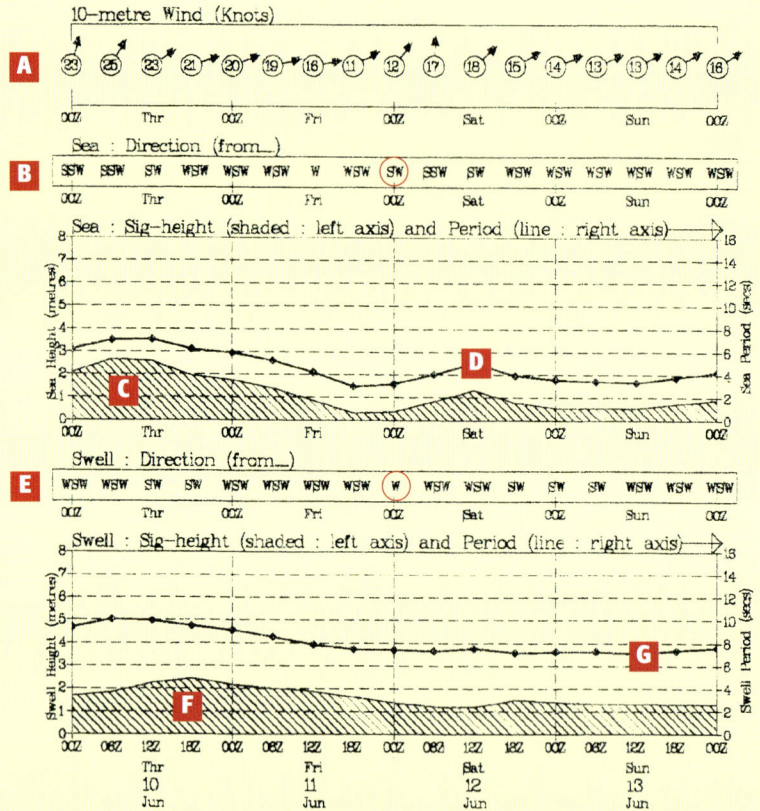

A Weatherdial fax: four-day forecast for 10-13 June 2004

Key

A Wind speed and direction

B Sea direction (wind driven waves)

C Sea (wave) height in metres

D Sea period in seconds (wave frequency)

E Swell direction (Notice that at midnight on Friday the waves are from the SW and the swell is from the W)

F Swell height in metres

G Swell period in seconds

The approach to Inishbofin is clearly marked with transit white towers.

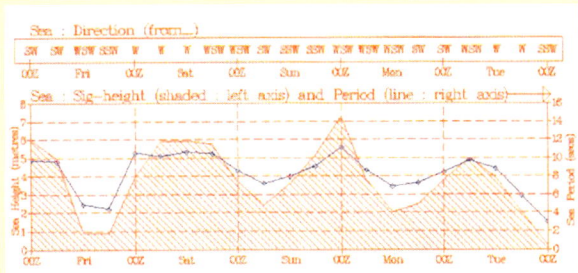

This red *Weatherdial* graph shows a rougher picture with 7m seas!

Buoy	Time	Location	Press	Wind Direction	Wind Speed	Temp	Dew Point	Humidity	Wave Period	Wave Height	Sea Temp
	GMT		hPa	o	Kts	°C	°C	%	sec	m	°C
M1 62090	7 Jan 10:00	53° 8'N 11° 12'W	1005.6	n/a	n/a	9.9	n/a	n/a	10	13.3	n/a
M2 62091	7 Jan 10:00	53° 28'N 5° 26'W	1007.4	210	24	11.7	10.0	89	7	2.7	10.1
M3 62092	7 Jan 10:00	51° 13'N 10° 33'W	1010.0	210	29 gust 43	11.1	9.9	92	9	6.7	10.9
M4 62093	7 Jan 10:00	54° 40'N 9° 4'W	1003.0	230	19 gust 35	10.6	8.5	87	9	3.7	9.5
M5 62094	7 Jan 10:00	51° 41'N 6° 42'W	1014.2	220	31 gust 47	11.2	10.4	95	8	4.5	n/a
Marathon 62023	7 Jan 9:00	51° 24'N 7° 54'W	1012.9	220	41	11.3	n/a	n/a	7	5.1	n/a

Met Éireann's Sea Area Forecast Map

Weather on the web

I also visited MET Eireann's Internet site www.met.ir with my second-hand laptop plugged in at various pubs, cafes and harbour offices. Usually, I offered them a few euros for a few minutes use. This then gave me the bigger weather picture, including data from weather buoys around the coast and satellite photos, that could be added to my synoptic charts that I received via laptop and SSB radio

had just started Dover HW +4 and I wanted to clear Slyne Head by 1100 when I would meet the first of the ebb at Dover HW −3. I would then close into Clifden Bay to avoid the worst of the tide. But when I was tacking out of Clifden Bay and closing on Inishbofin I noticed the sun's shadow move quickly across the chart table – my heading was changing. The autopilot was behaving erratically and doing its best to head me straight towards some rocks. So I had to rely on (damaged) hand-helming for the remainder of the passage.

By 1800, HW Dover +4, the tide had turned in my favour. On average, I found the tides on the West Coast ranged from half to one and a half knots, but on headlands you can expect up to three knots or more.

The passage went well and as there was very little ground swell I decided to make my overnight stop at Inishbofin. This is a small Island where Oliver Cromwell built a fort. It has good shelter but care is needed to avoid the rocks near the entrance. If there had been too much swell I would have gone to Clifden. Being spring tides +2 days my LW depth above chart datum was increasing each day, so being LW, I allowed that little extra depth then anchored in 2.5m. Anchoring was a problem as there was a great deal of kelp on the sea bottom. I moved east of the ferry pier, and I finally succeeded on the third attempt.

I would have liked to explore this beautiful island, but with good weather holding I needed to be on my way, because another gale was forecast within 24 hours.

North-west Ireland: Inishbofin to Portrush

Loch Swilly
Malin Head
Sheephaven
Bloody Foreland
Portrush
Torneady Pt
Stag Rocks
Loch Foyle
Aranmore I
Rosses Bay
Donegal Hbr
Donegal Bay
Sligo Bay
Broad Haven
Belmullet
Blacksod Bay
Achill Head
Clare I
Inishturk
Killary
Inishbofin
Edinburgh
Portrush
Belfast
miles
Inishbofin
Dublin
Cardiff
London

When Jalina (with red boom cover, far right) is tucked up safely, as here in Portrush, I can get on with making some good grub.

NORTH-WEST IRELAND: INISHBOFIN TO PORTRUSH 75

During the final part of my cruise up the west coast of Ireland I had some exhilarating sailing and discovered that the tidal stream atlases can be a little out. Off Malin Head, according to my GPS I covered four miles in 15 minutes – that's 16 knots over the ground!

Inishbofin to Broad Haven
Distance: 60nm
Passage time: 12hr

I rose at 0300 to take advantage of the tides, had a good breakfast and then signed on with the Coastguard with my passage plan. I weighed anchor at 0445 (HW Dover +3hr)

as I needed daylight to see the two white towers, in transit, to guide me out of the harbour. It was slack water and then I got a full period of fair tide to clear Achill Head. During the passage I called up *Merinda*, an Ocean Cat that had previously crossed the Atlantic – it was great to have some company. I also tuned into Northwood to get an update on the approaching gale and a synoptic chart on my laptop.

The ebb tide started here at 1200 (HW Dover −2hr) so I cleared Achill Head by 1230 and got about one knot of tide against me until I reached Broad Haven. As I was following the foul and fair tide with my rhumb line, I could log this easily, as it was the difference between my GPS and speed log. We entered Broad Haven at 1630 picking up a mooring adjacent to *Merinda* by 1700.

There are four moorings south of Inver Point, four south of Ballyglass Point and three south of the pier close to the lifeboat – all capable of taking up to 15 tonnes.

Mooring up for a gale
Getting a good weather forecast and synoptic chart not only confirmed that the gale would hit in the night but also said that it would change direction from NE to N then NW.

Secure mooring for a gale.

Mooring tip

When mooring I always assume there is no pick up strop and therefore run a line from the bow, outside the stanchions and rigging, to the cockpit. I also release the guard wires, on that side, so I can easily reach the mooring buoy eye with the boat hook. When it is within reach I thread the line through the eye, keep it tensioned, and give *Jalina* a little nudge astern with the engine. The buoy will run along the line to the bow as I go into neutral.

When the buoy is abeam I walk forward and thread the line through a fairlead and secure it to a cleat. This then enables me to shackle on a heavy chain strop, which in turn is shackled to two lines with hard eyes (metal thimbles). These lines are 14mm shore lines, which are long enough to reach the aft cleats for extra security. The original long line is left on the buoy, but kept slack, to act as a recovery line. This lets me winch the boat forward to check up on the chain and shackles. Where the lines go through fairleads I pad or 'parcel' them with heavy canvas, which has a short line sewn onto each end. This light line is threaded through the lay of the heavy line to lock it in place. I use two separate shackles for each mooring line, to allow each line to be serviced separately and also mouse each shackle with stainless steel wire.

Mooring for a gale

1 When the buoy is within reach I thread the line through the eye
2 I keep it tight and give *Jalina* a little nudge astern with the engine. The buoy will run along the line to the bow.
3 When the buoy is abeam I walk forward and thread the line through a fairlead and secure it to a cleat
4 Heavy weather mooring:
   A – Chain, B – Recovery line,
   C – Lines led aft, D – Parcelling

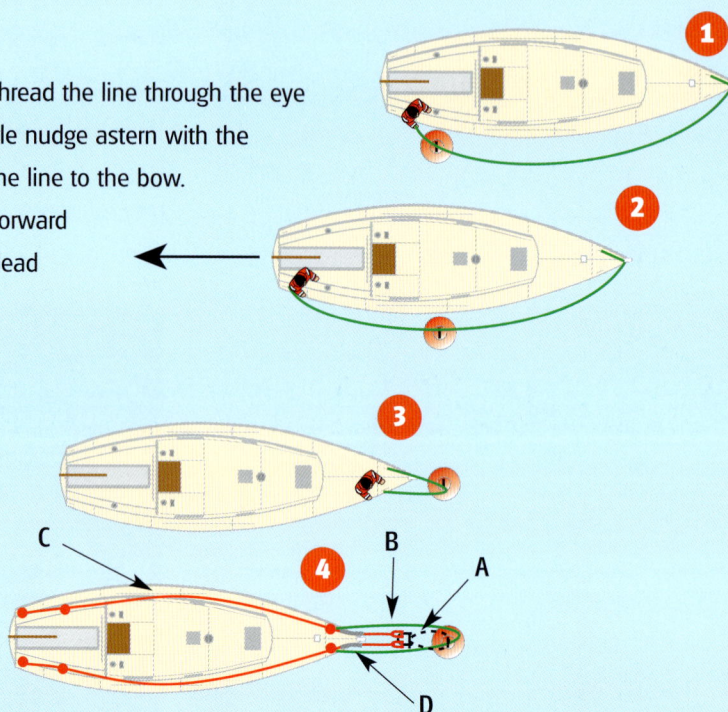

The gales came

Gale force winds blew for seven days and at times I was subjected to force 9 coming straight down the Haven on to the mooring. This was coupled with a deep swell which made it difficult to move about on the boat. When one of the gales eased, Joe the RNLI mechanic for Broad Haven Lifeboat came over to see how we were coping. I normally carry quite a reserve of supplies but I was running low on water and food. The nearest shop was six miles away so he kindly organised supplies for *Jalina* and *Merinda*. There is now a dredged buoyed channel constructed from Broad Haven to Belmullet.

The main problem on this coast is the big Atlantic swell with waves on top of it – so the Coastguard put out two levels of weather warnings; gale warnings and small craft warnings.

Broad Haven Harbour in a gale.

Broad Haven to Aranmore
Distance: 76nm
Passage time 13hr

The weather forecast was SW force 5, gusty veering W force 4–5 to force 6–7 overnight. So I prepared *Jalina* for the long passage to Aranmore – without the use of my Simrad autopilot which was not working. I called the Coastguard at 0400 for an update and they said the wind would reduce later in the day but there was still a small craft warning out. I decided to have a go, as the wind would be aft of my port beam.

With three reefs in the main and my high visibility orange working jib hoisted, I slipped my mooring in Broad Haven at 0600 (HW Dover –2hr). The wind was quite strong force 6–7. I knew it would be a tough passage. I often have to curb my frustration and force myself not to sail, but seven days of gales with another coming meant this was likely to be my best opportunity to get away. Once clear of the Haven I set a course for Aranmore on a good rhumb-line fetch. During the day *Jalina* and I had to contend with squalls, hailstones and driving rain, visibility that kept coming and going, and with the odd lump of sea that came over the stern. With no autopilot I had to jury rig the helm. I also had a bit of bad luck by being thrown and hitting my head against the reefing horns on the boom.

I made no allowance for the tide, as it would run fair and foul along my rhumb line, but I definitely wanted to arrive at the shallows near Aranmore in a wind-with-tide scenario to reduce the swell. By 1700 (HW Dover –3hr) the tide was slack. I spotted Aranmore Island but the swell was building as I closed the shoaling water near Torneady Point. The swell got steeper and as I went from a reach to a broad reach, the wind eased to force 5.

Drogue at the ready
But I needed to speed up *Jalina* to avoid being pooped and to keep steerageway. In these big seas I had my drogue ready, with a trip line, to slow the boat and keep my stern down.

Drogue tip

The theory is that with the drogue streamed to slow me down, if I'm only doing the same speed as the surf or swell, I'll lose steerage. So to correct her heading I just need to trip the drogue, then correct the helm and release the trip, I have practised this while dinghy sailing in Cyprus. When running towards shore in big surf, I used to fit a drogue with several bights in the line. To correct the heading I'd release a peg and let out about 4m of line. On one occasion, the drogue parted and I pitch-poled in the surf up the beach! It is important that the drogue is of a suitable size for your yacht and the main warp should keep it within the second swell astern.

I find the drogue works best if I can keep it in the second swell astern.

On the Aran Road

Luckily I did not need my drogue. But as it would be awkward to shake out a reef in these big seas, I started up the engine to give her the extra speed. I was then able to ride the tops of the swell and maintain steerageway. By 1830 we rounded Torneady Point and entered Rosses Bay. The flat calm of the sheltered bay was an anticlimax after riding the big seas throughout the passage. *Jalina* and I were encrusted with salt from the spray and feeling very wet indeed. We continued on to Aran Road, a sheltered anchorage east of the Island.

The visitors' moorings here have been removed, so I picked up a free fisherman's mooring – but as another gale was approaching, I fitted my heavy-duty mooring chain, made fast my lines and also set my main anchor, as I was not sure of the mooring's integrity.

For the passage we had averaged 5.8 knots, and at one point *Jalina* touched 9.8 knots. I felt very tired after the 76 mile passage and a little bruised, so I decided to get a hot meal and go to bed early – the black areas of bruising from my previous injuries had now turned yellow and I appeared to be on the mend.

Leabgarrow, the small village off Aran Road, has a small store and Post Office *bureau de change*. There are several pubs that serve food, and water is available at the slip near the obelisk. But for diesel you have to go by ferry to nearby Burtonport, which costs €10 for a return ticket.

Aranmore to Sheep Haven
Distance: 33nm
Passage time: 6hr

With one day before springs I could expect much stronger tides – so planning had to be done with care. Originally, I had pencilled in my arrival at Aranmore and Sheep Haven as being earlier, giving me a window of 14 days to round Malin Head and reach Portrush. From Rosses Bay I set a course to clear Stag Rocks and go through Gola North Sound, clearing Inishsirrer for Bloody Foreland. I decided to prepare for an early departure, so I made a casserole using some wonderful fresh Dunglow pork. I added two onions, carrots, parsnips, swede, and one tin of Scotch broth. It was topped with sliced potatoes, grated cheese and sprinkle of mixed herbs. It cooked for two-and-a-half hours at setting six on my Plastimo oven (turning every round 30 minutes to cook evenly) and provided two good hot meals and saved me cooking when I reached Sheep Haven.

The wind was still blowing and the Coastguard said the new area forecast would be issued after midday and they could lift the small craft warning. Before departure I called the Coastguard for an update, as there had been a number of gale warnings, plus a number of severe squalls. I slipped my lines at 1350 and as I cleared the shelter of Aranmore I met the swell coming in from the Atlantic.

With a strong fair wind from the west. Slack water at 1500 (HW Dover +3hr) and a fair tide to take me down to Sheep Haven, things were looking up – the blessing *Jalina* got at Crosshaven was kicking in. It was a sunny day with a good wind on the beam and fair tide so the passage was uneventful. By 2030 we were tucked up in Downies Bay, Sheep Haven.

Sheep Haven to Portrush
Distance: 53nm
Passage time: 8.5hr

The weather forecast was good: W force 4–5 veering NW to W force 2–4 occasionally force 6, with scattered showers. I was looking forward to seeing Malin Head with my own eyes, after hearing about it for so many years on the shipping forecasts. It was a tricky passage to plan, being the top of the spring tides. I needed to clear Malin Head by 1000 (HW Dover –3hr) and be in Portrush by 1330 (HW Dover).

The new ebb tide divides at Malin Head so once I was there it would sweep me down to Portrush. I would need to depart Sheep Haven at 0430 and make an average of 5.8 knots. If I were to be late into Portrush I would be met by the very strong foul tide coming north from around the east of Ireland.

I also prepared some tidal vectors to allow for different strengths of current coming out of Lough Swilly and Lough Foyle. On the day, with all the earlier rainfall, there must have been nearly four knots coming out of Lough Swilly and the water was brown. All along this coast I noticed that the tide was running much faster than the tidal atlas predicted.

As I cleared Malin Head I did four miles in 15 minutes – as I mentioned earlier that's 16 knots over the ground, so

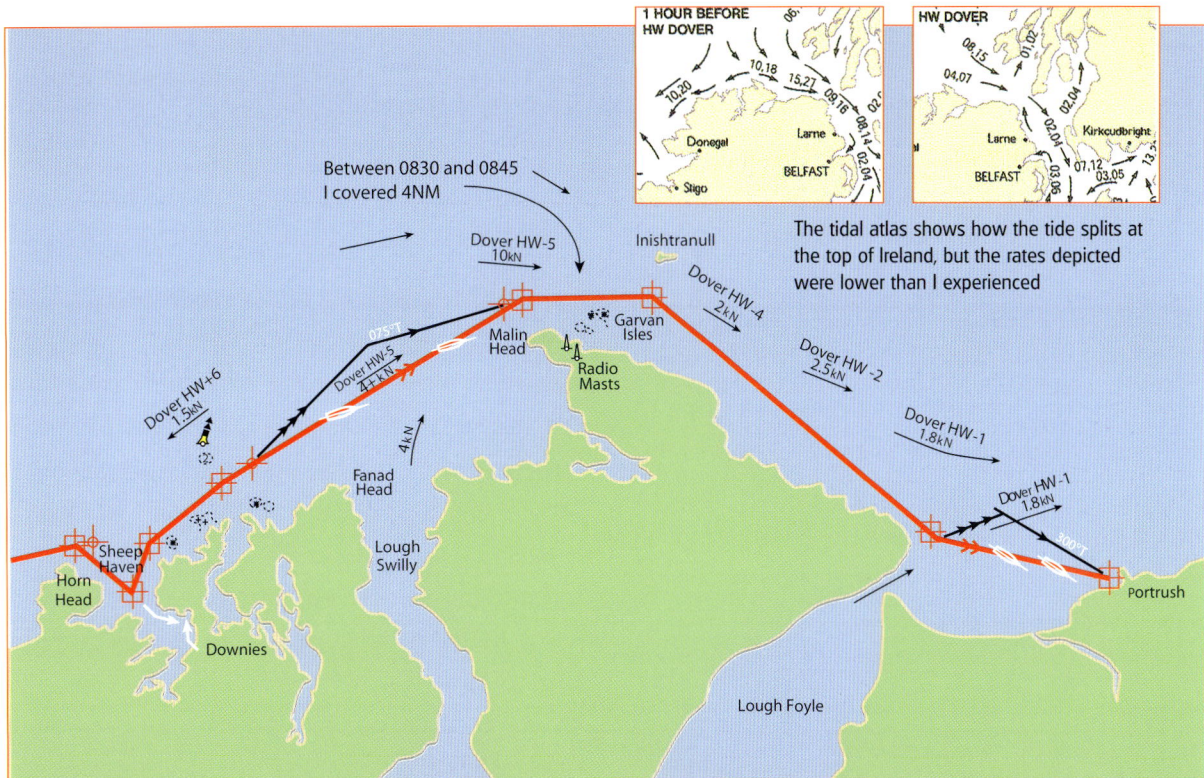

Sheep Haven to Portrush. The tide, combined with days of gales and water rushing out of Loch Swilly, meant that at one point I was sailing on a 10-knot current.

the tide must have been running at around 10 knots! With NW winds force 5–6 on a broad reach with two reefs in the main, plus the high-visibility orange working jib, I averaged 6.2 knots and arrived in Portrush at 1300. What a sail that was – the lack of the big Atlantic swell meant 100 per cent of my sail area was working rather than just the top bits poking out of the troughs. When I asked the locals about the strong tides they just smiled knowingly!

My stay in Portrush was really good. There is diesel and water available from the harbour master; plus a chandlery, post office, and a medical centre only a short walk away. The Portrush Sailing Club has new showers, good beer and a very warm welcome for all visitors.

Tranquil Portrush Harbour looking towards Lough Foyle.

On to Scotland: Portrush to Tobermory

After four days of rest and recuperation, sunshine and good hospitality in Portrush, I was ready to push on and cross the Irish Sea again – this time to Scotland. But while doing the boat chores I noticed that there was quite a build-up of algae collecting on the hull and, more importantly, in the engine filter which needed cleaning. I'd also fitted and tested the new Simrad TP22 autopilot that had arrived to replace my failed TP20. Believe me, after hand steering for 220 miles I was looking forward to the freedom and simple pleasure of being able to take a break to make fresh cups of tea and soup!

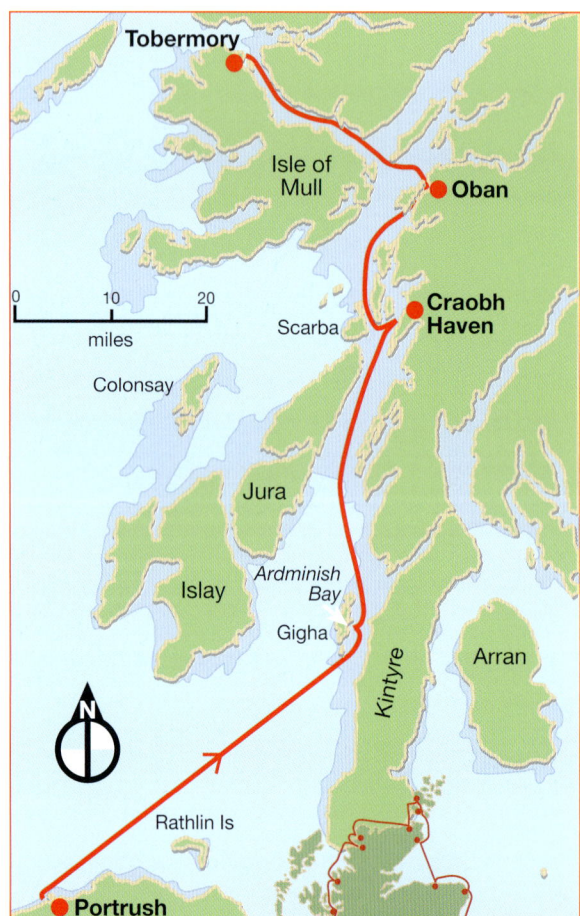

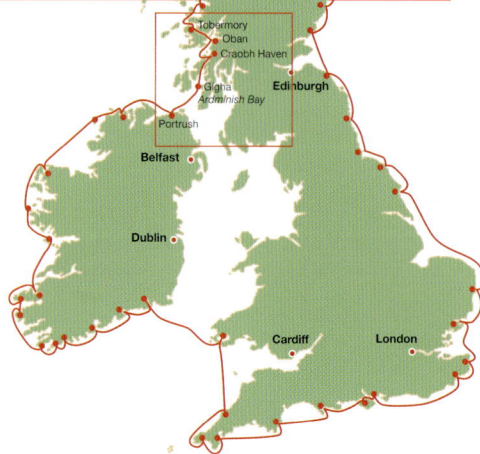

Portrush to Gigha (Ardminish Bay)
Distance: 46nm
Passage time: 9hr

The weather forecast was good: Malin Head NW force 3–4 occasional force 5; showers, visibility good, sea state slight, going around to WNW in the next 24 hours. I was looking forward to getting away from the big Atlantic swells that had given me such a beating on the west coast of Ireland.

The NW wind would give me a beam reach to the Sound of Gigha, west of the Peninsula of Kintyre, and I also had a TSS (Traffic Separation Scheme) to clear north of Rathlin Island. As I am not keen on crossing shipping lanes, I drew my rhumb line to avoid the end of the TSS. Then, as an extra safety margin, I worked out a tidal vector to give me a heading which would keep me west of the rhumb line. I slipped at 0900 (HW Dover +4hr) to give me three hours to get to a position six miles south-west of the TSS. At 1200 the tide would turn SE, assisting me towards the Kintyre. Once in the Sound of Gigha, the tide would be against me, but at no more than 0.5 knots. With the possibility of anchoring, I worked out the total tidal range. This was only 0.6m (2ft), unlike the 10m (30ft) I had experienced on the French coast.

With all prepared, I said my farewells and slipped my lines. Once clear of the Skerries, the course west of the TSS went well. I had full main and No 2 genoa with my high-visibility orange jib hanked on and lashed down on the foredeck (just in case). The wind was N force 3–4, the sun was shining and *Jalina* was sweeping along at five knots. With very little Atlantic swell, I shed my waterproofs and put on sunblock and sunglasses. I felt great excitement when I could see the beautiful mountains of Islay – it was good to be back in these fantastic cruising waters.

In my passage planning I had plotted a WP 'Guard' to keep me north of the west side of the TSS. For simplicity I chose one with rounded minutes (55° 28.00N, 06° 04.00). I marked this with chinagraph on the cockpit bulkhead and kept an eye on the GPS to be sure I didn't stray too far. By 1330 we'd cleared the shipping lanes and could bear away

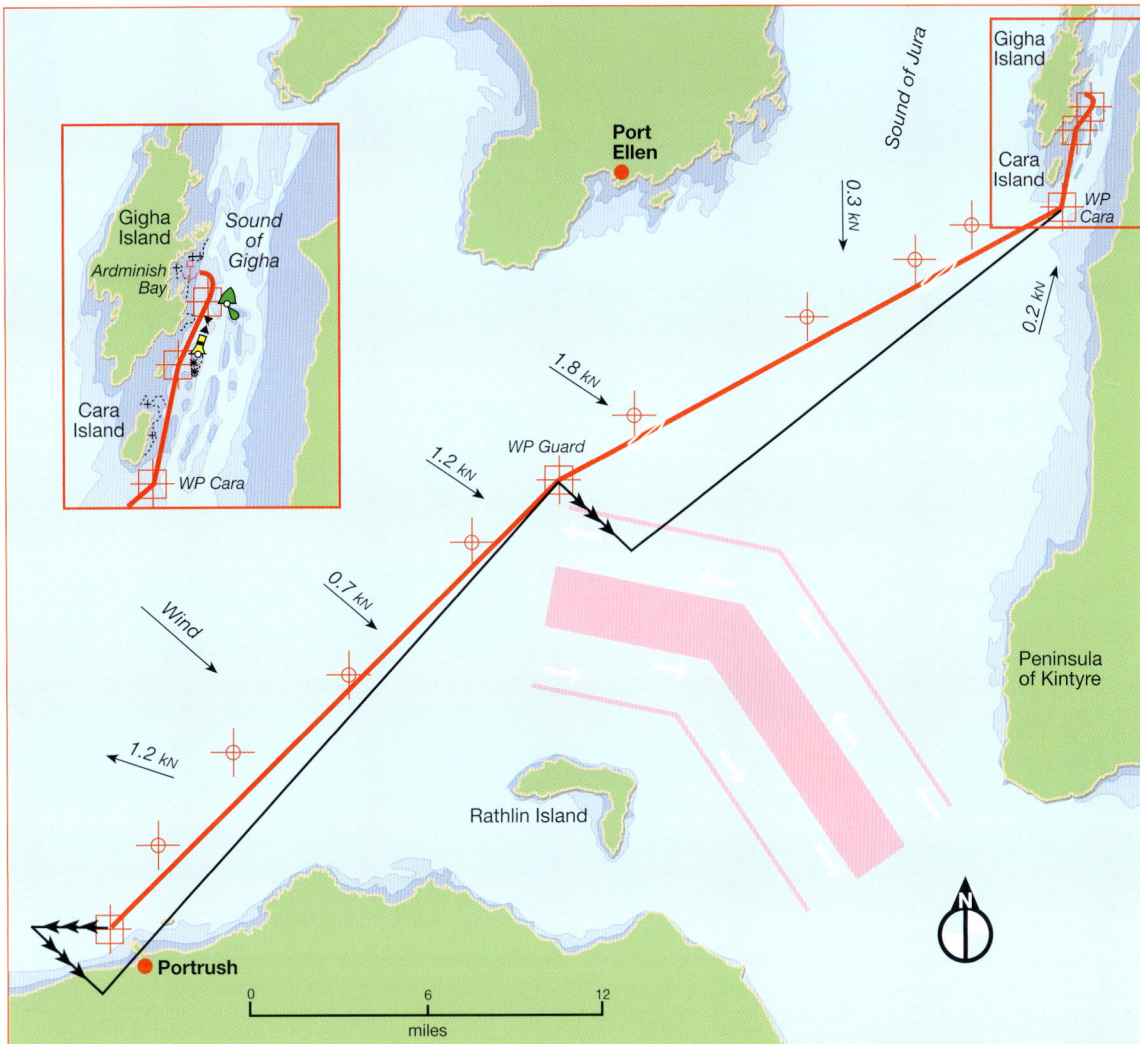

I plotted a course to avoid the end of the TSS (Traffic Separation Scheme), but if you do have to cross one, you must obey the rules and do so in the quickest possible way. If you can, try to keep your heading roughly at right angles to the traffic – and if anything holds you up, call the Coastguard so they can warn approaching shipping.

on a broad reach. Within the hour we had covered 6 miles and were soon into the Sound of Gigha.

Here we had very little foul tide (0.4 knots) and within 10 miles of Gigha the wind fell away so the sea looked like a mirror. With power from the ever faithful Yanmar, *Jalina* steered herself while I prepared an evening meal of fresh fish, potatoes and salad followed by a fresh fruit salad. By 1630, the tide turned fair and we arrived into Ardminish Bay at 1830. This entrance is straightforward but does need some care as reefs extend off both points and the southerly reef is only marked by an unlit, port-hand marker buoy.

Within the bay there are many HIE (Highlands and Islands Enterprise) visitors' moorings, to encourage sailors to drop in, or you can anchor in the hard sand. It was amazing how clean and clear the water was – I could even count the fish! The bay is open to NE winds and ashore

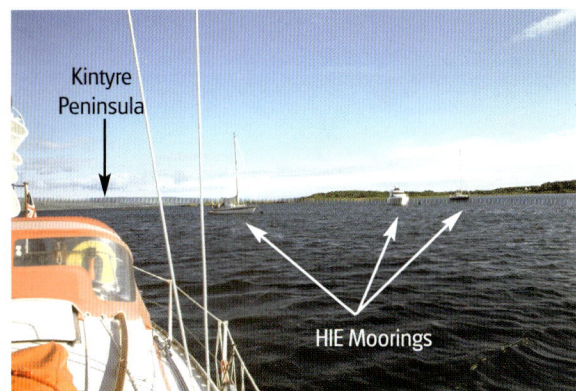

Highlands and Islands Enterprise (HIE) moorings in Ardminish Bay, Gigha.

there is a shop and hotel for creature comforts. There's a wooden landing jetty where you can leave your dinghy and then it was a pleasant walk across the island to see the breathtaking mountains of Islay and Jura.

Gigha to Craobh Haven in Loch Shuna

Distance: 36nm

Passage time: 6hr

This passage would take me up Loch Shuna to a small marina called Craobh Haven – a very pretty harbour with all the facilities you could wish for. The brightly-painted houses and the backdrop of green mountains make it a lovely place to visit. The weather forecast from the Coastguard for the Clyde to Kintyre area was NW force 4, locally force 5, showers, sea state slight. But after looking at a synoptic chart from Northwood, taken from my SSB and laptop, I reckoned the wind could go more northerly. This, coupled with the funnelling effect of the mountains, meant that instead of a reach I could be beating. I prepared my charts, marking up a rhumb line to clear any danger points through the Sound of Jura to Loch Shuna. To draw my attention to dangers such as underlying rocks I drew a circle around them in pencil. I would take bearings and then confirm these with the GPS. The tide was fore and aft along the rhumb line, so a tidal vector was not necessary.

This passage through the Sound of Jura to Loch Shuna is one of my favourites. I slipped my lines at 0615, heading for just south of Craobh Haven and east of Eilean Arsa Isle where there is a good anchorage that is open to southerly winds. By 1230 I was abeam of the entrance to the infamous whirlpools of the Corryvreckan and The Great Race, and amid the breathtaking scenery of Loch Shuna I was tied up by 1400 in plenty of time to pay a visit to the bar at the local hotel.

With the possibility of force 5–6 winds in the next 24 hours I also needed to top up with water and diesel and do a little shopping.

I telephoned Oban Yacht Marina in Ardantrive Bay, on Kerrera, across the bay from Oban – but they had no vacancies and no space to anchor. However, they said I may be able to pick up one of the eight visitor's moorings off Oban, or one of the six east of Northern Lights Wharf, SW of Oban.

Craobh Haven in Loch Shuna to Oban

Distance: 16nm

Passage time: 5hr

I decided to plan an early departure in the half-light so I could use the sectors of the Fladda lighthouse to guide me through the Sound of Luing. The sectors are the usual red, white and green, and as long as I kept in the white sector I would be OK.

Because of the eddies, overfalls and strong tidal streams of over seven knots it is necessary to watch your course at all times – particularly if under sail in light winds when it would be easy to be carried off course. It also makes sense to have your engine ready to pop into gear. This passage would be eyeball pilotage combined with both GPS sets – just in case one failed at the wrong moment.

The fixed set would monitor WP 'Binn', inbetween the two rocks, and the handheld GPS would be on WP 'Lunga'. In case the GPS signal should shut down I could concentrate on two clearing lines with the hand-bearing compass.

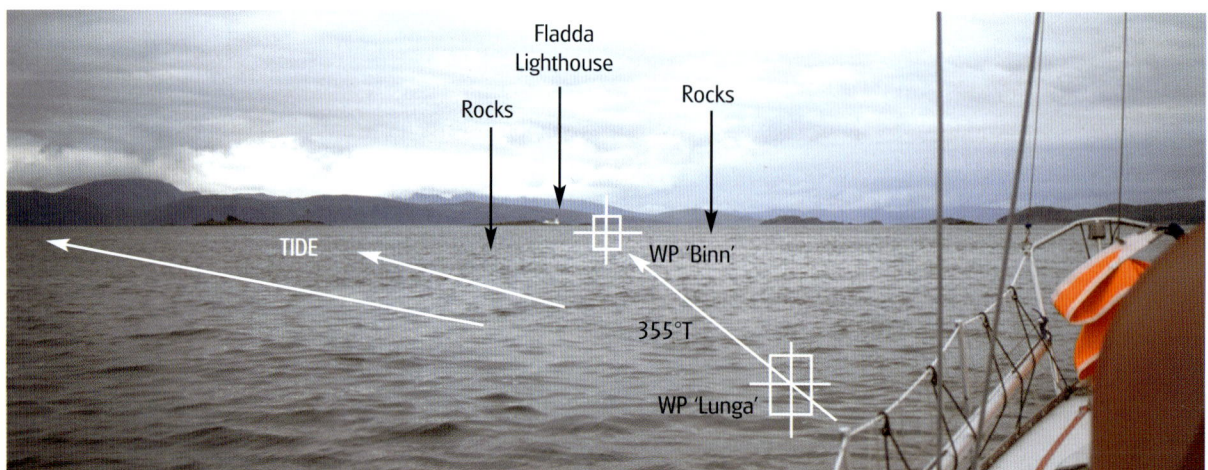

You can see how we were crabbing across the tide in the Sound of Luing.

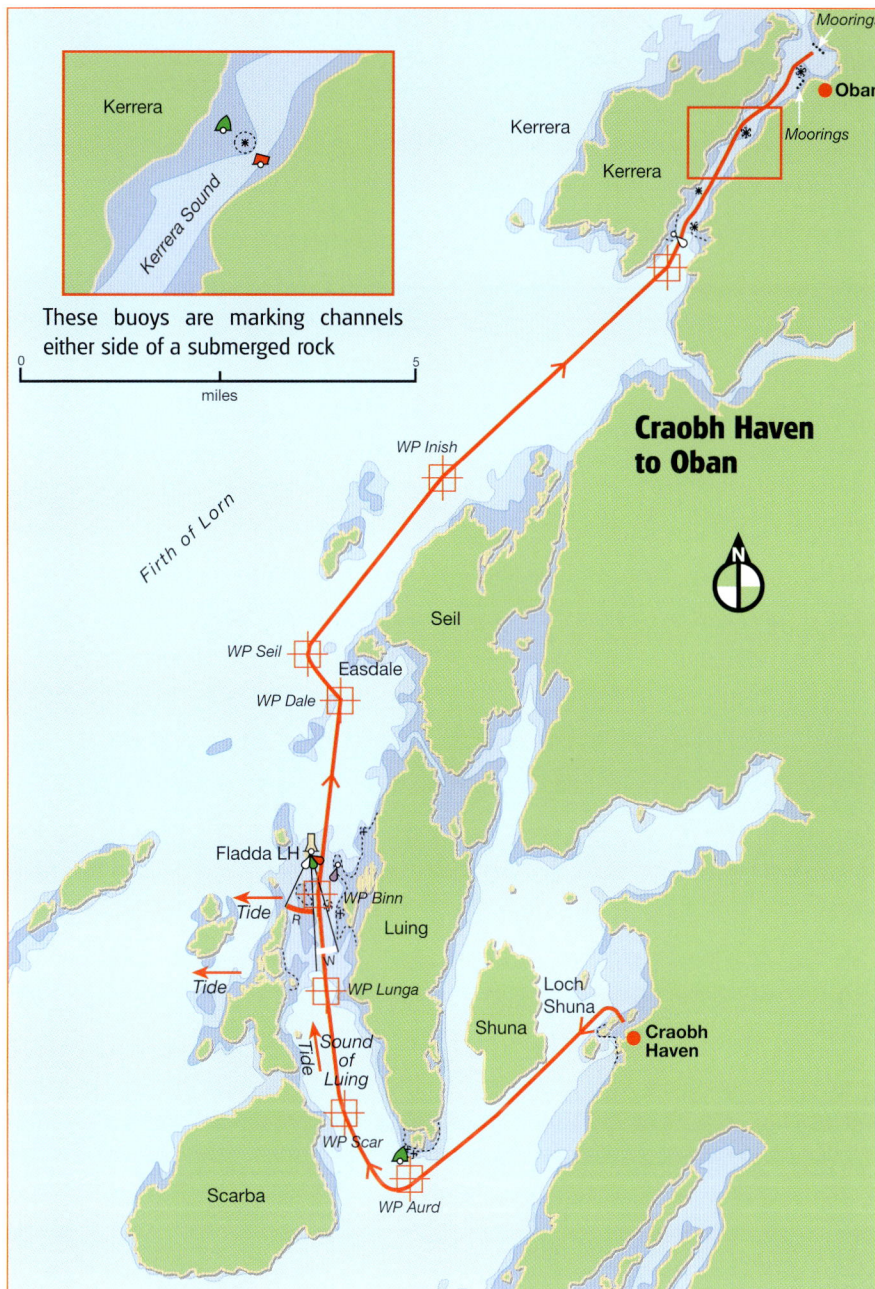

Kerrera

Kerrera Sound

These buoys are marking channels either side of a submerged rock

0   miles   5

Moorings

Oban

Kerrera

Kerrera

Moorings

WP Inish

Craobh Haven to Oban

Firth of Lorn

Seil

WP Seil

Easdale

WP Dale

N

Fladda LH

Tide

WP Binn

Luing

R

W

Loch Shuna

Tide

WP Lunga

Shuna

Craobh Haven

Sound of Luing

Tide

WP Scar

Scarba

WP Aurd

My plan was to slip early (0420 HW Dover −2hr 30min) to reach the dangerous rocks at slack water and clear Fladda Lighthouse (HW Dover −5hr) I would then avoid the strong tide and should the wind be NW F 5, as forecast, I would avoid the wind- against-tide problem. As a precaution I also flaked out my main CQR anchor ready to use, just in case the wind dropped and I picked up a pot line on the prop.

This may all seem over-cautious, but I experienced the loss of GPS satellite signals three times when going around Britain, and the locals told me that the underlying rocks in the Sound of Luing had wrecked one German and two Swedish yachts that year.

When I slipped and cleared the marina, the weather was overcast so the Fladda lighthouse white sector would stand out even better. The first obstacle was to clear a starboard-hand mark Ardluing where skippers have hit the submerged rocks by trying to cut the corner. At 0600, 2NM from Fladda lighthouse, I could see the white sector light. I then lashed the jib down to give me an unobstructed view ahead for navigation. As I approached the submerged rocks, the tide kept setting me off to port and the odd eddy pushed me to starboard − so I used the engine to correct my heading. This probably sounds more dangerous than it really was, but as I've said before I love to take controlled risks. We were really moving apace − a good 11 knots over the ground as WP 'Binn' grew closer. I watched the countdown on the distance-to-WP and held my breath as we swept past the rocks. Then the world became calmer, and the passage went well as I sailed up towards Kerrera Sound. However, in the Sound be aware that there is one set of red and green buoys that look as if they are marking channels on either side of a submerged rock – which is hit regularly by yachts! I picked up a mooring off Oban at 0830.

Oban to Tobermory
Distance: 31nm
Passage time: 6hr

This passage would take me through some of the most beautiful sailing waters I have ever seen. The weather forecast for Ardnamurchan area was NW force 4–5, locally force 6, visibility good, sea state rough – but I was well rested, and ready for a good thrash up the Sound of Mull. With these high mountains I had to be ready for the winds to be funnelled in different directions producing nasty squalls. With two reefs in the main and a slab in the jib, it would be a beat – a long port tack and short starboard tack. If I kept two cables from the shores I could manage without too much chart work, but I took the precaution of circling any danger areas with pencil. I rose to be greeted by heavy rain and a strong wind, then slipped at 0800 (HW Dover) as this would give me a full six hours of fair tide – and being neaps, the maximum foul would only be half a knot.

By 0900 I cleared Eilean Musdile lighthouse and Lady's

Lady's Rock and Eilean Musdile lighthouse

Rock, by 0930 we had cleared Glas Eileanan light and its rocks, and the remainder of the passage was straight-forward. I encountered quite a heavy swell due to the force 4–5 winds with some stronger gusts in different directions but Tobermory itself is sheltered by Calve Island. The harbour is quite magnificent, its colourful houses shining in the sunshine. There are more than 20 swinging moorings here and still more are to be laid. But this does make anchoring more awkward and there is a charge to drop your hook. Just in case there was no room I'd also made plans to anchor in Loch Sunart, five miles to the east.

I arrived in good time giving me a chance to clean down *Jalina*, carry out some housework and check the engine. Tobermory has all the facilities you need and you can get alongside, for a short stay only, to pick up fuel and water. There is now a new harbour office and a number of pontoons.

I then settled down to plan the passage to Mallaig.

North-west Scotland: Tobermory to Loch Inver

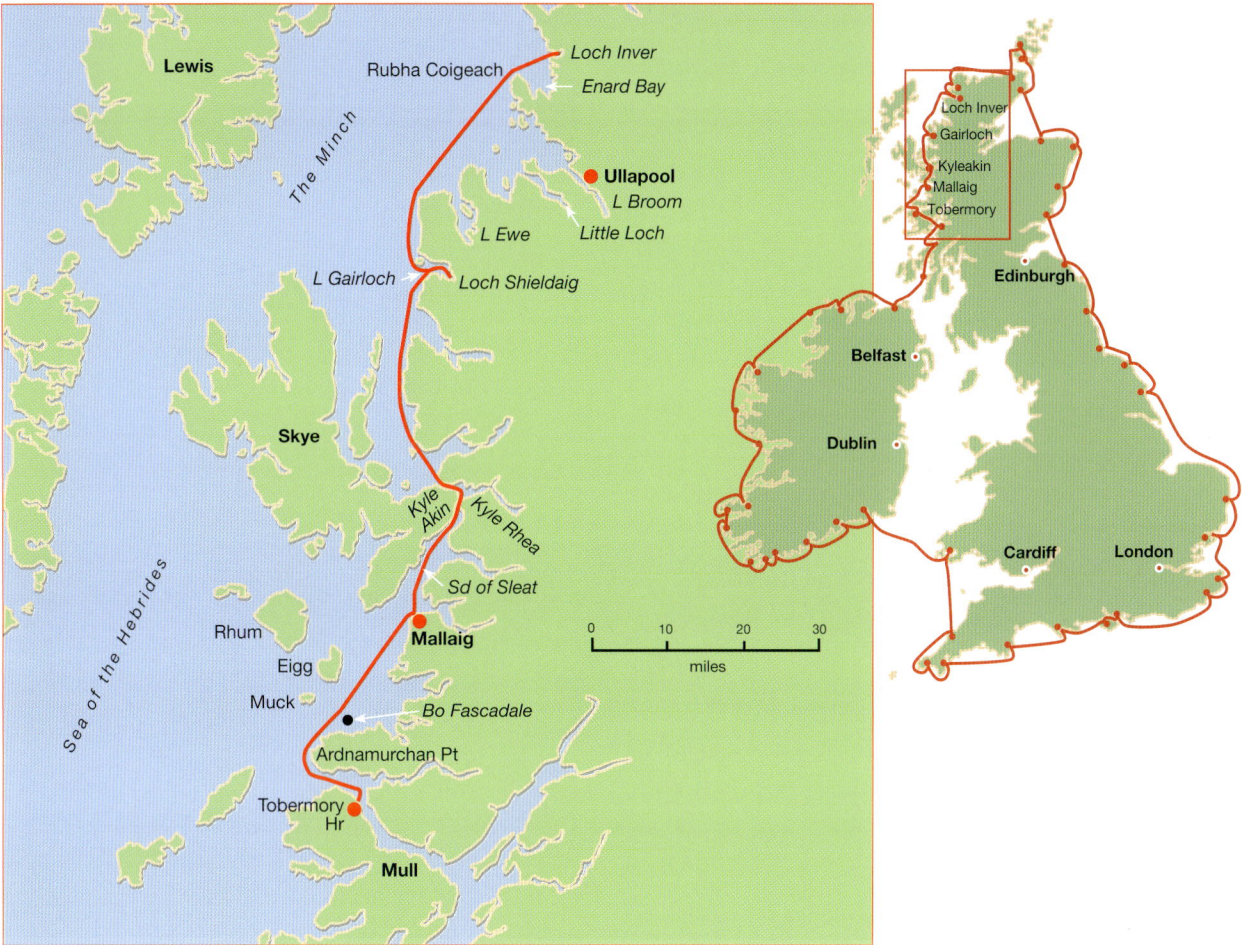

Tobermory Harbour and anchorages.

My next passage from Tobermory to Mallaig would take me around Ardnamurchan, the most westerly point of the UK mainland, and earn me the right to display a bunch of heather that can be worn on *Jalina*'s bow. I've no idea why and when this quaint tradition started – it is said that it was a way of identifying boats to show they were local, and not hostile.

Once round Ardnamurchan Point I will dress Jalina *with her bunch of heather.*

Tobermory to Mallaig
Distance: 33nm
Passage time 7hr

As much as I wanted to linger in Tobermory I was three weeks behind my schedule and needed to press on. The weather forecast for Ardnamurchan to Cape Wrath was force 2–3, occasional force 4, backing to SSE force 3–4, occasional force 5, with a risk of mist or fog patches, sea state moderate – so it would be a beat from Tobermory to the point of Ardnamurchan and then a fetch or reach to Mallaig. However, after looking at several synoptic charts from my SSB I was concerned that there was a series of deep lows approaching from the Atlantic that could reach me in the next three days, so I needed to work a sheltered haven into my plan.

But this should be a comfortable passage with very little tacking and only three main dangers to consider; fog patches, Bo Fascadale Rocks, and rocks at the entrance to Mallaig Harbour.

I called Clyde Coastguard, first on Ch16 and then Ch10 to sign on with my passage plan, and was asked to sign

off later with Stornoway Coastguard on arrival at my destination. I now had the feeling of going towards the peaceful isolation of the north.

I slipped my mooring at 0715 (HW Dover −2hr) and planned to be at Ardnamurchan by 0900 with 0.3 knots of foul tide, after which it would ease to a fair tide by midday.

I'd noticed the engine's water pump had developed a slight leak, so as we approached the totally isolated Ardnamurchan Point, I decided to try to order a replacement from the agent at Burseldon near Hamble on the South Coast. After a quick call on my mobile phone, the order was sorted, and it would be delivered to the Mallaig harbour master – the wonders of modern communications!

Sailing north, the mountains and scenery became even more breathtaking and the low broken cloud emphasized their height. For a time I shed my waterproofs and enjoyed the cool breeze through my first layer thermals. I even put on my sunglasses – it was chill-out time!

On the approach to Mallaig Harbour, there are rocks on the starboard side guarded by a small lighthouse marker and a small green can. The harbour master was there to assist me by taking my lines; I moored among the local fishing boats and lifeboats.

Mallaig Harbour where I serviced Jalina's *engine and fitted a new water pump.*

Mallaig to Kyleakin
Distance: 20nm
Passage time: 4hr

The water pump arrived just 29 hours after the order was placed – what a service! It was quickly fitted and I decided to give the engine a full service.

Mallaig is mainly a fishing port but there are swinging moorings available by contacting Harbour Slipways Engineering tel: 01687 462303. Diesel is available from the

SUBMARINE SHADOW

You may come across submarines in this area. During my last visit here I found that in charted depths of over 100m, my depth sounder suddenly recorded 20m! Some of my charts may be 'cancelled' but you don't lose 80m in five years. So I changed direction and immediately the depth registered 100m again. Then after a few minutes I would be back to 20m again. For fun I zigzagged for a few miles – the only thing it could have been was a submarine shadowing me – practising hiding from satellites under the surface disturbance, I guess.

In Kyle Rhea the tide can run at around eight knots and eddies can be a problem.

nearby garage, there are several small supermarkets, a chemist, bars and restaurants. The harbour master will provide a five-day weather report and showers and meals are available at the Fisherman's Mission.

The weather forecast for Ardnamurchan Point to Cape Wrath given by Stornoway Coastguard at 1010 for this passage was winds WSW force 3–4 backing SW force 3–4 occasional 5, later. Showers, visibility moderate to good, sea state slight to moderate. Looking ahead, the forecast for the following day and the day after was not good: SW force 6–7, sea state rough with rain. Looking at synoptic charts from the laptop, the force 7 could be a force 8 gale. I decided to go but not before I had selected some suitable bolt holes if things turned nasty.

The passage to Kyleakin would take me down the Sound of Sleat, which is sheltered from the sea, but can be subject to squalls and the tide can run up eight knots in the narrow passage of Kyle Rhea. There are eddies along the shores and care should be taken during the second half of the flood so as not to be carried towards the covered rocks on the western side – you need to keep a cable off to avoid drying rocks.

The passage was straightforward, reaching a SOG of 10.7 knots through Kyle Rhea – accompanied by heavy rain and squalls. Once in Loch Alsh it was a short beat in driving rain and a rising wind to the shelter of Kyleakin just east of the Skye Bridge. I was tucked up in the small pool east of, and between, the old ferry slip and the half-tide rocks to the east of it. The ferry slip extends for some way, so take care when entering. The weather forecast was spot on, and

I tied up alongside *Morning Star* from Belfast and was invited on board for a piece of their daughter's birthday cake. There is only one small store and a water tap here and mooring on the pontoon cost £11 for the night, although there are Highlands and Islands Enterprise moorings to the north of Kyleakin and east of the bridge.

Poor communications

My next intended anchorage was to be Loch Shieldaig, a small, very well sheltered loch within Loch Gairloch. In the past I have had communications problems within some of the lochs, including broken reception on my NAVTEX, and being unable to contact the Coastguard on VHF or mobile phone. This is where getting the long-wave shipping forecast via my NASA SSB receiver comes into its own and has never failed. I was not happy with the weather forecast for the next few days with strong winds forecast among the mountains. Winds can be funnelled in different directions and can increase well above their forecast strength. When entering some of the lochs, I have experienced an open sea force 2–3 suddenly rising to a force 5–6 katabatic wind. Stornoway Coastguard gave SW force 6–7 in four days time, sea state rough, and much the same for the following few days. I wanted to get into Loch Inver where there is good shelter, stores, diesel and pubs as well as a Seaman's Mission. Here I'd rest up and let the weather clear a little before tackling Cape Wrath. The last time I was here, I surfed into Loch Inver and sat out a four-day gale – I could see the same happening again.

Loch Shieldaig.

Kyleakin to Loch Shieldaig in Loch Gairloch

Distance: 33nm

Passage time: 7hr

The main consideration for this passage was the weather: – SW force 3–4 increasing force 6, backing SSE, force 3-4 later. The wind backing to SSE force 3 and easing would make it better to enter Loch Gairloch, so should I slip later? A SSE wind would give me a weather shore rather than a lee shore and an added safety margin. I wanted to slip at 0500 (slack water in Loch Alsh) when there would be only 0.3 knots of foul tide. But I rose at 0400 to find thick fog and heavy rain, so it would be a later start. I went back to bed and at 0600 cooked myself a bowl of porridge with mixed dried fruit. I left at 0800 and passed through Skye Bridge against 0.8 knots of foul tide. Once clear, the foul

tide fell to less than 0.3 knots and for much of the passage it was slack water for hours on end, due to a choke point further south. The sky looked very threatening with heavy rain showers, but when Loch Torridon was abeam the sun came out to show off the swathes of brightly-coloured heather glistening in the distance. Before entering Loch Shieldaig, I called the Coastguard to sign off in case my signal was shielded by the mountains. Care has to be taken entering as there is a covered rock a half a cable to the east of Eilean ant-Sabhail. In fact there were several 'new' rocks discovered by aerial survey that I had to add to the chart. During the passage I had taken weather reports from Stornoway Coastguard knowing that I might not pick up their transmission once within Loch Shieldaig. The winds were picking up; so I needed an early start to cover the 41 miles to get into the good shelter of Loch Inver.

New port and starboard buoys had been laid in Loch Inver since my last visit.

Loch Shieldaig to Loch Inver
Distance: 41nm
Passage time: 8hr

My planned points of refuge en route were Loch Ewe at 15 miles, Little Loch Broom at 26 miles and Loch Broom at 32 miles. Ullapool is in Loch Broom and has diesel, petrol, gas, stores, a bank and a rail link.

I put two reefs in the main and as it was a lee shore, I had the engine ticking over until I cleared Longa Island. In the open sea there was a good force 4–5 blowing and we cleared Longa Island around slack water. There was a fair tide and wind, so progress was swift, with many white tops. For the next two hours we had heavy rain with squalls and even though I had put in a third reef we were still making a SOG of 6.7 knots.

Streams of water cascading off the mountains glistened in the broken rays of sunlight, and even the angry grey swirls of cloud looked great. Navigation was made more difficult with the dripping waterproofs and wet glasses.

The weather forecast from Stornoway Coastguard gave force 7 and a rough sea state, so I was pleased with my early start. If the sea had built up as I approached Loch Inver I planned to round Rubha Coigeach headland and approach in its lee from Enard Bay.

I got into the loch by 1200 (HW Dover) and found new port and starboard buoys had been laid since my last visit. But within 30 minutes the heavens opened and by 1700 the predicted strong wind came, creating a heavy swell in the harbour entrance.

The facilities are good with two pubs, a café, a hotel, a small supermarket, a butcher, hardware/chandler's store plus a bank. Diesel and petrol can be bought at the local garage and there is water at the pontoon. The Fisherman's Mission serves food and has a laundrette and showers.

The area is also a ramblers' paradise with some of the finest views I have ever seen – and with the weather worsening, it looked as if I would be joining them for a few days.

Looking across to the pontoons and Loch Inver.

Rounding Cape Wrath: Loch Inver to Stromness

The synoptic charts that I'd downloaded from my SSB warned of the coming storms, so I was well prepared to spend several days in Loch Inver. And it was not all bad news, because once I had doubled up all *Jalina*'s lines, added extra fenders and removed anything that the wind would shred – I headed for the hills. After sailing for so long, I needed some other form of exercise to stretch my legs and get my heart and lungs working harder. So with a packed rucksack I set off, believe it or not – in a taxi! I was dropped off 10 miles away and the walk back was quite breathtaking. From Ledmore junction I passed Mt Suilven, with its distinctive round dome top, to the delightful Loch Culag and back to Loch Inver. The moss was springy, the rain was cold and the gale was in full swing – but I loved it, taking in the fantastic sounds and colours of this exciting area.

A break from the boat and a 10-mile hike through the countryside of Loch Inver and Culag provided some healthy exercise and beautiful scenery.

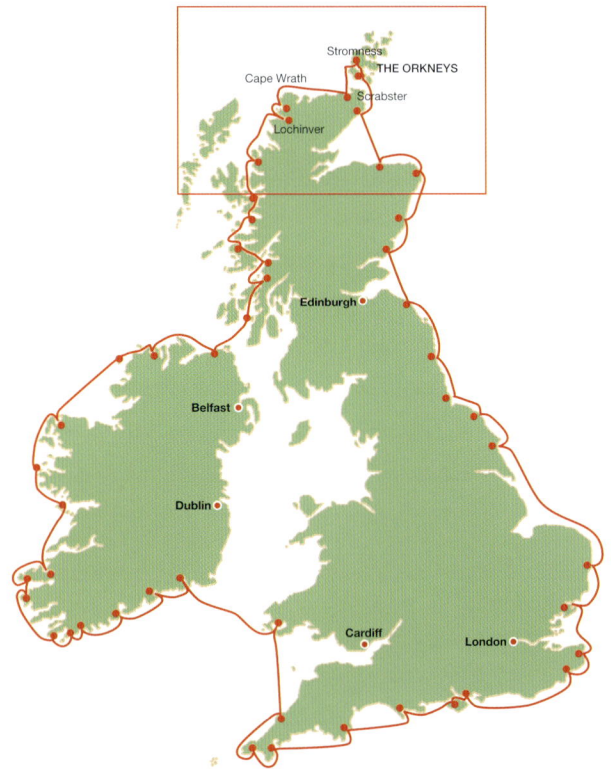

Loch Inver to Kinlochbervie
Distance: 30nm
Passage time: 5.5hr

The weather forecast for sea area Ardnamurchan to Cape Wrath was SW to SE force 4–5, force 6 locally with scattered showers; sea state slight to moderate. We were on high spring tides and slack water was at 0730 (HW Dover –6hr).

Along this part of the coast the maximum tide will be 0.6 knots at springs and I would have the wind with tide once around 'Old Man of Stoer' (Point of Stoer). But then my stern would be open to any build-up of heavy swell, so as a precaution I flaked out and fitted the drogue.

I rose at 0400 and breakfasted on porridge, dried fruit, and marmalade on homemade bread. It would be short passage and the wind was blowing a good force 5–6 out in the Loch. Even though it would have been shorter to go between Soyea Island and Rubha Robha, I tacked to clear Soyea Island. The shorter route would have put me on a lee shore and there could be breaking swell from the SW. The tide was to run fair along my rhumb line for the whole passage, but along a lee shore a good offing of two miles was needed.

I hanked on the heavy orange No 1 jib and put three reefs in the main – these can be dangerous waters so you must spend time making careful preparations. Out at sea these lonely waters and rugged coastlines fill me with excitement – with sails pulling hard and water rushing down the deck it was shaping up to be a good day!

I called Stornoway Coastguard to sign on with my passage plan. 'Can you confirm you said one person on board?' 'Yes, one person,' I replied, suddenly feeling very isolated. Once clear of the breakwater, the engine was off and I met a full force 6. Wow – these are the moments to savour. Mind you, everything was streaming with water. Once clear of Soyea Island I bore away onto a reach and shook out a reef to maintain five or six knots. The sea was quite rough, with the odd dollop finding its way into the cockpit and occasionally we rode a quartering sea, which caused the autopilot to work much harder. Some of the spray found its way down the hatch onto the chart table and I was constantly drying off my navigation plastic bits and pieces. Even though paper charts don't pack up in the

At Loch Inver I doubled up all Jalina's lines, added extra fenders and removed anything the wind would shred.

wet, next winter I'll make a rigid plastic cover for the chart and use a chinagraph pencil to mark up the plots. The swell was quite steep so I decided to stand out to sea into deeper water. This paid off and by 0830 we were off 'Old Man of Stoer' and bearing away for the west of Handa Island. The wind eased to force 4–5 and we were now running with one reef in the main. Jalina was going like a train, but with little personal protection from the weather coming over the stern, I put on two full body thermal layers with neck protection – but could still feel the chill of the sea and rain through my waterproofs.

Along this wild coast I also use Ordnance Survey maps, as they are geared up for GPS and, unlike Admiralty charts, show handy distinctive landmarks like campsites and the mountains well inshore. However I always view information from pilots, almanacs, charts and maps with a jaundiced eye as I have found so many discrepancies along the way.

Top: Ordnance Survey maps are useful for showing distinctive features on land.
Right: On passage to Loch Inver using 728m dome-topped Mount Suilven as a handy landmark.

Mount Suilven 728m

With a SW wind and swell it is easy to mistake Loch Clash, north of the entrance to Loch Inchard, for Loch Inchard itself. The only navigation mark on the approach is a light on Rubha na Leacaig that is also painted white and a cardinal marker guarding a rock within the entrance to Loch Inchard. By 1210 we were tied up safely alongside the harbour wall. There are now pontoons and plans to build a new marina here. Facilities include diesel, water, a seven-ton crane, a launderette, showers and meals at the Fisherman's Mission. There is also a small well-stocked shop and Kinlochbervie Hotel provides 'carry out food'.

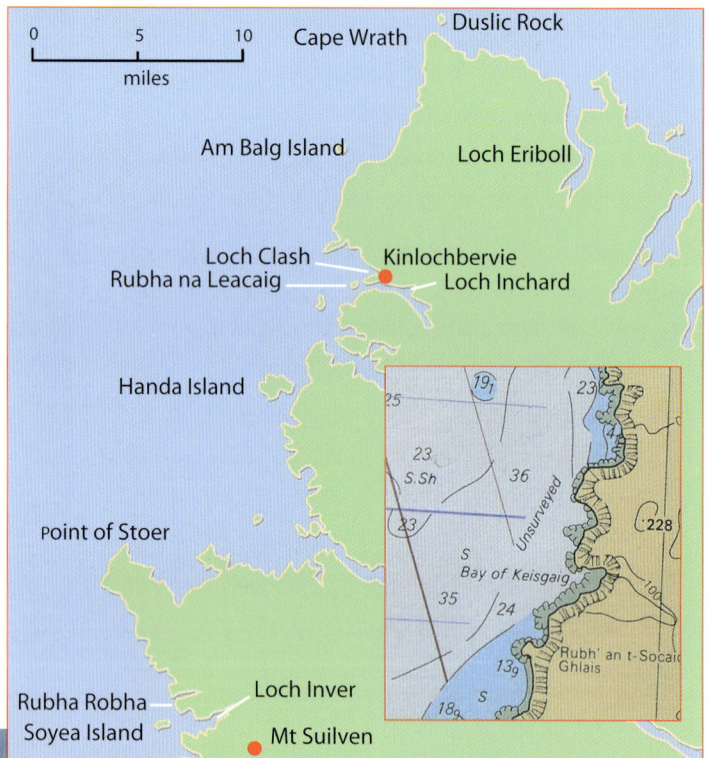

Cape Wrath
Duslic Rock
Am Balg Island
Loch Eriboll
Loch Clash
Rubha na Leacaig
Kinlochbervie
Loch Inchard
Handa Island
Point of Stoer
Rubha Robha
Soyea Island
Loch Inver
Mt Suilven

Take care if closing the coast to find favourable eddies as there are many unsurveyed areas.

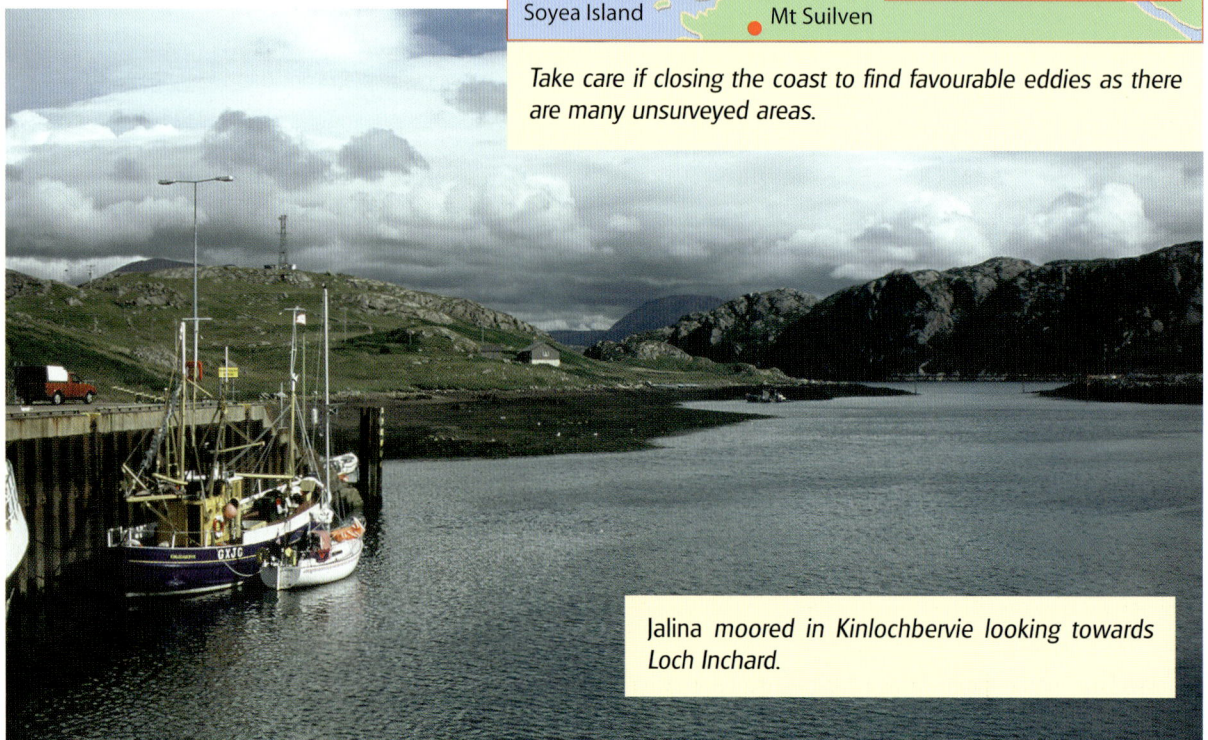

Jalina moored in Kinlochbervie looking towards Loch Inchard.

Kinlochbervie to Scrabster
(first attempt)
Distance: 36nm
Passage time: 8hr

My first attempt to round Cape Wrath was aborted, but the reasons are well worth explaining.

Throughout my passage to Kinlochbervie I'd recorded weather forecasts from my SSB LW and from Stornoway Coastguard every four hours. But for my departure around Cape Wrath to Scrabster, I wanted a synoptic chart of the approaching bad weather fronts. Stornoway reported SE force 5–6, occasionally force 7, with a SW force 3–4 later. Visibility moderate to good; sea state slight to rough. The following 24 hours was forecast SE force 5–7, reducing to force 3–4 for a time then increasing to force 5 later, sea state moderate to rough.

My first response to this was good: a south-easterly would be a fetch and I could close the weather shore for some protection, but if the wind went more into the east, I would abort the passage. Kinlochbervie harbour master John George was a great help providing me with a five-day weather forecast, because within the harbour I could not receive a VHF signal. I also phoned Stornoway Coastguard for a forecast, and checked my NASA Navtex, which worked well.

I rose at 0300 and called Stornoway and Aberdeen Coastguards by mobile phone. The forecast for Ardnamurchan to Cape Wrath: no gale warning; SE force 3, with force 5–7 in SW later, visibility moderate to good. Cape Wrath to Scrabster SE force 3 to force 5–7, sea state slight to rough in open water.

I slipped at 0500 with a foul tide to Cape Wrath and a little in hand with some fair tide to come back and round Cape Wrath should I have to abort the passage. If I continued then I'd get a full fair tide for the passage.

As I cleared Cape Wrath at 0815 all looked fine, so I decided to go for it – then Stornoway Coastguard put out a forecast that the wind would change to the east force 7. The sea was already building, and I could not contact Stornoway so I called Aberdeen Coastguard to report I was aborting the passage.

I also had another problem. As I approached Cape Wrath

The second attempt to round Cape Wrath on passage to Scrabster was successful.

I spotted what I thought was a man waving on Duslic Rock. I was some distance off but was convinced it was not a seal, so I altered course and went around the rock for a look – there was nothing there! I decided I must have been tired, or worse – hallucinating. For the first time I started to doubt myself.

At 0900 the tide had started to turn foul, so I closed the coast to keep out of it, staying about a half mile off (some sections inshore have not been surveyed). It was a weather shore with very little swell, and once clear of Am Balg Island, the foul tide eased to less than half a knot, so we got back to Kinlochbervie by 1330. I sat tight for 36 hours and monitored the weather.

Kinlochbervie to Scrabster
(second attempt)
Distance: 59nm
Passage time: 13hr

Through my SSB and laptop I obtained synoptic charts showing that a gale was on its way, but there was a window for me. I phoned Stornoway and Aberdeen Coastguards to check the weather reports before slipping at 0400 (HW Dover +1hr). It was still dark as I cleared Loch Inchard. At first light it looked very menacing towards the SW. At 0640 I called Stornoway and they confirmed a gale warning imminent – the wind was now S force 3. At 0700 I called Aberdeen and they confirmed SSE force 4, locally force 2, showers and good visibility. At 0730 (HW Dover

Sailing from Cape Wrath to Scrabster with Holborn Head and Thurso Bay in the distance.

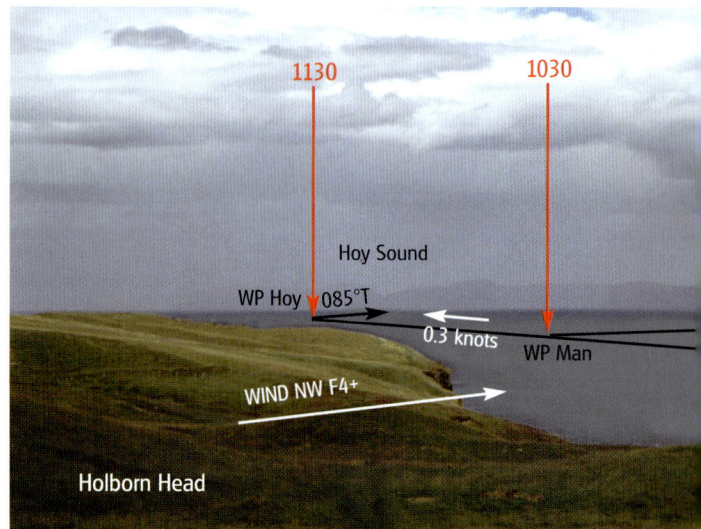

+5hr) the fair tide turns east at Cape Wrath. Looking east it was bright and clear but to the west it was very menacing. However from the synoptic charts I knew that the front would keep to the west of Cape Wrath so I decided to go for it. I called both Coastguards to confirm my intention and gave them my passage plan. Stornoway came back and issued me the same gale warning. I confirmed I had received it and was pressing on – I had a full fair tide taking me east. As I cleared the Cape I felt the total isolation of this lonely place, the wind was S force 3–4 and I pressed *Jalina* hard under full sail.

I put the cooker on and made some hot soup and toast – but kept looking aft towards the weather from the west! The adrenaline was pumping so I soothed my isolation with some music – Beethoven and warm food helped me join the world of reality. My last and only safe refuge, Loch Eriboll, soon passed but the barometer was steady (1002–995mb during a 10hr period) so all seemed well. Progress was good and by 1330 we were off Strathy Point with the sky clearing. At 1500 the old Dounreay Atomic Power Station was abeam and as we closed on Thurso Bay I could see the Orkneys to the NE and the Pentland Firth. By 1700 we were tied up in Scrabster's inner harbour. Diesel, water, and stores are all available and the Fisherman's Mission provides meals and showers. There is also a good bus service to Thurso for banks etc.

Scrabster to Stromness
Distance: 28nm
Passage time: 5.5hr

It's not wise to cross over to the Orkneys in strong winds and tides so I waited four days to get neaps and favourable winds. This passage would take me across Thurso Bay, then to the west of the Pentland Firth and due north, west of the Orkneys past the Old Man of Hoy. On entering Hoy Sound, round Skerry of Ness, I had to keep clear of the rocks and take care not to cut the corner before changing course for Stromness Harbour. I prepared a tidal vector for Dunnet Head to Hoy Sound starting from 0800 (HW Dover +2hr) to 1130 (HW Dover +6hr), when the tide would turn east and fair, to take me into the Sound. I calculated approximately five knots of west-going tide for the 15 mile stretch, and my course would be 015°T. If entering Hoy

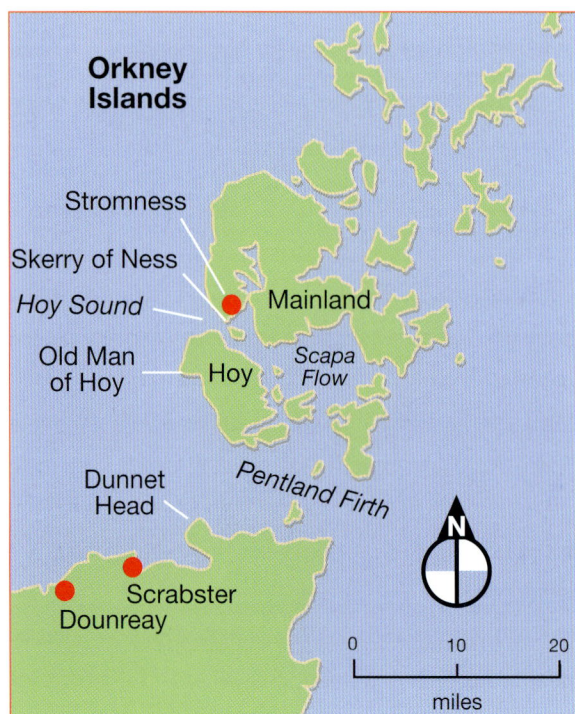

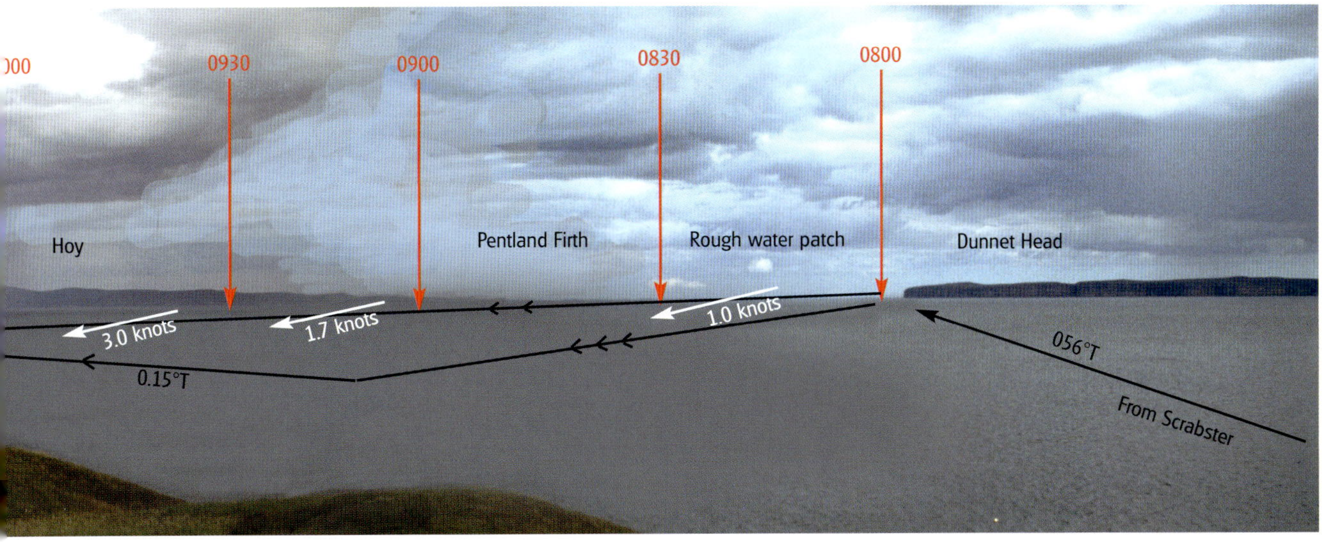

0930   0900   0830   0800

Hoy   Pentland Firth   Rough water patch   Dunnet Head

3.0 knots   1.7 knots   1.0 knots

0.15°T   056°T

From Scrabster

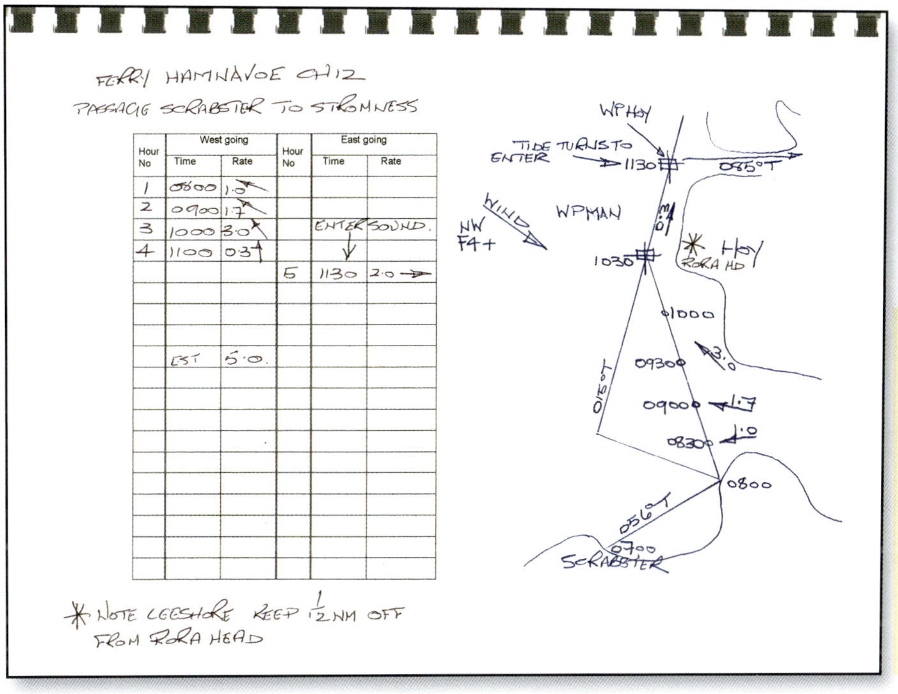

FERRY HAMNAVOE CH12
PASSAGE SCRABSTER TO STROMNESS

Hour No	West going Time	West going Rate	Hour No	East going Time	East going Rate
1	0800	1.0			
2	0900	1.7			
3	1000	3.0		ENTER SOUND.	
4	1100	0.3			
			5	1130	2.0
	EST	5.0			

* NOTE LEESHORE KEEP 1½ NM OFF
FROM RORA HEAD

WP HOY
TIDE TURNS TO ENTER   1130   045°T
WIND   WP MAN
NW F4+   1030   Hoy RORA HD
1000
0930   3.0
0900   1.7
0830   1.0
0800
056°T
0700
SCRABSTER

For the trip from Scrabster via Dunnet Head to Stromness I worked out a combined tidal vector to allow for the strong ides. The photo at the top of the page shows how it would roughly look.

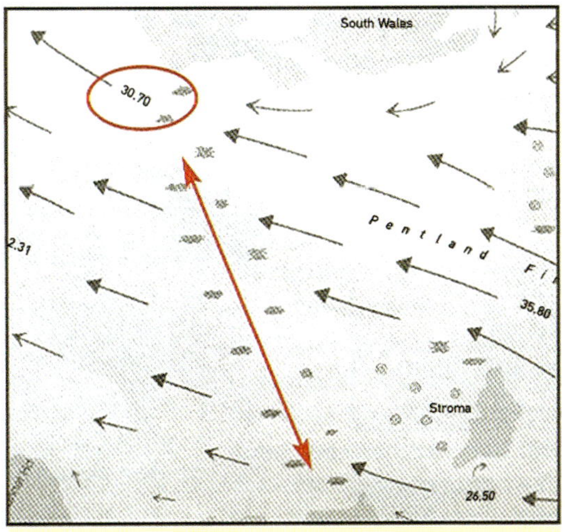

South Walas
30.70
2.31
Pentland Fi
35.80
Stroma
26.50

This compression point can cause rough waters with overfalls and the tide can run up to seven knots at springs. So I waited four days to get only three knots at neaps.

Sound looked difficult, I had arranged that I could ask for local advice, on Ch12, from the captain of the ferry that plies between Scrabster and Stromness, via Hoy Sound. This passage has its problems. First you have to crab across the west-going ebb tide to Dunnet Head, and there the strong tide from the Pentland Firth reaches a compression point which makes the sea very rough for about two miles offshore – similar to the Alderney Race. Once you are through that patch of water the seas usually ease a little. The weather forecast for Cape Wrath to Rattery Head was NW force 3–4, backing SSW force 2–3; showers; visibility fair to good and sea state slight to moderate. I had rested enough and was champing at the bit to go for a sail.

I slipped my lines at 0700 (HW Dover +1hr) to leave an hour in hand, and planned to be off Hoy Sound at 1130

The impressive stack of the Old Man of Hoy makes a useful landmark.

(HW Dover +6hr) when the new flood would take me in. All went well; the wind was more than the forecast. It was blowing about force 4–5 as we cleared Skerry of Ness, and by 1230 we were safely tied up in Stromness.

There is so much to visit and explore in this area and I have always had a warm welcome from the community – especially the harbour master who will help with local knowledge and weather reports. There have also been great improvements in the facilities for yachtsmen – there is now a well-equipped marina with showers, laundrette, diesel, water, slip, a 30-ton lift as well as banks and a supermarket.

Cruising the Orkneys: Stromness to Stonehaven

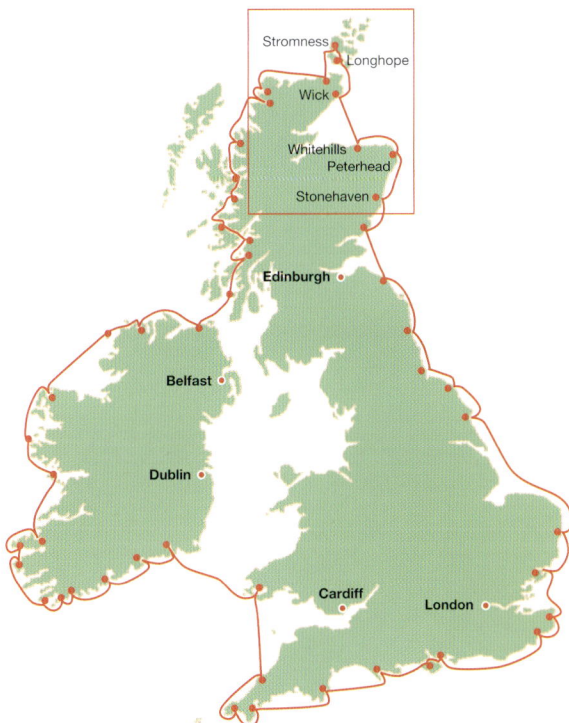

The Pentland Firth overfalls can be tricky at the best of times.

A short morning's sail would take me the 12 miles from Stromness to Longhope, but that didn't mean I could relax – great care is needed in these tricky waters around the Orkneys, and especially crossing the Pentland Firth back to mainland Scotland where tides reach 12 knots. I wasn't to be alone, however. I met a number of sailors in the Orkneys who had read about my previous trip through the Pentland Firth, in *Practical Boat Owner* and wanted to cruise in company with me.

Sunrise at Stonehaven.

Stromness to Longhope on Hoy via Scapa Flow

Distance: 12nm

Passage time: 3hr

I slipped at 0830 (HW Dover) and made my way with the south-going tide to arrive at Longhope at 1230 (HW Dover +4). I made up waypoints just in case they were needed, and my passage took me south through Hoy Sound and Gutter Sound, leaving Fara to port and then turning SW into Longhope at The Ruff red can buoy.

We'd had thick fog for two days, but it cleared enough to make the 12-mile passage to Longhope possible. I was longing to see the many friends I had made during my last circumnavigation because the community there is very special to me.

The sail down was a mixture of moderate visibility together with the odd ray of sunshine trying to break through. I rounded into Longhope and the wind dropped.

As there was only a mile to go I stowed my sails, prepared lines and fenders and motored towards the harbour. A new breakwater has been built since my last visit so visitors can tie up in complete safety.

I was given a very warm welcome by the Kirkpatricks whose son Kevin has featured many times in the RNLI Magazine as the coxswain of the Longhope lifeboat *The Queen Mother*, now replaced by *Helen Comrie* a Tamar class boat. It was great to see them all again with the new RNLI doctor, Tony, who kindly checked out my hand, which I had damaged in the Atlantic swell off of Ireland.

Yachtsmen will not get a better welcome anywhere than here in Longhope, and it is the ideal point to cross the Pentland Firth. The Aith Hope Lifeboat museum is a must to visit, and the village has stores, diesel, water, a first class pub and showers. The shelter is good within the new harbour and many of the locals are professional men of the sea willing to help with advice on the weather and crossing the Firth.

A warm welcome awaits visitors to Longhope Harbour.

Longhope to Wick via the Pentland Firth

Distance: 30nm

Passage time: 6hr

There can be tides up to 12 knots here so I had planned to go through on neaps. I needed to clear Cantick Head lighthouse and then head as far west as possible on the last of the ebb tide. I could then head south on the slack and be ready to ride the start of the flood between Swona and Stroma Islands. The flood would get up to six knots and carry me SE towards Duncansby Head.

I wanted to catch the early morning tide but the visibility was poor so we had to wait until the afternoon. The passage through the Pentland Firth must be done with care and in settled weather. This day was fine, but with two other yachts coming with me I felt like mother hen.

We cast off at 1530 (HW Dover +5) cleared Cantick Head lighthouse at 1615, reached Aith Hope at 1700 (HW Dover −6) then headed south on the slack. I plotted several WPs and several clearing bearings to check my position to keep clear of the islands.

It is best to keep in deep water when clearing Duncansby Head as the overfalls can be quite severe. _Jalina_ and I tried cutting the corner – which was quite

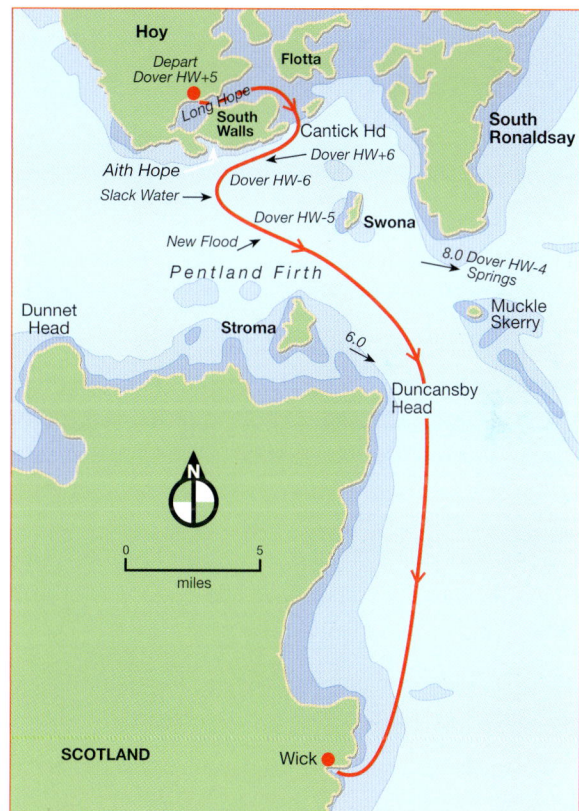

Crossing the Pentland Firth meant timing the flood to carry _Jalina_ round Duncansby Head.

safe but proved very rough, despite the good weather.

It was a good passage, and as I cleared Duncansby Head, I looked back to Hoy and was filled with great sadness at leaving the islands. However, by 2130 we were tied up in Wick, our first port on the mainland, and _Jalina_ and I were homebound once again.

Wick to Whitehills

Distance: 49nm

Passage time: 10hr

I had come through the Pentland Firth in company with *Athena* and *Shardik* and, as they were staying on in Wick, John and Carol on *Athena* invited us all on board for a glass of wine. These are the moments to savour – you can be in the loneliest of places but a common love for the sea draws people together. We were now on the east coast of Scotland and although clear of the big west coast Atlantic swell, we would instead experience very different sea conditions: the shallower depths form short, sharp seas that can build up very quickly.

There are few all-weather harbours with 24-hour access, so if you are caught in strong winds with a building sea, and the only available harbours are on a lee shore, you could be in deep trouble. During this east Coast part of my circumnavigation I experienced the hazard of a lee shore, the need to close a weather shore in a gale and suffered severe local weather patterns that were not forecast. They may have only lasted for a few minutes, but to be caught unprepared can be life-threatening. The importance of weather information is always prominent in my mind but now it takes on a different meaning – to close the coast, on a lee shore, you run into shallower water where the seas build steeper with a vengeance.

Some east coast harbours have also lost their commercial importance: some have silted up, but positive efforts are now being made to turn them around by investing in dredging and installing marinas to encourage the leisure craft industry.

Whitehills, my next port, offered good shelter within the harbour. Depth at the entrance is 1.8m MLWS, 2m MLWS in the outer harbour and 1.5m in the inner harbour. There has been 36m of new pontoon fitted in the outer harbour and shoal area to the NW of the outer harbour has now been dredged – but there can be a surge in the narrow entrance when a NW/N force 4 has been blowing for some time. If in doubt contact the Harbour Master and he will advise on local conditions (tel: 01261 861291, VHF Ch16 or 14, www.whitehillsharbour.co.uk). I called here during my last trip and it's a good example of what can be done to replace the

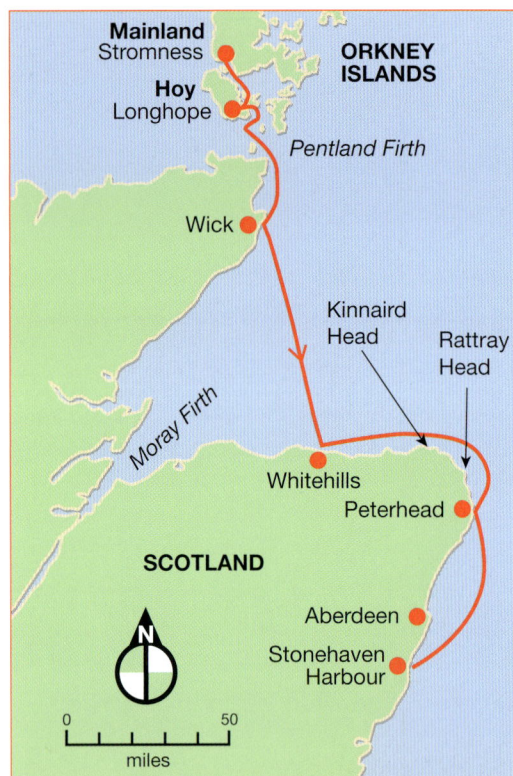

From Stromness in the Orkneys to Stonehaven on Scotland's east coast, Jalina *covered 166 miles in five days.*

fishing industry with a fine marina and excellent facilities.

The weather forecast from Aberdeen Coastguard for sea area Cape Wrath to Rattray Head was for no gale warnings; variable WNW backing to SE or veering into the NW force 3 or less; mist or fog patches, visibility moderate to good, poor in fog patches; sea state smooth to slight. For the past two days the barometer had been consistent at 1012/1015mb, so it looked like a motoring passage. As a precaution I checked the water intake filter and the engine and gearbox oil levels – all looked fine.

I always build into my planning an alternative harbour and here on the east coast I had several possibilities. Should the wind go into the NW and increase to force 4–5, I would change my course for Fraserburgh Harbour, adding 7 miles to the passage. Here the northern breakwater would give me shelter, the entrance is wide plus there is a greater depth of water. Then there is Peterhead Harbour, a good deep water harbour 15 miles further south which I estimated at worst I would reach no later than 2200 – although I had to bear in mind that a foul tide would start at 1638 (HW Dover +5) so a NW force 5 against an ebb tide, two days off springs, would build quite a sea.

Looking down onto Whitehills Harbour and marina.

I made up a tidal vector for the 50-mile passage and found there would be only 1 mile more east-going tide to allow for, magnetic variation was 5.3°W, and with the possibility of no wind, I would not have to allow for any leeway if cruising under engine. However, I reminded myself that 1° in 60 miles could put me adrift by one mile, and if the visibility should go down, and if I lost both GPS sets, then I would need to build in a discrepancy to put me up-tide of the harbour entrance.

We slipped at 0650 (HW Dover −5) in visibility of approximately half a mile with the prospect of it improving. It did, but the wind fell off, so I had to motor until 1100 when a force 2 breeze came in from the SSW. I sailed and adjusted the course to allow for leeway of +3°. The vector to allow for a slight 'S' shape for the tide both sides of the rhumb line worked out well.

I still had the company of *Shardik* who had also been circumnavigating the UK with the help of some pilotage notes from myself. We'd been sailing together for two days and it was great to have company after being alone for several months.

The approach into Whitehills Harbour was straight-forward with the white pillar of the breakwater light standing out well. Once within the breakwater you go hard to port to get into the outer harbour.

The marina offers diesel, water, a laundrette, showers, a meeting/tea room, and there is a well-stocked supermarket, restaurant and bar nearby.

Whitehills to Peterhead
Distance: 41nm
Passage time: 11hr

The weather forecast given by Aberdeen Coastguard for Cape Wrath to Rattray Head area was WNW backing SE force 4–5; occasional force 6 later, with fog patches at first. Forth Coastguard gave SE force 4–5; showers, fog patches for south of Rattray Head area. This wind direction would give me a fetch to Kinnaird Head, then from there it would be long tack down and short ones out to sea.

I was tired and left late. The morning was grey and overcast when I headed out into an easterly wind − not SE as forecast − so it was to be a beat to Rattray Head. At this point I knew it was to be a grind. As we cleared Rattray Head the wind was now force 4 and gusting, and at 1730 the tide turned foul 1.3 knots (HW Dover +5) with the wind now from the SE.

The final seven miles took three hours, and I was a little cross with myself. The wind had veered early from E to SE and I had not been tracking the fronts with my laptop and my SSB. If I had spotted the wind change I would have set off much earlier.

I think it is important to sign on with the Coastguard, with a passage plan, and sign off on arrival. Then they can keep you informed of any severe weather changes through your MMSI number – mind you, it's a bit of a shock when your alarm goes off!

As I approached the harbour I called up the port control on Ch14 and was given permission to enter – by 2050 *Jalina* and I were tied up safely. Unfortunately I had not been able to do any meal preparation on passage, because of the rough seas, so I set about making a salad,

potatoes, chicken in foil, and a fresh fruit salad. I would not slip until 0930, so I left the washing up and passage planning until the morning – sleep was more important as I was so tired.

Peterhead to Stonehaven
Distance: 34nm
Passage time: 7hr

The forecast for Rattray Head to Berwick-upon-Tweed was SE force 4–5 variable NW force 3–5; rain, showers, cyclonic; sea state slight.

My course would be influenced by the visibility; if poor I would close the coast to keep clear of any bigger vessels. A tidal vector was not necessary as the tide would run along my rhumb line.

The two obstacles on this passage are a firing range, 15 miles south of Peterhead extending two miles out to sea, and the busy approach to Aberdeen harbour. If my approach had been close to either I would have given the Coastguard a call to let them know my position and they could warn other shipping if they thought it necessary.

I slipped my lines at 0930 (HW Dover −4.5) and called Port Control for permission to clear the harbour and Aberdeen Coastguard to sign on. As it was one day before high springs, I would have one knot of tide against me easing until 1200 (HW Dover −1). But in the event the flood

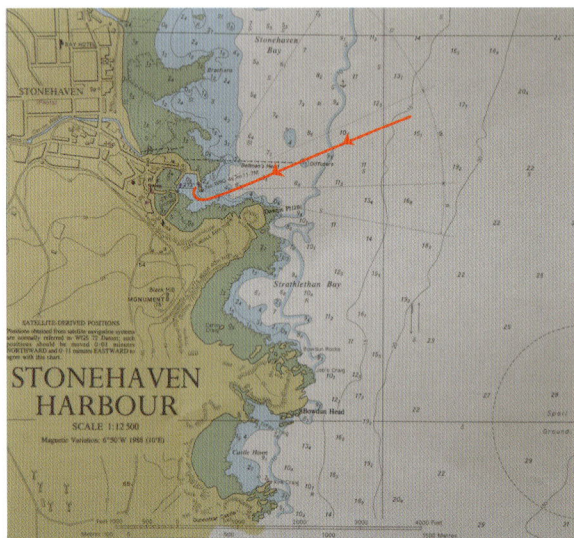

STONEHAVEN HARBOUR
SCALE 1:12 500
Magnetic Variation 6°50'W 1988 (10'E)

The approach to Stonehaven. Entry is aided by using the white sector light (see chart above left).

White sector light

started one hour early and the visibility was not too bad with the odd ray of sunshine coming through.

Stonehaven has been a busy fishing harbour, but it is tricky in strong N, NE to E winds when a swell comes in. Your approach has to be done with care so as not to cut the corners at Bellman's Head and Downie Point. Entry into the harbour is aided by a sector light and the white sector was easily spotted in the overcast light as I approached the entrance out of the mist. Within the outer harbour, dredging has been done with a long-arm JCB, so there is more depth close to the inner walls.

For the next few days I was stuck in harbour as the weather changed from the odd ray of sun to thick fog and rain – at times you could not see the opposite harbour wall. But I was surprised by the number of yachts coming and going in these conditions without radar.

Mind you, as a walker, being fog-bound has its advantages, as this is one of the most beautiful coastlines in Scotland and the monument on Black Hill is well worth the trip.

Jalina delayed by fog in Stonehaven.

Showers are included in the mooring fee; the local Stonehaven Ship Inn serves good food and beer; there is water, stores, banks, diesel by tender and rail links.

An ominous-looking storm brews over Stonehaven harbour.

Down the north-east coast: Stonehaven to Whitby

It was a frustrating few days stuck in Stonehaven harbour due to the fog. This tests a sailor's patience to the limit, but on this hostile coast fog and rocks are best not mixed. However I made the best of it by putting on my walking boots and heading for the hills. I made it to the ruins of Dunnottar Castle (the location for *Hamlet* starring Mel Gibson) and the beautiful RSPB reserve at Fowlsheugh, so my enforced stay was not without its merits.

Stonehaven to Arbroath

Distance: 31nm

Passage time: 7hr

At 0705 I received the Coastguard forecast for Rattray Head to Berwick-upon-Tweed for the next 24 hours: SE force 3–4, variable south-west later; thundery showers, visibility moderate, fog patches, sea state smooth – and the following 24 hours was much the same. So I sat tight to see if the fog would clear by 1000, which would let us make Arbroath by teatime. The tide would be fair by 1400 (HW Dover −2) and the worst of the foul would be one knot. My course would be the same as the fore-and-aft tide, so it looked like a motoring passage.

I rang the harbour master at Arbroath to ask about getting into the inner-gated harbour and was told the latest time would be 1945. Access to the marina is approximately 2.5 hours either side of high water, and outside these times you can either tie up alongside the harbour wall under the

The new marina at Arbroath has plenty of room.

299°T – Leading lights in transit

Rocks

299°T
Leading lights in transit

Arbroath leading marks are clear (top) and keep you off rocks near the entrance (above).

Watch House (Lazy Hole) in the outer harbour, or alongside the fish market. I slipped at 1015 (HW Dover –6) with a Jaguar called *Aluco* and motored all the way to Arbroath.

The two white transit markers for Arbroath Harbour stand out to the right of the prominent signal tower, but care is needed as there are underlying rocks about 100m either side of the transit. The bar was dredged in 1999 to 2m CD,

although the entrance can be dangerous in a south-easterly swell. As we turned into the inner harbour I was surprised to see two Viking longboats coming out of the mist – a Viking raid re-enactment was underway! This really was worth seeing, with duelling, archery, and displays of traditional crafts like chain-mail making all taking place – and the highlight was a torch-lit procession that concluded with the burning of a longboat.

But even better was an invitation to go out on exercise with the Arbroath lifeboat – named *Inchcape* after the rock that the Bell Rock lighthouse is built upon. The slipway launch was a skilled task, because just ahead of us was the harbour wall! I had a tremendous time with the crew.

Arbroath is famous for 'smokies' (cured haddock) that are processed in the fishing quarter, and the hot 'Bridie' meat and onion pies from the local town of Forfar.

Other facilities include supermarkets, launderettes, banks, restaurants, pubs, rail links, diesel, water and marine engineers.

I was most impressed with the professionalism and seamanship of the lifeboat crew aboard Inchcape.

Arbroath to Eyemouth
Distance: 44nm
Passage time: 10hr

I was tied up in Arbroath for over a week because of fog and gales. At last the weather forecast gave N force 4–5, occasional force 6 easing, but there was still a big sea running due to the gale. My main concern was the entry into Eyemouth harbour, which is exposed to the north with rocks each side of the approach.

I prepared my drogue because if the northerly wind

The carnival atmosphere of the Arbroath Viking raid re-enactment included Crusaders as well as Norsemen.

increased to a force 6 I wouldn't be able to see the tops of the swell, as it would be breaking away from my direction. I also checked to see if the tidal movement in and out of the Tay made any difference to my passage.

During the winter I'd planned this passage by spreading out the charts against each other, on the carpet at home, and drawing up my passage rhumb lines – all so much easier than trying to do it onboard.

At 0330 I contacted the Forth Coastguard by mobile phone for a weather update. I decided to go and slipped my lines at 0530 (HW Dover −6). If the entrance at

Gale force winds and fog kept us in Arbroath Harbour for over a week.

Eyemouth was too dangerous to enter with a big sea running from the north to north-east I would carry on to Blyth. This would be a long passage but the best option, as I could enter in all but strong winds from the east and south-east when the seas break across the bar.

I was a little concerned that the fog, which had been plaguing the Tay area might return while I was on passage, so I called the Forth Coastguard and asked them for any shipping movements. They said they could also give me ships' AIS (Automatic Identification System) positions should the visibility fall.

In the past, in fog, I have also put out a general call to ships giving my position and heading. On the whole I've found they are quite happy to help, giving their position, heading etc and warning me if any other ships are coming my way.

It was good to be free and out to sea again, settling down to the navigation I enjoy so much. A number of ships passed by and I phoned the Eyemouth harbour master who said there were breakers on the surrounding rocks but that it should settle a little later. I knew the entrance well, having been close to hitting the rocks off the entrance during my last circumnavigation; on that occasion the yellow on the north cardinal had been masked by a number of red buoys used to stop it from sinking.

As I approached Eyemouth entrance, I could see the white of the swell and spray breaking onto the rocks at either side, but the centre looked fine. One thing the pilot books don't tell you about is the noise of the swell crashing onto the rocks, which is hard to block out of your mind.

I checked my heading, clearing lines and waypoint, and all looked fine. I spotted the north cardinal guarding the rocks to the east of my track, but there is only about half a cable clear each side of your track. I could see the red transit, and once clear of the rocks, lined up and pressed on under sail and engine. Once in the harbour I handed and stowed the sails and got the lines and fenders ready – in rough conditions I don't fit shore lines until I enter the shelter of harbour just in case they are washed overboard and foul the prop.

Since my last visit, when I tied up onto the harbour wall, they'd fitted a pontoon the full length of the upper harbour wall on your port side.

Eyemouth to Blyth
Distance: 55nm
Passage time: 12hr

The weather forecast was SW force 3–4, so the passage would be a fetch with no tidal vectors needed. I informed the Forth Coastguard of my passage plans on Ch16 and was asked to sign off with Humber Coastguard on my arrival. I did not slip until 0530 (HW Dover +6) to use the daylight to clear the rocky entrance, with a full main, orange working jib and genoa lashed down on the foredeck.

To clear the entrance, I plotted a reciprocal course to my entry, plus a WP to clear north of the cardinal marker, then a course due east for one mile, followed by a course towards the 'Goldstone' green can between Holy Island and the Farne Islands.

I also made up extra WPs to take me east of the Farne Islands (58m) in case the wind changed and a heavy swell

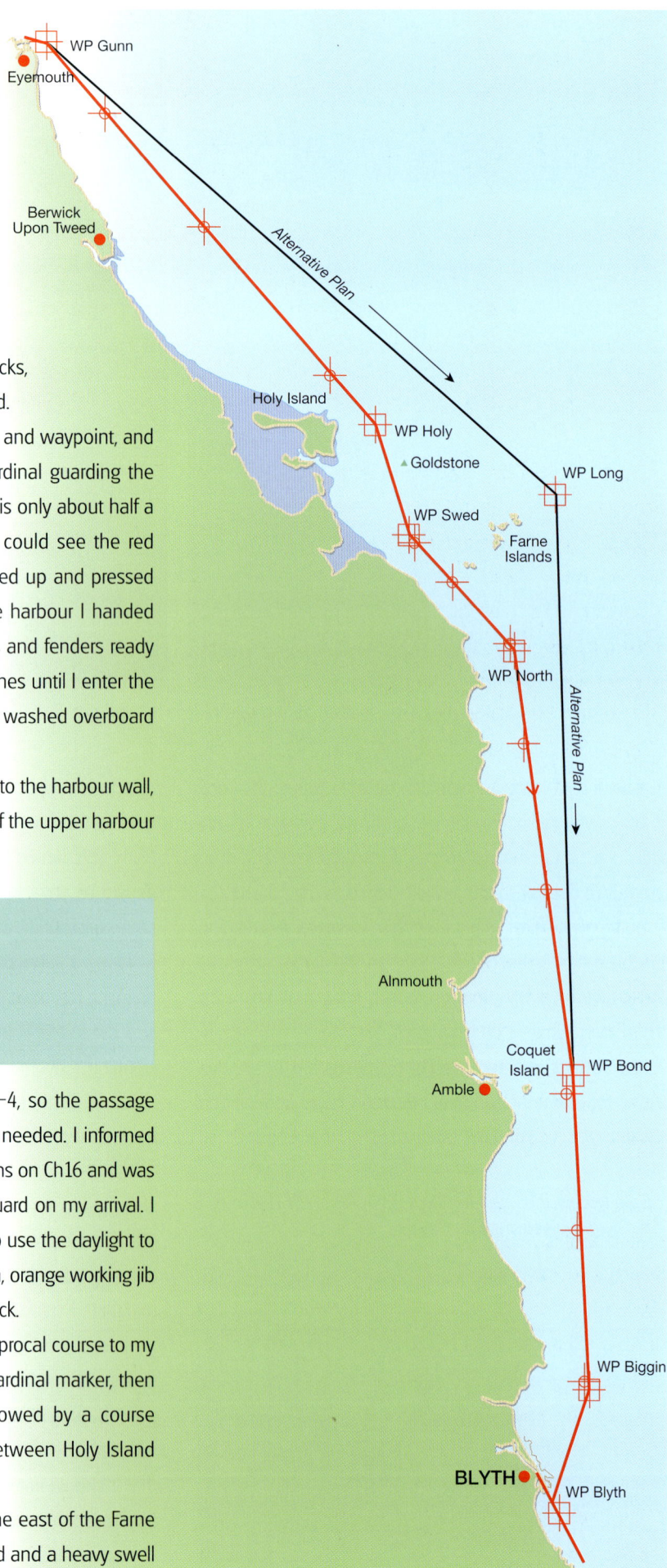

On the approach to Eyemouth Harbour, the navigation red transit posts stand out well.

developed, making the Inner Passage shallow water (11m) dangerous.

Once clear of the entrance, I hoisted the No 2 genoa and we were making five knots in a force 3 – I was well pleased. It was great to be moving and I was looking forward to meeting up with my good friend Mike, a fellow circumnavigator, on his yacht *Kes* off the Amble.

By 0900 I was off the distinctive Holy Island (Lindisfarne) with its castle standing high, then passed Goldstone and Swedman green cans to clear the inner Sound to the Farne Islands.

Bamburgh Castle and village stood out against the otherwise flat coastline and once clear of Grimstone red can, south of North Sunderland Harbour, I set a course for WP 'Bond' one mile east of Amble Coquet Island. Rocks stretch nearly a mile from the shore at this point. At 1300 (HW Dover +1) as the tide turned slack, then fair, I spotted *Kes* approaching – his timing was perfect. Five miles north of Blyth the chimneys of the Lynemouth aluminium works stand out well and we soon spotted the wind turbines lining the east pier of Blyth harbour.

Our approach from the north was along the 10m contour as this would keep us clear of rocks Pig, Sow, and Seaton, east of the pier. The old Sow Rock buoy has been removed, so once past the eastern pier head we bore 280°T and called the harbour control on Ch12 for clearance to enter. The orange transit diamonds stand out well and once off the Royal Northumberland Yacht Club (RNYC) marina there is plenty of room to round up and hand the main and set lines and fenders.

The clubhouse is an old wooden lightship with showers, bar and a restaurant, and you are guaranteed a very warm

welcome. Fuel is available in cans, and there is also water and gas. Banks and supermarkets are just a short walk away from the RNYC, but they close early on Wednesdays.

Blyth to Hartlepool Marina
Distance: 31nm
Passage time: 6hr

The weather forecast was SSW force 3–4, rain showers, visibility moderate to good, sea state slight. I only needed WPs off South Shields Harbour entrance and Hartlepool Bay. The only dangers for this passage were rocks close to St Mary's lighthouse, three miles south of Blyth entrance, and crossing the shipping near South Shields Harbours.

After checking the weather with NAVTEX and Humber Coastguard, *Kes* and *Jalina* were ready to slip by 1000 (HW Dover −3.5). By 1200 the skies darkened as a squall approached. We saw shipping crossing our path, on passage into South Shields Harbour, so we shortened sail and headed further out to sea. Within minutes the winds were up to force 7, the visibility down to a few yards and the rain was heavy, cold, and streaming off the main like a waterfall. The ships would have no chance of seeing us visually, or on radar, so we needed to keep well clear. The squall passed in a few minutes and we both hardened up back on course.

Due to the heavy rain, rivers were turning the water brown for miles out to sea, carrying flotsam like I have never seen before – huge trees large enough to sink a yacht.

We were soon in Hartlepool Bay (HW Dover +3). Access is through a dredged channel with a sector light and a lock

You can charter HMS Trincomalee *for special events.*

with traffic signals. The marina is one of the best along this coast with everything nearby. There is even HMS *Trincomalee* of 1817, that can be chartered for special events, together with Royal Marines in full dress uniform.

Mike soon took me to a great local drinking hole called Smallies (Small Craft Club) and kindly invited me for a meal and a real bed for the night. However I was a little reluctant to leave *Jalina* and not sure of how his wife Rose would greet the man who encouraged Mike to leave her for a few months while he circumnavigated the UK! I needn't have worried – we had a great time.

Hartlepool to Whitby

Distance: 24nm

Passage time: 5hr

The main obstacles for this passage were crossing the shipping using the River Tees, Salt Scar Rocks to the southeast of Tees Bay, and the narrow entrance of Whitby harbour itself. The weather forecast for Hartlepool to Whitby was SE going SW force 4; showers, visibility good, sea state moderate.

Whitby entrance is set into the coastline a little, giving some protection and the south-west wind would give me a weather shore.

I departed Hartlepool at 1445 on a fair flood tide for a five hour passage. By 1730, the flood tide had increased to one knot and, as it was 'wind-against-tide', the building sea was not helped by the shallow waters of the east coast. *Jalina* was soon digging her nose into the swell and the sea was running down the deck and over the spray hood. This made it hard to spot the many crab pot markers, even though they were well flagged.

On the approach to Whitby harbour there are rocks to the eastern side guarded by a north cardinal buoy one mile north of the entrance. By 1900 we closed on the entrance, with very little swell, and I called the bridge control who have to open the road bridge to give access to the marina.

By 1940 *Jalina* and I were tied up in one of the most beautiful marina settings along this coast. I spent my early childhood around here and remember buying freshly

Shoal water — Brown scouring of seabed — Rocks — Rocks

The water was churned up and brown off Whitby due to storms. The entrance can be tricky with rocks stretching out to the east of the harbour.

smoked kippers from the shop that is still on the hill path to the Abbey.

My mother, who still lives nearby, visited to check that I was still in one piece – mums never let go! We had two days walking and caught up with all the gossip until it was time to go. Her parting gift was a beautiful fruit cake to be eaten with slabs of cheese – an old northern tradition.

Sunrise over Whitby.

Gales on the English east coast: Whitby to Felixstowe

Bridlington – Y class yachts prepare to race.

The east coast of England has a beauty of its own, but it can be hostile. Shoal waters create breaking seas in a force 6 and closing a lee shore when a force 4 has been blowing for several days can hold a few surprises. After being at sea for several months your senses become heightened and more sensitive to developing weather patterns, but at this point in my circumnavigation, I was concerned at becoming complacent – weather forecasting is hardly an exact science, after all.

On the Bridlington to Lowestoft leg, I encountered busy shipping lanes and gale force winds.

Whitby

Scarborough

Flamborough Head

Bridlington

North Sea

Hull

Squall

Spurn Head
Fl.21M

Grimsby

Gale warning

R. Humber

Shipping Lane

Inner Dowsing
Fl.24M

Race Bk

F7

F8

Skegness

The Wash

F7

Wells

Cromer
Gp Fl(5)20M

F6 gusting

N

0   20
miles

BRIDLINGTON TO LOWESTOFT

Great Yarmouth

Lowestoft
Fl.28M

Whitby to Bridlington
Distance: 39nm
Passage time: 10hr

Whitby lies between two Coastguard weather forecasting areas. The forecast for Berwick-upon-Tweed to Whitby was NW force 3–4, going SW force 2–3, showers; visibility good, sea state moderate. For Whitby to the Wash it was force 4–5, going SW force 2–3; sea state slight to moderate. However, the five-day forecast was not good with strong easterly winds for the next four days, so I decided to get going.

This passage would take me past Robin Hood's Bay, Scarborough, and Filey with its distinctive headland of Filey Brigg – some of the busiest holiday resorts on this coast. Beyond Flamborough Head lighthouse, the only danger was the shallows of North Smithic, which are guarded by a north cardinal mark. A number of big racing yachts were preparing to leave the harbour, so I asked for their ideas on coping with the deep swell that was running through the entrance. 'Keep over to the port side with full main up, gun the engine and go for it,' was the advice.

So, I taped up the hatch with two-inch tape, made sure my orange heavy foresail was well lashed down and slipped my lines at 0920 (HW Dover −6hr), two days after springs.

Bridlington before the storm.

Wow – what a swell! This really peaked my adrenaline. The main was pulling, I kept over to port, gunned the engine and we were off. Why go to Blackpool for a big-dipper ride when they have an even better one at Whitby? Once outside the entrance I cleared the north cardinal buoy and set a course for Flamborough Head. Bridlington is just inside the Head and the earliest I could enter was 1900 (HW Dover +4hr), two hours before HW Bridlington. To the south of the Head I could just make out the sea breaking over the shoals of North Smithic.

Shallows to the east of the harbour entrance had built up the seas and rain had reduced visibility, but as I approached the harbour entrance on a weather shore, the swell died down. By 1915 I was tied up safely against the southern harbour wall, near the crane. I made sure I closed off all the sea-cocks because as the harbour dries, you sink completely into the soft mud. I also had to fit my running snatch block onto a masthead line to keep *Jalina* against the wall as she went down.

Facilities here are adequate, with the best showers being at the Royal Yorkshire Yacht Club RYYC) close to the harbour. Fuel, water, banks, stores, restaurants and bars are all nearby.

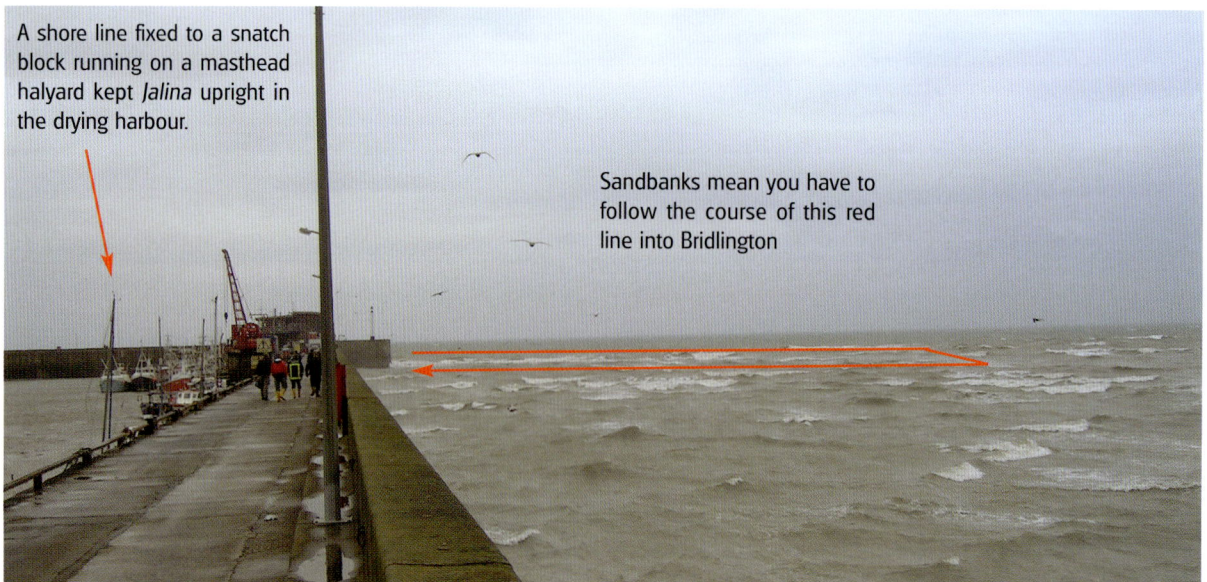

A shore line fixed to a snatch block running on a masthead halyard kept *Jalina* upright in the drying harbour.

Sandbanks mean you have to follow the course of this red line into Bridlington

Cut the corner into Bridlington harbour entrance and the chances are you'll run aground on the sandbank.

Bridlington to Lowestoft
Distance: 126nm
Passage time: 26hr

This passage from Bridlington to Lowestoft turned out to be the longest and the most demanding in my circumnavigation. I monitored the weather forecasts from a number of different sources: my Navtex, the Coastguard's four-hourly bulletins, LW 198, and synoptic charts from my NASA SSB radio via my second-hand laptop.

The Coastguard forecast for Humber to the Wash was SE veering S to SW force 4–5, occasional force 6; showers, some rain, visibility moderate to good, sea state moderate. The following 24 hours was forecast S to SW veering W force 4–5. The weather looked OK for the next 48 hours, so I decided to go for it, but at the same time I was hesitant – it was unsettled. I would monitor the weather while under way on my approach to the Humber (my last bolt hole), I would make a decision whether to go on or not. I prepared a tidal vector for the passage Humber to Lowestoft, which worked out at one knot more east-going tide for The Wash section, but I was more concerned about the swell. If it got up it could have a greater effect on my heading, and I would have to keep within the deeper water of the channels. (See chart on page 113.)

Before slipping I checked that the seacocks were clear of mud and then made my way into the open sea. The wind was SW force 2, so progress was slow, and in six hours we only covered 20 miles.

Storm clouds gather
On all these passages I book in with the Coastguard, giving my passage plan, ETA and DSC Maritime Mobile Service Identity (MMSI) number so they can call me easily. Six miles north of the Humber, I booked in with Humber Vessel Traffic Services (VTS) on Ch12–14, and then called Humber and Great Yarmouth Coastguard for weather information. As both gave me good weather reports, I told them that my plan was to continue down through the Dowsing and press on to Lowestoft. The tide was with me but I had no bolt hole. Humber VTS gave permission to cross their Traffic Separation Scheme, visibility was good, the wind was SW force 3–4 and the barometer had been steady all day at 990–999MB. But about five miles NE of the entrance to the Humber, I spotted a large, dark cloud approaching. During the afternoon there had been several squalls, but with the setting sun behind this one, it looked particularly menacing.

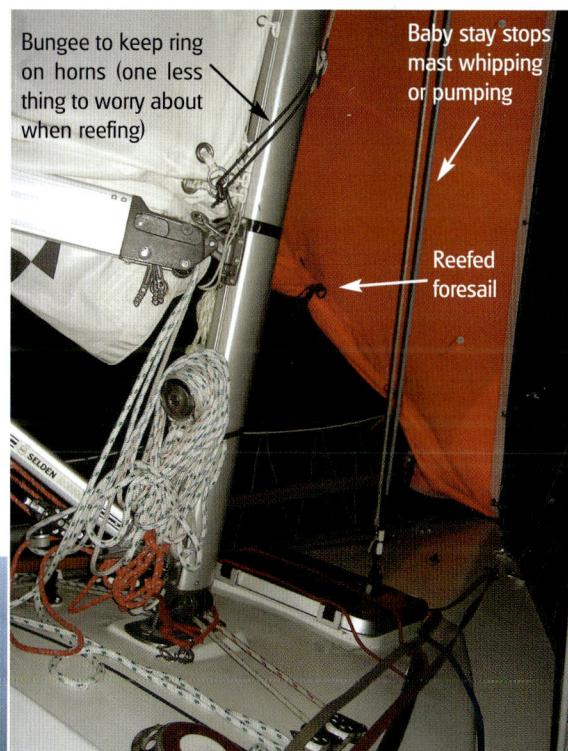

Bungee to keep ring on horns (one less thing to worry about when reefing)

Baby stay stops mast whipping or pumping

Reefed foresail

This foreboding cloud on the horizon was a squall and a precursor to rough weather.

I started the engine and lashed down all the sails, and all the while I could hear the sound of the wind and waves increasing dramatically. We were then hit by a tremendous force that I'm sure would have shredded the sails, if they had still been up. Luckily, it was soon over and later on I discovered that these violent squalls might have been caused by the remnants of Hurricane Charley in the Atlantic.

After a few more bursts of high wind, conditions improved enough to allow me to have a wash and shave. I managed to heat up a chicken casserole – food, rest and warm, dry clothes can do wonders for morale. There was no turning back now, so I prepared for a long night passage. I lowered the topmast pennant (to avoid obscuring the tricolour masthead light), checked all the torches, plugged in the search light, checked the spare GPS, and put the liferaft into the cockpit. I changed down to my orange, heavy-duty jib (as it is easier to see ahead under the high-cut foot) and put a reef in the main.

At 2030, the night was closing in and the sky looked very angry. Travelling at 6.1 knots, I put in a second reef in the main – but was still doing 6 knots!

Water over the decks

The wind was gathering strength from the west and at 2130, Yarmouth Coastguard put out an imminent gale warning. I called them back for confirmation and they asked for my position, number of persons on board, safety equipment, DSC MMSI number and who held my CG66 (ship's and personal details). A general discussion took place, ending with, 'don't hesitate to call us if you need help – we will

Good wet weather gear proved an essential accessory.

WP preparation: when I work out a Lat and Long, I write down the bearing to the next WP at the end of it. This is a good check that you have transferred the data for the WP correctly. (Bearing to WP circled.)

keep in touch'. I prepared for the worst. I needed to close the Norfolk weather shore to get a bit of a lee as quickly as possible – but it was still about 10 hours away. I put a slab in the orange heavyweight jib, three slabs in the main and replaced the top sail battens with flexible ones which allows the roach to bend out and spill the wind in a gust.

The wind increased quickly, driving water over the deck, so I was glad that I had earlier taped up all the hatches and lockers. The violent gusts were driving a heavy sea before them, so I eased the main to reduce weather helm and to help my autopilot. I had two thoughts; one to drive her hard to my next heading change, which was more to the east, so if the gale got any worse I could bear away and take the seas on the quarter; the other plan was to take it steady and slow her down for comfort. In the event I pressed her on and we reached 8.7 knots at times. *Jalina* lifted well on the swell and surf, but every so often the cockpit filled, so I dropped the sprayhood to reduce windage and to allow the sea a clear run over the top.

Weathering the storm

The wind increased to force 7, gusting force 8, and I was thankful *Jalina* had a low freeboard and heavy displacement. Her lee side was hardly dipping and she kept a good steady course. Throughout all this we also had to avoid a few ships and I often shone my searchlight onto the main-sail to draw us to their attention. Flasks of hot soup and tea were stowed in my sea bucket in the cockpit for refreshment, and several slices of toasted bread kept me going.

Then above the tremendous noise of the wind and sea the Coastguard announced a downgrading of the gale to a strong wind force 7 warning – thank goodness!

At 0400 we were closing the weather shore of the Cromer coast and the shore lights were a welcome sight. The wind was still force 7 but at least the seas had eased and were no longer running into the cockpit. This meant I could make a cup of fresh tea and have a good slice of my mum's cake and cheese.

By 0600 the wind had eased to force 3. As the sun started to come up I felt a bit bruised and drained – it had been a long night and one hell of a sail. Then my DSC alarm went off. Surely not another gale warning? But no, it was the Coastguard. 'How are you faring – is all OK?' They were changing watches and wanted to maintain contact – it was good to hear from them again. The remainder of the passage was in a gentle breeze and we tied up in Lowestoft at 0730. I thanked Great Yarmouth Coastguard and signed off, relieved to have come through a testing trip with no gear failure.

Lowestoft to Felixstowe (Shotley Marina)
Distance: 39nm
Passage time 9.5hr

I stayed two nights at Lowestoft to rest and recover and stock up with enough stores to last a week. Fresh fruit, vegetables and salad items were kept aired in net bags and the cans were all marked up in coded shorthand so they were easy to identify. *Jalina* was so encrusted with salt that I gave the decks, sails and saloon a good wash down with fresh water. The warm breeze soon dried her out and after doing a load of washing, I was ready to move on.

I planned to slip at 0600 (HW Dover −2hr 30min) to use the last three hours of the flood to take me down towards Shotley. Being one day after neaps, I would get a total of 5.9 knots of foul tide, and 5.2 knots of fair for the passage. The weather forecast for The Wash to North Foreland was good; NW force 4–5 to force 5–6, easing. I called the Great Yarmouth Coastguard (Ch16–67) with my passage plan and permission to clear their harbour. By 0730 we were abeam of Southwold; the wind was WSW force 3, gusting force 4, and we were on a fine reach with one reef in the main

Ten miles to go, the sea was brown after the gale.

CG66 FORMS AND DSC ALERT

When you call the Coastguard using their MMSI (Maritime Mobile Service Identity), your own MMSI number, name and call sign come up on their screen. Using their International Telecommunications Union Database, they can then run a search for your CG66 details. CG66 has personal details, a description of your vessel, sail number, Small Ships Registry (SSR) number, colour etc, and other contact information.

When filling in the CG66 form, most skippers apparently give their home as a contact – which is not much use when everyone is at sea. So they prefer this should be a neighbour or a friend to whom you have given a passage plan. A mobile phone number is also useful. Form CG66 can be downloaded from the MCA website www. mcga.gov.uk. You can then write, e-mail or fax the Coastguard a pre-set passage plan, which they feed into a 'working log' or 'electronic diary'. Using this they can keep track of your movements – all you need to do is keep them informed of your progress by radio.

When I faced the gale crossing The Wash, I'd already been in touch with the Coastguard giving my passage plan, so they were aware of my presence. As a result of my asking for confirmation of the gale warning they set up a 'watching brief' or 'minor incident'. As they had my MMSI number, they were then able to contact me periodically to check on my progress.

Don't press the button

NEVER press the red distress button to test the DSC set – there is no test facility and the authorities will assume you are in trouble. What you should do instead is to send a routine call to the Coastguard using their MMSI number. They can then tell you your DSC signal strength on a scale of one to five.

and my trusty orange working jib. At 0900 we were abeam of the Sizewell atomic power station with its distinctive silver dome, and in the distance I could see the Orford Ness lighthouse.

When approaching the busy shipping harbour of Felixstowe, yachts must keep to a recommended track. Coming from the north you cross to the south of the main channel between Platters south cardinal and Rolling Ground green can, and then keep outside, following the red cans. Once round Andrews Spit, take care not to stray too close to the shore (as my depth alarm warned me I had done) as it shoals.

On my approach to Felixstowe I called Shotley marina (Ch80), as I could see in the distance that there were yachts going into the lock. 'Yes we'll wait for you,' he said. By 1530 we were tied up and signed off with the Coastguard.

Shelter is good in Shotley Marina. It has access at all states of the tide via a dredged 2m channel, which is well lit, with 24-hour access through the lock. There are all the facilities you need: diesel, water, a laundrette, meals with a good pint of beer, and even a ferry to Harwich.

The Thames Estuary and the Goodwin Sands: Felixstowe to Dover

Ramsgate – one of my favourite harbours. I like its continental-style shops and cafés.

During my four months circumnavigation of the UK, I have dealt with all sorts of harbours; some dried out, some with limited access and others which were open all hours – but they were all tranquil compared to those encountered in the south-east. Having arrived at Felixstowe I was still in need of sleep after my 26-hour passage crossing The Wash, so I rested up for two days in the shelter of Shotley marina.

Felixstowe to Ramsgate

Distance: 43nm
Passage time: 9hr

I enjoyed walking along the rivers Orwell and Stour – it was peaceful and the weather was getting better by the day, so I was soon firing on all cylinders again.

My arrival at Felixstowe had been timed to cross the Thames close to neap tides. If I arrived at North Foreland before the tide turned fair I could close the coast a bit more to get out of the adverse stream. Also, the ideal time to use the Medusa Channel out of Felixstowe is at low water just before the flood. Mind you, with a deep swell running in this shallow channel, you have to wait to allow some of the flood to bring more water in. Alternatively, you can take the recommended yacht channel, which takes you out to the north of Cork Sand yacht beacon, then the north cardinal to clear Sunk Head Tower and on to Black Deep – but this would add an hour to your passage.

An alternative route would be to clear Long Sand Head and through Knock Deep to North Foreland. Although the majority of my charts are 'cancelled' and updated by me, for crossing the Thames I splashed out and bought a second-hand one updated by the supplier. I last crossed the Thames Estuary in a westerly force 7, but the forecast for this passage was WNW force 3–4 backing SW force 2–3; visibility good, sea state slight. So it looked like a full main and No 2 genoa – but because of the traffic in the Thames, to be on the safe side I used the orange working jib to be as visible as possible.

Shotley

Dover HW-6

Harwich

Harwich Deep Water Channel

Cork Sand Yacht Bn

Alternative Route

Dover HW-5

Medusa Channel

Dover HW-4

11,20

Dover HW-3.5

Heading

Track

Longsand Head

Mersea Island

Sunk Head Tower

09,17

Gunfleet Sand

Black Deep

Dover HW-3

Wind

09,17

Long Sand

Alternative Route

Sunk Sand

Dover HW-2

Fishermans Gat

N

Maplin Sand

Dover HW-0.5

0   10

miles

13,24

North Foreland

Dover HW+1

17,30

Margate

Elbow

Ramsgate

Edinburgh

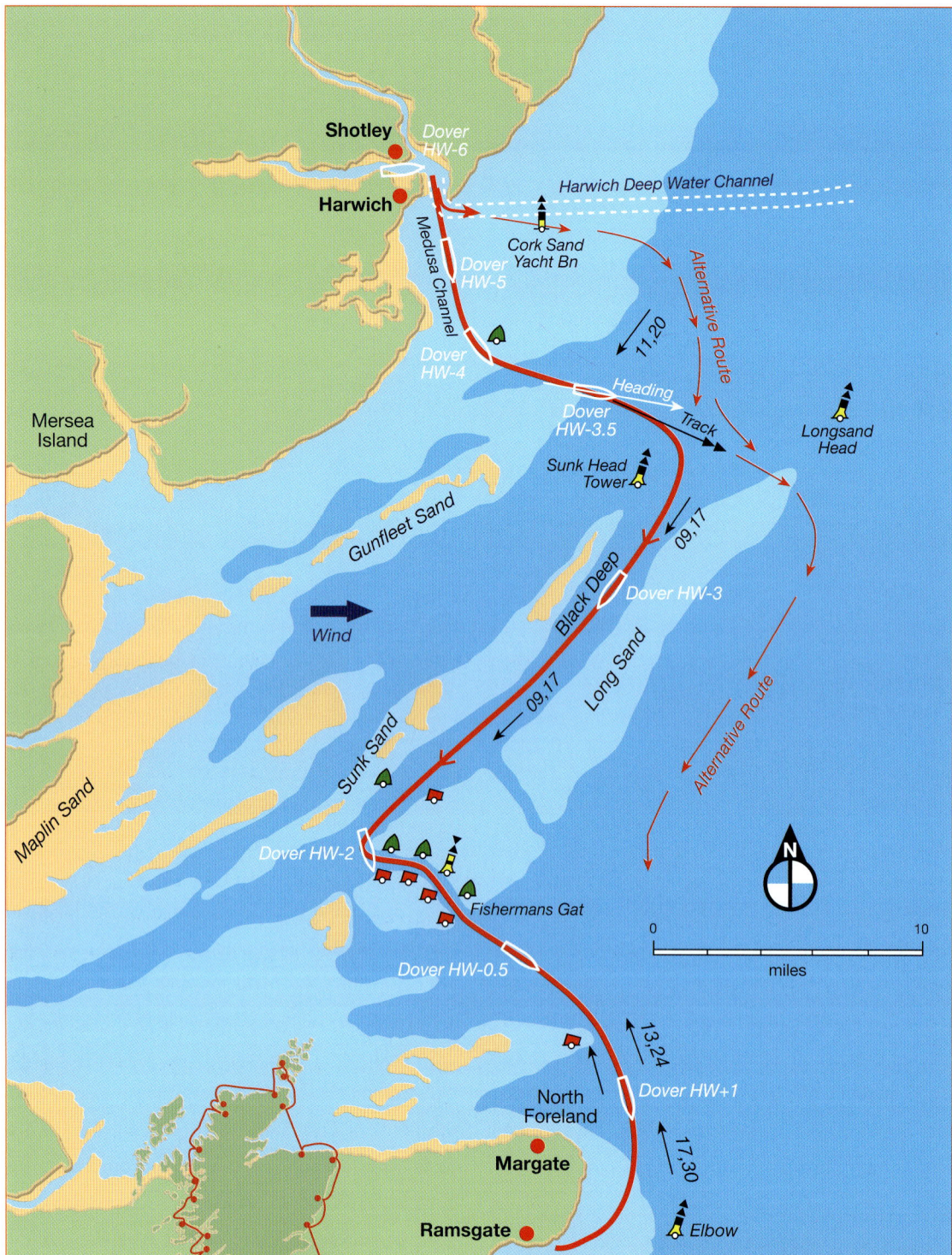

I plotted two alternative routes from Felixstowe (Shotley marina) to Ramsgate.

Belfast

Dublin

Cardiff

London

Shotley
Harwich

Margate   Ramsgate

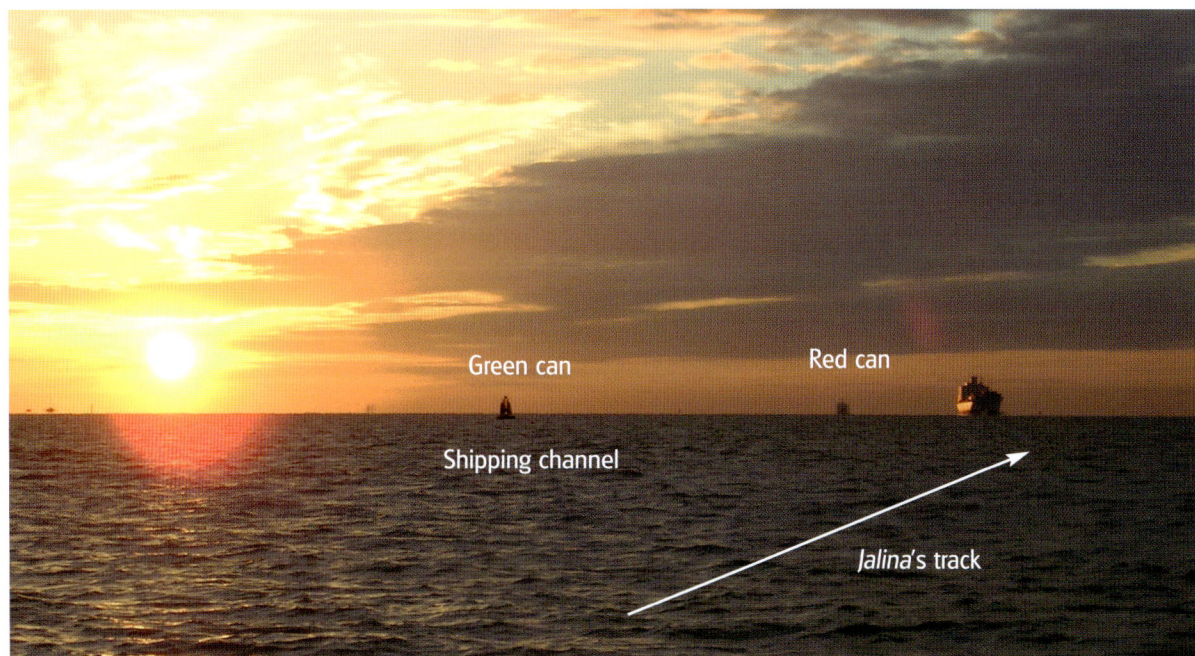

Green can

Red can

Shipping channel

Jalina's track

Clearing Felixstowe entrance and bound for Ramsgate with the rising sun.

I cleared Shotley Marina lock at 0530 (HW Dover −5hr), to give me one hour of the new flood for my passage down the Medusa Channel. At the same time I also called Thames Coastguard to sign on with my passage plan. Care has to be taken when entering and leaving this very busy shipping port and it is important to keep to the recommended yacht channel.

Proceed with caution

One thing I have learned about sailing down the UK's east coast is to treat the charted depths and sandbank positions with caution. I have encountered so many differences − probably caused by storms − that I keep a note of depths as I pass buoys and check their position with the GPS. A new chart can very quickly become out of date, even though I check it against the *Notice to Mariners* and *BA NP74 Lights and Fog Signals.*

For a passage through shoal areas I make up a 'passage plan logbook' to include depths for each hour. I used this to clear the Medusa Channel and to see if it was safe to cut across the Long Sand. In the event I ruled this out because as I approached Long Sand there was too much swell − in the troughs the depth sounder was showing depths of between just one and two metres, and over the shallows there would be even less water. The direction of the tide is influenced by the sandbanks and can change dramatically between high and low water. At HW the tide

passes over the sandbanks, but when the water level falls, the tidal streams follow the channel more. There can be crosscurrents in the channels (more pronounced at springs) particularly between HW −1hr and HW +1hr, so a constant check on the GPS highway is necessary to maintain an accurate course. I also think it's a good idea to have another GPS up and running to double-check your position. When sailing short-handed, well marked up charts and a good passage plan logbook can reduce the time spent at the chart table when eyeball pilotage is more important.

To help keep alert, I had flasks of soup and tea, together with toast and sandwiches in the cockpit − I love dunking strips of toast in soup and it always tastes better in the open! I was soon through the Medusa Channel and by 0800 I was in Black Deep.

Track and bearing indicators help to show that you are heading for the WP and that you are on course.

KEEP A GOOD LOOKOUT

Ships have very little room to manoeuvre in the channels so you need to keep a good lookout. The last time I was here I had a ship closing from astern on the same track, and when I managed to raise him on Ch12 he said it was difficult to see me in the broken water and that my radar image was lost in the clutter on his screen. This time when I called a ship giving my position he said he'd seen my bright orange sail from miles away – 'a good idea' he said. At some time in the future I will also have an orange upper panel fitted to a mainsail.

By 0930 *Jalina* and I were in Fisherman's Gat, going well in a westerly force 2–3. My next fair tide would be 1543 (HW Dover +5) but it was only 1300 when I arrived at North Foreland (HW Dover +2hr) so we had 1.3 knots against us. This is where my pre-calculated tidal depths came into their own, as I knew I could sail close inshore, along the 2m contour line, This is a simple technique – just match the depth shown on the depth sounder to the pre-calculated depths, and sail along the contour. My depth sounder is set to water depth and the alarm is set to depth under the keel.

With a westerly wind force 2–3, and nearly two hours of foul tide to contend with, it was a compromise, since the more we close the weather shore, the more we lost the wind. The approach to Ramsgate harbour had to be done under power and there is a recommended yacht channel to keep you clear of the ferries. From the north you should cross the shipping channel just west of No 3 green can. On my approach I called port control on Ch14 for permission

to enter the harbour. I had to wait for a short while in the Small Craft South Holding Area, just off the South Breakwater, while a ferry departed.

I entered, keeping a listening watch on Ch14, and once inside the harbour I called the Ramsgate Marina on Ch80. I tied up at 1430.

> Ramsgate is my favourite harbour along this part of the coast, as it is very Continental with street cafés and open-fronted fruit and vegetable shops. Facilities include diesel, petrol, gas, banks, launderette, and some of the best-stocked small shops I have seen.

The pressures of the populated South Coast were soon evident; I had left the peace and quite of the north and east coasts to be sitting under the flight path of the aircraft flying low into Ramsgate airport. And after being at sea for so long I even had to re-learn how to cross the road and deal with the busy traffic of Ramsgate. I was not looking forward, to Dover harbour with its heavy sea traffic of fast cats and ferries.

Ramsgate to Dover
Distance: 17nm
Passage time: 3hr

I had rested for two days so I needed to press on. A new strong wind warning was issued for late morning; SW force 3–4 increasing to force 5–6. I decided to slip immediately because even though it was only a short passage, the sea around Dover can build to a very uncomfortable swell. I'd prepared my waypoints and charts the night before so I only had to sign on with Dover Coastguard with my passage plan, and call Ramsgate Harbour Control for permission to clear the harbour via the Small Craft Holding Area. I cleared east of North Quern north cardinal by 0630 and set a course for South Brake red can, taking care to clear the shoals of Cross Ledge and Brake. Even though it was only a short passage, care was needed not to go off course. With the last three hours of fair ebb tide I would be heading through the inner passage of the Goodwin Sands – a graveyard for ships!

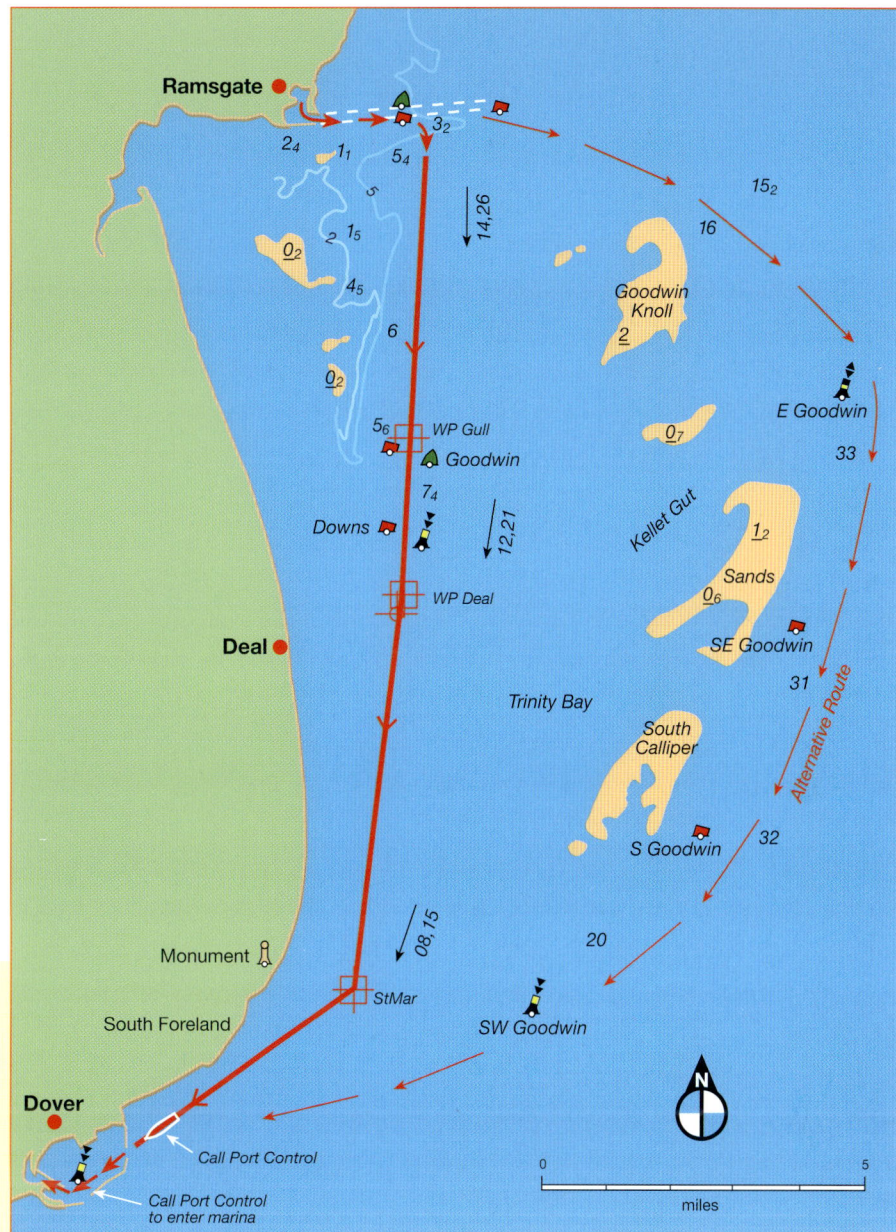

Ramsgate

2_4 1_1 5_4 3_2

5

$14,26$

15_2

0_2 2 1_5 16

4_5

Goodwin Knoll
2

6

0_2

0_7 E Goodwin

5_6 WP Gull 33

Goodwin

7_4 Kellet Gut 1_2

Downs Sands 0_6

WP Deal SE Goodwin

$12,21$ 31

Deal

Trinity Bay

South Calliper

$08,15$

S Goodwin 32 Alternative Route

Monument

20

StMar

South Foreland SW Goodwin

Dover N

Call Port Control

Call Port Control to enter marina

0   5

miles

Ramsgate to Dover. Strong winds can build a dangerous sea in the inner Goodwin Sands; so plan an alternative route east to give plenty of sea room.

As a precaution I made sure the anchor was ready to let go just in case I found myself without sail or power in these treacherous waters (some years ago I was in the area on a bigger boat, and had to give assistance to a yacht that was drifting towards the Goodwins with its sails jammed and a rope around her prop).

A few minutes into the passage I saw dark, heavy clouds approaching; I quickly put two reefs in the main and the wind picked up to a SW force 4. In these shoal waters, the sea quickly develops a short, sharp chop, so I eased the main a little to take some strain off the autopilot. By 0730 I had cleared both Goodwin Fork south cardinal and Deal with its distinctive water tower, and I decided I'd put a third reef in the main as I could see the increasing white

tops of the oncoming weather. As we rounded the Monument off South Foreland, there was less than three miles to go; heading for Dover's East Harbour entrance, the wind picked up to force 5 with force 6 gusts.

The route through the inner Goodwin Sands is quite shallow in parts and stronger winds could have built dangerous sea, in which case I would have taken an alternative route east to give myself plenty of sea room.

Seeking shelter

As I approached Dover Harbour I called Port Control on Ch74 for permission to enter. But as I had to wait 20 minutes I closed in on the 5m contour line to shelter under the harbour wall while the ferry traffic cleared. Once given

Sailing through the inner passage of the Goodwins, I had to reef the main as the dark clouds rolled in and the wind picked up.

clearance to enter, I had to wait again at the north cardinal buoy until Port Control gave permission for me to enter the inner harbour. I then called the Marina on Ch80 and was directed to Granville Dock, where you have to lock in and out.

I was now only a little more than 100 miles from home and feeling in good form. I had been at sea for four months and was settled into a pleasant routine of looking after myself and *Jalina*. There was to be a full moon in two days; a clear sky and a steady SW wind would tempt me to make my final passage to Portsmouth in one 26-hour leg and complete my second circumnavigation of the UK.

Yachts wait for a ferry to pass before entering the shelter of the north-east entrance to Dover Harbour.

Homeward bound: Dover to Portsmouth

With the right weather, the final leg of my trip could be done in one go, so I had to study the synoptic weather forecast charts. I had planned to leave the day before I actually did, but this would have given me a westerly wind on the nose.

The charts showed a low north-west of Scotland and a new high coming in from the Atlantic, so if I waited a day, the low would be off Norway, moving the airstream in the channel from the south-west to north-west, which is what I wanted. Also, a change from a warmer south-west airstream to the cooler north-west airstream would give me clearer visibility, which was important as I might be sailing through the night.

The Coastguard weather report for North Foreland to Selsey Bill was for W veering NW force 4–6; showers, visibility good, and for the following 24 hours; NW force 3–4 backing SW force 2–3, good visibility, sea state slight. This was fine, because if the wind got up I could close the weather shore where there would be very little swell.

As part of my planning, once all the waypoints are completed, I also check the charts and circle in pencil any points of danger that I need to keep an eye on.

During this passage, there were the Royal Sovereign shoals, six miles east of Beachy Head, where strong winds can create a nasty sea. So if the wind got up to more than force 4, I planned to sail an alternative route, in deeper water, south of Royal Sovereign.

The second danger was the passage through the Inner Owers, south of Selsey Bill. Here there are the Malt Ower rocks and Mixon Rocks guarded by a red post. On clearing the Mixon, you have to pass two navigation buoys: Bolder and Street, to avoid the other surrounding shoals. As this area is very shallow, the wrong combination of tide and strong winds can provide heavy breaking seas, so as a precaution I planned an alternative route south of the Outer Owers south cardinal mark. But this would add eight miles to my passage and I would then have the wind on the nose for my final leg up the Solent to Portsmouth. This would add at least three hours to the passage and I could miss the tide to take me into Portsmouth Harbour. I could decide on-passage whether to go non-stop to Portsmouth, or pull into Sovereign Harbour at Eastbourne. But with the prospect of a clear sky, good visibility and a full moon to light the way, a night passage looked most attractive.

I get a real buzz from night sailing but I need plenty of sustainance, so I prepared a chicken casserole and flasks of hot soup and sandwiches. I do, however, always try to make fresh tea as it never tastes the same from the flask. Luckily, I still had some of Mum's wholesome fruitcake and cheese left that she gave me at Whitby.

Dover to Portsmouth
Distance: 107nm
Passage time: 27hr

With winds forecast from force 4–6, I hanked on two foresails; my working orange jib, which can have a slab reef, and my No 2 genoa. My plan was to keep *Jalina* moving and as my genoa is a heavyweight cloth it would

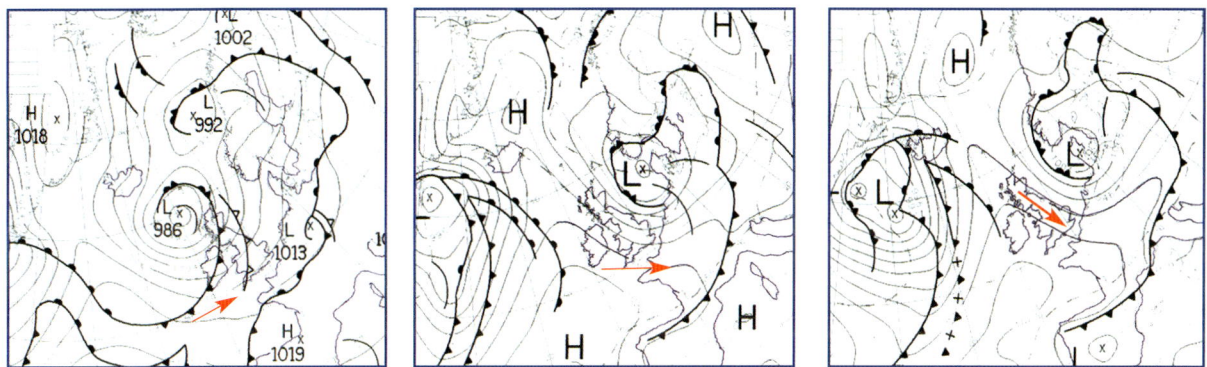

The synoptic charts show how the wind should veer, from west to north-west, as the low moves towards Norway.

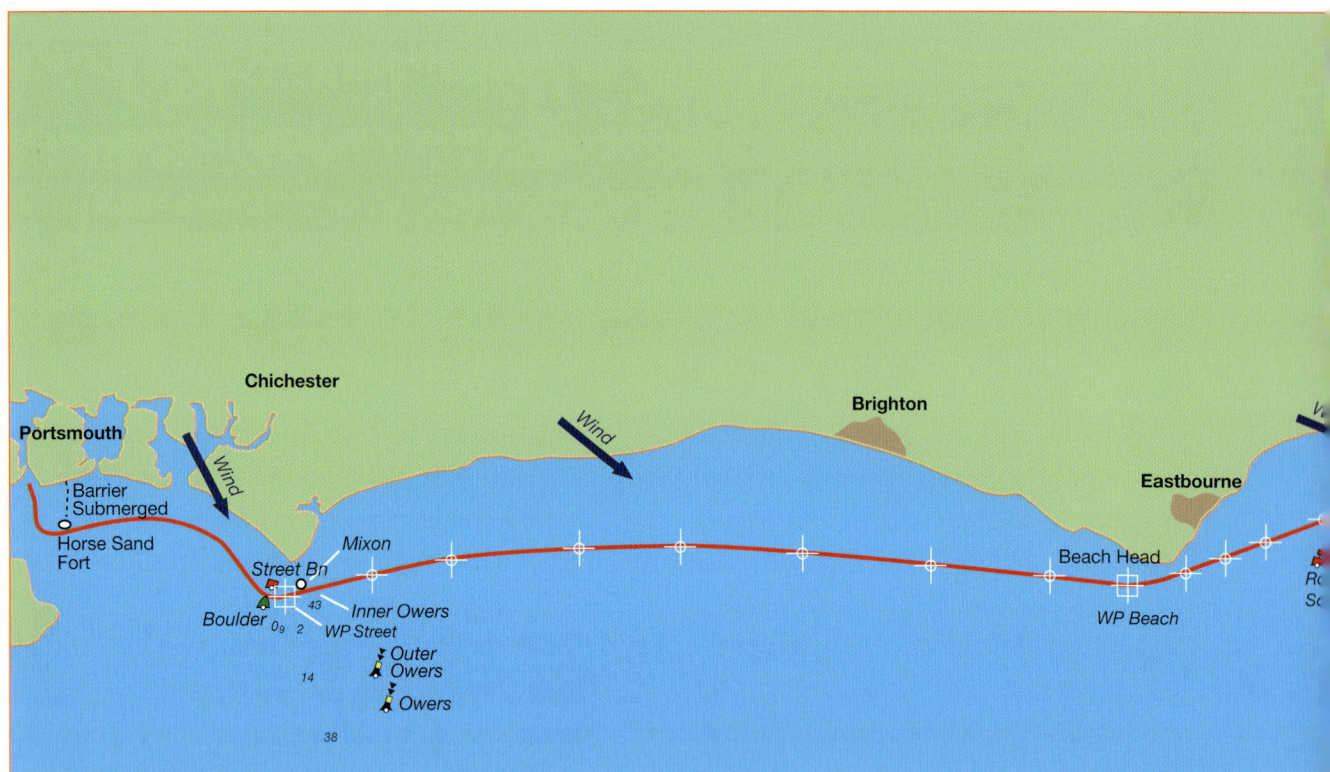

be fine up to force 3–4. As the wind rises, before changing down from my No 2 genoa, I reef the main and keep the benefit of the slot effect formed between the foresail and mainsail. In order to keep an even airflow through the slot, I usually trim the foresail first (until it disturbs the luff of the main) and then I trim the main. I find that using my genoa like this gives me far more lift to windward than changing down, too early, to my working jib. I love tweaking sails and throughout the whole circumnavigation I managed to average four knots.

I slipped my lines and cleared Granville locked harbour at 0915 (HW Dover –3hr). I had two hours of fair tide and called Dover Coastguard to sign on and give my passage plan: Dover to Eastbourne. Then I called Dover Harbour Control for permission to clear the western entrance, but had to wait for a Fastcat ferry to enter and dock.

Once clear, the wind was still westerly but I could just sail my rhumb line of 230° for Dungeness. However, it was not long before there were some very menacing clouds gathering from the south-west, which soon developed into a nasty squall with gusts of force 5–6. These had not been mentioned in the weather forecast, but did create some magnificent rainbows.

Progress was good. By 1300 I'd rounded Dungeness and had to harden up on the new course of 259° for Beachy Head, but the best I could hold was 242°. However, I couldn't

have held that if *Jalina* didn't have a fin keel and a good set of racing sails. I was confident the expected north-westerly would come in, as the low moved east, so I decided to put in short tacks to keep close to my rhumb line.

By 1640 the wind started to veer and I could make 253°. With a force 2–3 and the No 2 genoa we were making five knots off Hastings, so when the wind slowly veered north I reckoned I could reach and clear the Inner Owers on the last of the fair tide at around 0700, so I decided to press on through the night. I called Dover Coastguard with my revised passage plan.

A FRIENDLY VOICE

Over the past months, my daily reports to the Coastguard had become part of my routine and it was often the only human contact that I had for many hours. In remote places with not much going on, it felt like I had a mate on board when the Coastguard were able to talk. But in the crowded English Channel I felt more alone than I had ever been because they were far too busy to chat.

By 2100 we were off the Royal Sovereign Light and the wind moved round – as if to order. *Jalina* picked up her skirts and reached 7.3 knots over the ground with a fair

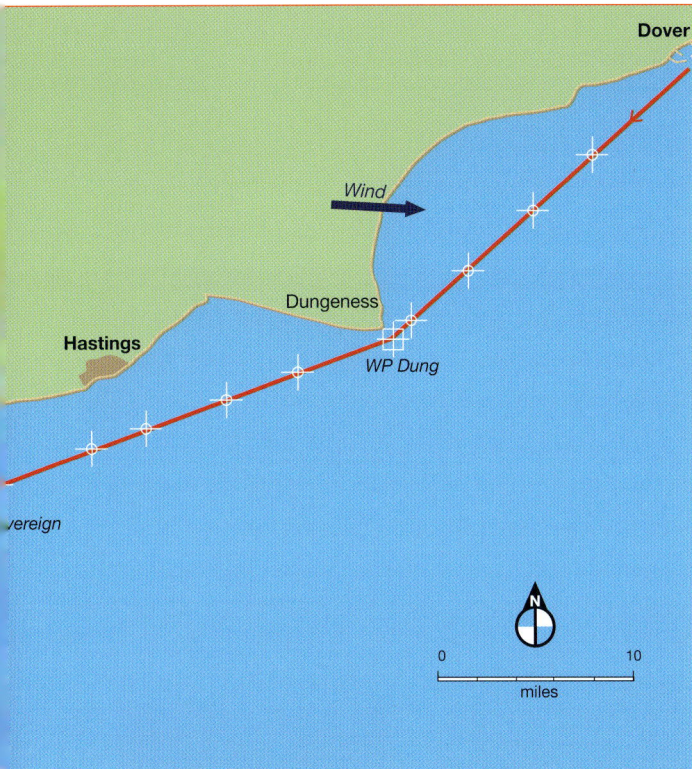

Be sure not to mistake the Mixon for Street red can.

The tides can run very fast through the Inner Owers.

tide. We were making good progress and the miles seem to slip away very quickly.

I prepared for the night passage by changing to my orange heavy-duty jib (it is easier to see under its high cut foot), and, as usual lowering the mast pennant to avoid obscuring the tricolour masthead light; plugging in my faithful searchlight; checking my torches and finally adjusting my clothing for the cool of the night.

As we approached Beachy Head, enjoying a wonderful sunset, I was feeling good; I was warm, dry and on the final passage of my adventure.

At midnight I settled down to a helping of hot casserole and put the kettle on. The wind was now picking up from the north-west and brought with it a beautifully crystal-clear sky with a full moon. What a perfect night!

At 2300 my DSC alarm sounded, which always gives me a shock as I fear it is an imminent gale warning like the one that gave me a pasting on the east coast. This time, however, it was only warning of a French fishing vessel drifting near the east-going shipping lane.

The autopilot kept a good course close to the wind, just in case the wind went south, I could then always

As we approached Beachy Head the orange sunset was magnificent, almost beckoning me on.

give that heading away. As we closed the Owers inner passage buoys, Bolder and Street, I gave away the heading to increase my speed and catch the last of the fair tide. It was now 0630 (HW Dover +4hr 30min) and we were on time. The sunrise was bright in a clear sky and I could feel the warmth beginning to permeate my layer of waterproofs.

Once through the Owers, I turned a little north to lee-bow the slackest of the foul tide, which cancelled out my leeway. Then I headed to the south of Horse Sand Fort (as there is a submerged barrier to the north of it) and soon let the new flood take us into Portsmouth Harbour. On my approach, I switched to VHF Ch11 as in Portsmouth all vessels come under the control of the Queen's Harbour Master. You must have your engine running and use the small boat channel, as the winds at the entrance can be fickle and the tides run hard.

Home at last

With the engine ticking over, I entered the harbour under sail, and it was with mixed emotions that I handed *Jalina*'s sails. I had never taken so much time over such a simple task as it was both exciting – and sad – that another great adventure was coming to a close. By 1130, I was alongside, having completed my second circumnavigation of the UK.

I had a very warm welcome home from my wife Liz, and from many sailing club members. I would like to thank everyone who helped me during this long trip – particularly all the RNLI staff, harbour masters, marina staff; and the doctors who patched me up.

It was with mixed emotions that I handed Jalina's sails at the end of my voyage.

Up the Irish Sea: Milford Haven to Gigha, Scotland

This section is part of my first circumnavigation, going from Milford Haven to the Island of Gigha in Scotland via the Irish Sea, giving useful pilotage information for sailors wishing to circumnavigate round the UK only.

I had considered crossing over to Ireland from Milford Haven, then sailing north along the coast of Ireland, making use of the prevailing south-westerly winds; I would also be on a safer weather shore. However, over the years I had spent many weeks walking the Welsh hills, so I decided to revisit old haunts, and opted for the Welsh coast.

In 2002, I had sailed from Padstow to Milford Haven; it had been a rough passage, wind NW force 4–5, a head wind, with a heavy swell in the Bristol Channel. I entered the Haven at 2100 and there were gale warnings for the next few days. I decided to seek a good shelter so I sailed to Neyland Marina, approximately nine miles from the entrance; we arrived at 0130, 20 hours after leaving Padstow.

Two days later, the forecast for the next 48 hours was good, I planned to slip from Neyland Marina and stay that night at Dale Bay; I would then take a full fair tide the next morning and sail to Fishguard.

Moorings and facilities

There are visitor's moorings in Dale Bay, for which there is a charge; there is a chandlery and a good pub in the village.

Neyland Marina: ideal if you want to spend time visiting Pembroke.

Milford Haven to Fishguard

Distance: 38nm

Passage time: 7hr 20min

My main concern for this passage were the many rocky hazards to clear on this stretch of coastline. Another was the weather window; I needed 48 hours of settled weather. The next 24-hour forecast for St David's Head to Colwyn Bay and St Georges Channel was SE force 4-5; sea state slight to moderate; visibility good. For the following 24

hours it was SE force 3-4 backing SE by E force 2-3, increasing force 4-5, fair, cyclonic, with fog patches.

The wind direction would give me a weather shore for this passage, but a lee shore to enter the shallow waters of Pwllheli Harbour. The synoptic charts at Neyland Marina indicated the possibility of westerlies in 48 hours, with isobars narrowing.

After studying the charts in detail, I circled danger areas in pencil, and added waypoints to the course to keep me to the outside of hazards, giving them a reasonable offing; I had plenty of time and seven hours of fair tide. With a

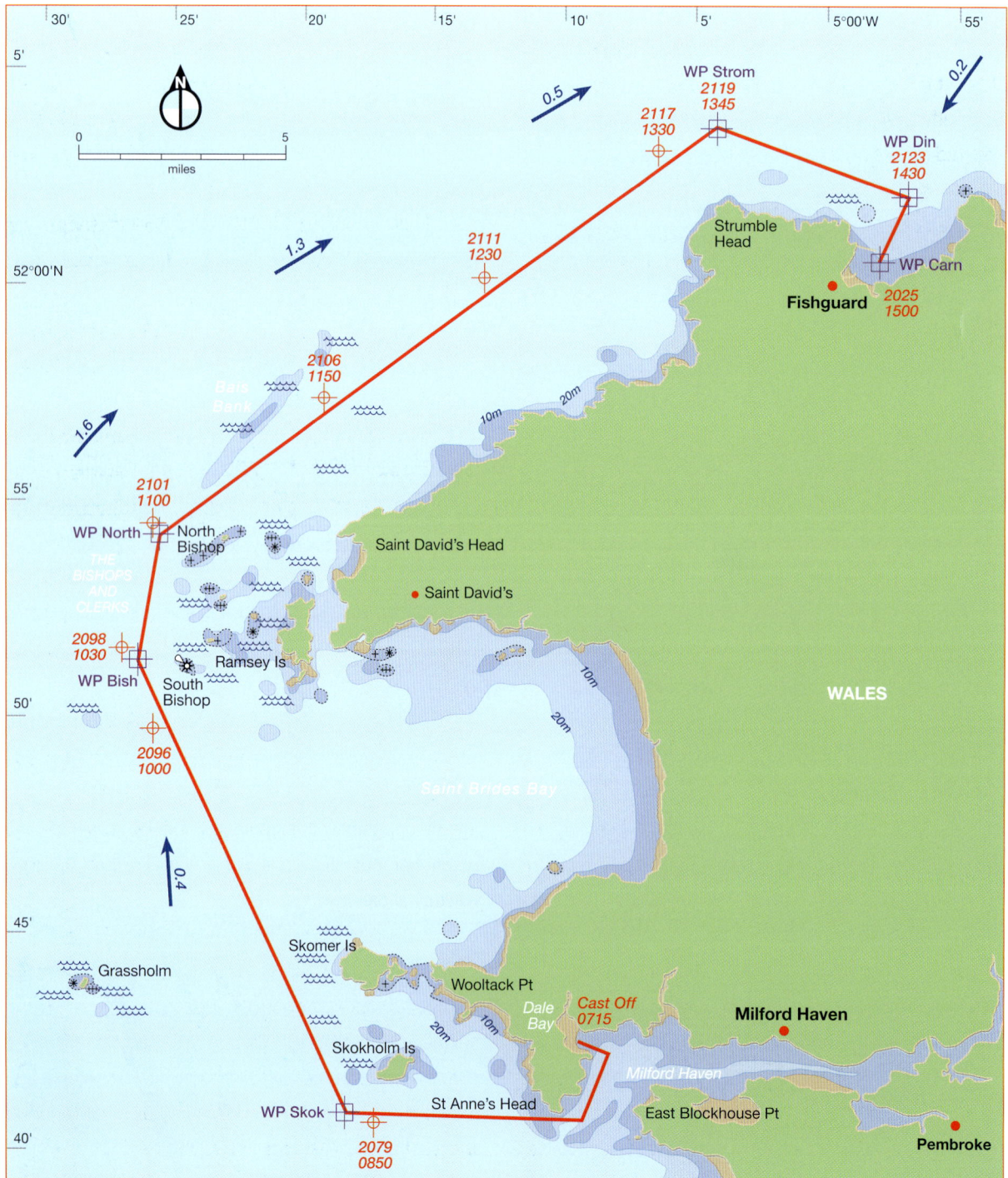

Jalina was getting a good lift with the fair tide.

Once clear of Skokholm Jalina was on a broad reach.

long adventure ahead, I had no intention of taking any short cuts to save the odd hour.

Overfalls are numerous around the peninsula so care is needed to avoid these.

Proceeding with caution

I did not sleep very well as there was a little swell running into Dale Bay against the concrete pontoon, causing *Jalina* to have an uneasy motion.

At 0530 I enjoyed a good breakfast and prepared sandwiches, hot soup, and tea in flasks for the passage.

The wind was easterly force 3; the barometer had been steady for the past 24 hours with clear skies, and all looked good for the passage. As I would be anchoring in Fishguard, off Castle Point in Lower Harbour, I calculated depths of water for six hours from 1400 onwards to save having to do that task on arrival.

I called Milford Haven Coastguard on Ch16–67 with my passage plan; I slipped at 0715 and cleared Dale Bay with full main and No 2 genoa; as a precaution, No 1 jib was also hanked on and lashed to the deck.

Visibility was good with the rising sun. There were a number of shipping movements; all craft within Milford Haven Port Control boundary must maintain a listening watch on Ch12.

By 0900 we had cleared Skokholm Island, reaching under full sail, with a weather shore; the sun was warming my waterproofs. The autopilot was doing its job, as we cleared Skomer Island. I poured out a cup of tea, opened the 'treats' box and cut a slice of fruit cake, then settled down to the gentle motion of *Jalina* reaching and gradually closing on South Bishop Rock, topped with its bright white lighthouse.

Care has to be taken on the approach to South Bishop Rock as the tide tends to sweep you towards the dangers of Ramsey Island. To assist me I used the track and bearing indicators of my GPS NASA repeater to show me that I was heading for the WP and on course.

As I cleared WP Bishop, WP North helped to keep me clear of North Bishop Rocks; I was making 7 knots over the ground aided by 1.6 knots of fair tide.

As a precaution I had loaded all the WPs for the passage into my portable hand-held GPS; this is usually stored in the emergency grab bag.

I had prepared a back-sight clearing bearing to Bishop Rock so that if the GPS went down, this would keep me clear of North Bishop Rocks; another check ensured that the tide was not setting us down.

Progress was good; Bais Bank was soon cleared, and I was closing Strumble Head. WP Strum would keep *Jalina* well clear of the headland and give an open approach to the entrance off Fishguard.

As *Jalina* approached WP Din, approximately 1.5 miles from the entrance, I noticed a large ferry approaching, so I held back to give him a clear run into Fishguard. This gave me the opportunity to prepare *Jalina* for our approach into Lower Harbour off Saddle Point; here I would be on a weather shore.

I prepared the CQR anchor and deployed it from the stern, driving it in under engine (see illustration on page 00); the holding was good.

By 1600 I had signed off with the Coastguard, then settled down to prepare a passage plan for the passage to Pwllheli. After a good wash down, I prepared a good wholesome hot meal, then went to bed early.

Fishguard to Pwllheli

Distance: 59nm

Passage time: 12hr

I was woken at 0330 by the noise of thunder and lightening, and the rattle of large hailstones. The storm was persistent and I could not sleep but the alarm was set for 0400; I decided to prepare an early breakfast, make sandwiches and fill flasks for the day. It was raining heavily

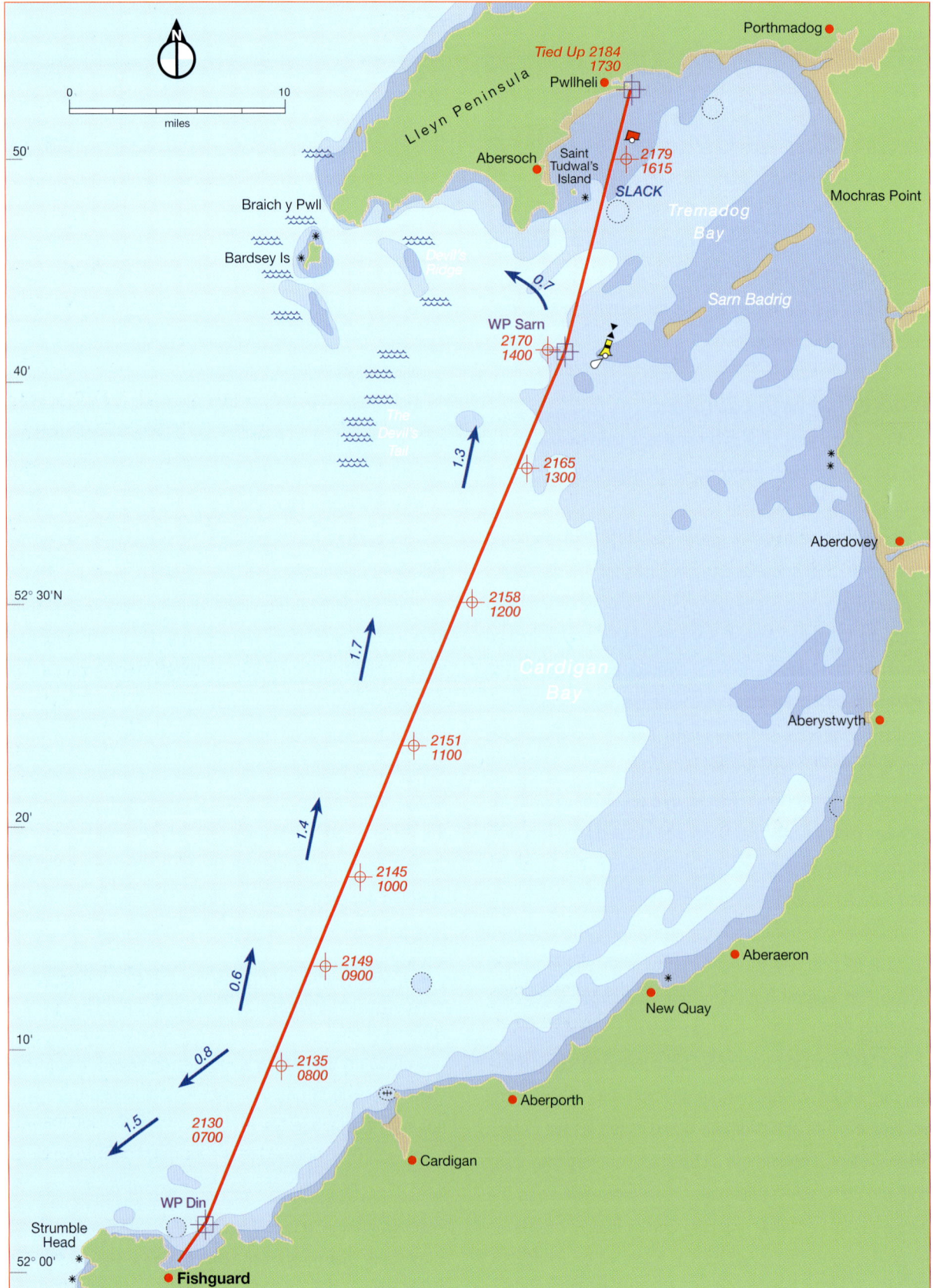

Care is needed to identify the training arm, when approaching Pwllheli entrance.

so I donned waterproofs. *Jalina* was prepared, with two reefs in the main and the working jib reefed.

The weather forecast was mixed: variable SE force 3–4 occasional force 5; later SW force 4–5; fog patches and scattered showers.

There was only one danger point I circled in pencil on the chart: the shallows of Sarn Badrig; this I would clear west of Causeway cardinal, from there on to the Pwllheli fairway the water becomes more shallow. My concern, if the wind picked up, was that there could be very shallow troughs in the final approach to the harbour entrance.

As a last resort I would clear to the west of Bardsey Island and press on to Holyhead: a total passage of 24 hours. I had noted the telephone numbers of the harbour master, and marina so, if necessary, I could ask for advice on the condition off the entrance to Pwllheli. There are no other harbours nearby with 24-hour access.

With anchor weighed, the sky still dark and thunder and lightening all around, *Jalina* slipped slowly out to sea, I called Milford Haven Coastguard to sign on with my passage plan.

The passage started well with *Jalina* making 5 knots or more over the ground, 4 knots through the water. Being a little early, the tide was against us; we had picked up an eddy. The rain was still quite heavy with the storm moving southwest.

Just after 0900 the wind died completely; the sea was like a millpond so on went the trusty Yanmar diesel. With a steady 5 knots, plus one knot of fair tide, progress was good. At 1200 it was still raining heavily and visibility was down to ¼ of a mile. By 1230 the wind had got up with a vengeance; within a few minutes it was force 5 with force

6 squalls. In anticipation, *Jalina* was well reefed, with three reefs in the main and one slab in the jib; she was now better balanced for the squalls.

By 1630 I spotted the fairway buoy off the entrance. On the approach, care has to be taken to clear Pwllheli point to the south and the training arm to the north of the entrance; the entrance was not difficult, but it did have quite a surge.

Facilities

The marina facilities are first class, with good showers. On arrival I was given a four-day weather report, and the Pwllheli Sailing Club next door will give you a warm welcome. There are chandlers nearby, plus diesel, water, supermarkets and good rail links.

I spent the next two days resting, walking, and enjoying the company of PYC members; meanwhile I had prepared my passage plan for Holyhead.

Pwllheli to Holyhead (aborted)
Distance: 5nm
Passage time: 2hr

I had prepared the charts with care, WPs listed and marked up; any danger points circled in pencil, and clearing bearings drawn. I had prepared sandwiches the evening before.

The weather forecast was SW force 4–5. It was a good forecast for the passage; it would be a fast reach. It was an early start to catch the tide. The evening before slipping, I put one reef in the main, and hanked on the working jib (this can be slab reefed).

I rose at 0430 ate a good breakfast: two eggs, marmalade on toast and tea. I prepared flasks of soup and tea, checked the Navtex for any new weather warnings and donned waterproofs. I called Holyhead Coastguard to sign on with my passage plan and I gave them my MMSI No. I slipped my lines and cleared the harbour at 0630 and the fairway buoy by 0645, and set a course for Bardsey Island. The VHF alarm went off; it was Holyhead Coastguard calling to tell me that there was an imminent gale warning so I aborted the passage. On arrival back in harbour I informed the Coastguard that we were safe in Pwllheli harbour. The Coastguard apologised for the bad news, but suggested that I should go and enjoy a good pint of Guinness at the Pwllheli Sailing Club.

For the next 7 days, there were gale warnings of up to force 9 for 16 sea areas. It was a case of waiting for a window to sail.

The strong wind pushed *Jalina* so hard up against the pontoon that the fenders were tending to ride up. So I decided to fit a weather spring on the windward side from a strong point at the stern back to the pontoon. When the wind eased from a gust, the weather spring lifted the boat off the pontoon allowing the fenders to drop back down.

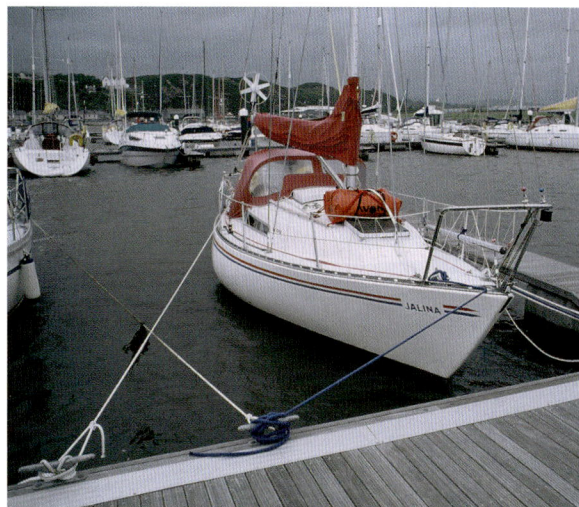
A weather spring may avoid damage to the gel coat, and no squeaking fenders at night.

Pwllheli to Holyhead
Distance: 58nm
Passage time: 11hr 20min

After being pinned down for nine days of gales, I became a little wary of watching the weather. The forecast for St David's Head to St Georges Channel for the next 24 hours was S–SW force 3–5 variable NW; showers, visibility good, occasionally moderate, sea state moderate.

I was now losing the window for a daylight sail, as the tides to clear Bardsey Island were getting later. I would be getting into Holyhead at night, so I had to make sure I had all the correct lights; I checked this with BA NP37 against my BA charts and all was fine.

The main dangers for this passage are: clearing St Tudwal's Islands, Bardsey Sound, finally South Stack and the overfalls.

Being one day before springs, timing was critical. My plan was to slip at HW Dover, go through Bardsey Sound HW Dover + 3, then I would have one hour or so of foul tide, then fair tide for the remainder of the passage.

I had many days to prepare my passage plans during the gales and update them daily. Eventually the forecast was good so we could go; there would be light winds but as I was likely to be in the centre of a high with variable winds, I was prepared to use the engine.

After nine days of gales it was good to be under way.

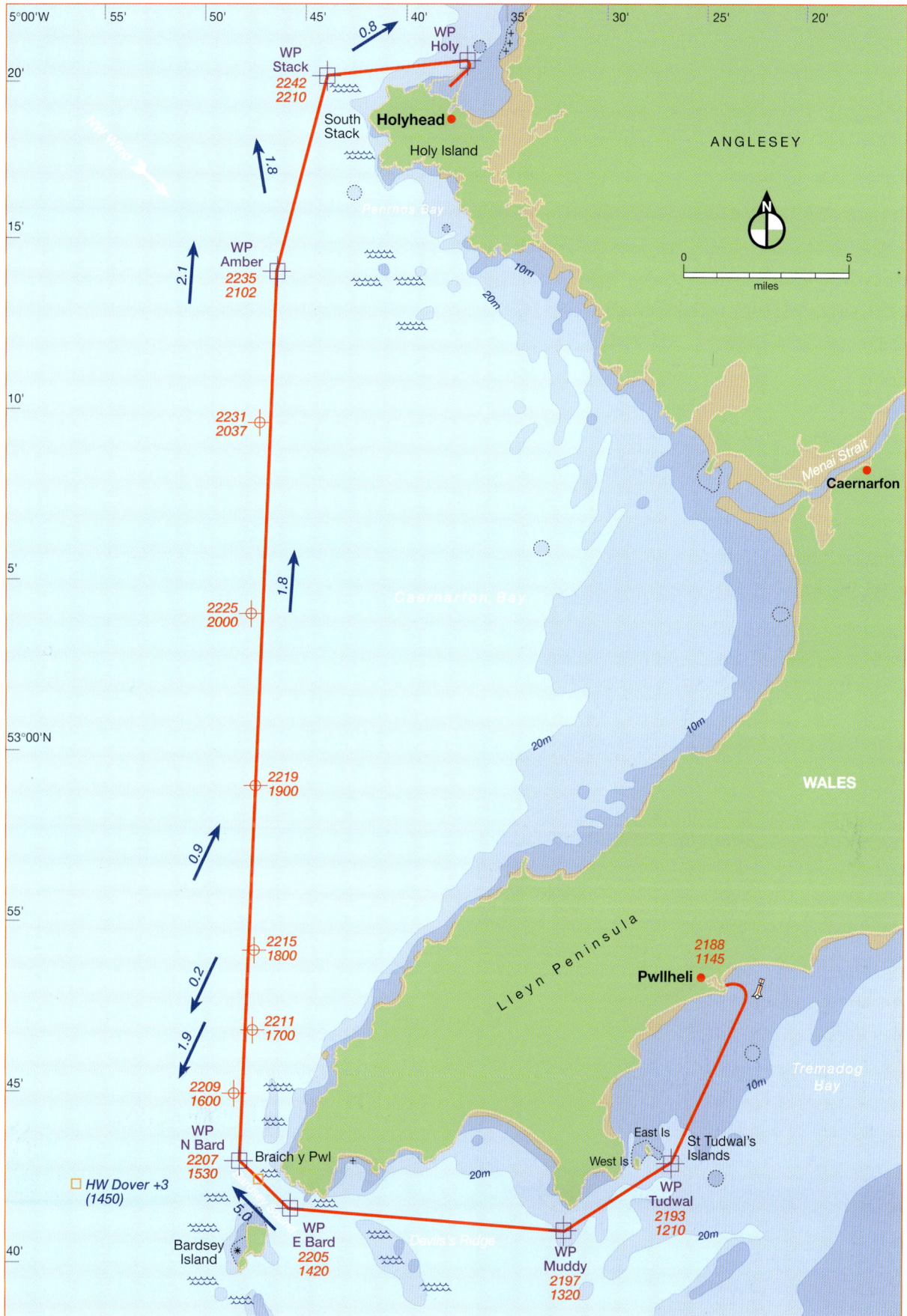

5°00'W   55'   50'   45'   40'   35'   30'   25'   20'

0.8

WP
Holy

WP
Stack
2242
2210

20'

South
Stack

Holyhead ●

Holy Island

ANGLESEY

1.8

N

Penrhos Bay

0   5
miles

15'

2.1

WP
Amber
2235
2102

10m

20m

10'

2231
2037

Menai Strait

Caernarfon ●

53°00'N

1.8

2225
2000

Caernarfon Bay

20m

10m

2219
1900

WALES

0.9

55'

2215
1800

0.2

Lleyn Peninsula

2188
1145

Pwllheli ●

*Tremadog
Bay*

1.9

2211
1700

10m

2209
1600

45'

WP
N Bard
2207
1530

Braich y Pwl

East Is

St Tudwal's
Islands

□ *HW Dover +3*
(1450)

West Is

WP
Tudwal
2193
1210

5.0

20m

WP
E Bard
2205
1420

Davis's Ridge

20m

40'

Bardsey
Island

WP
Muddy
2197
1320

BARDSEY SOUND (AC 1971)

(c) 2.5k   6k (a) 2.5k   4.5k (b)

The tide turns to the NW or NE (flood) as follows:
at (a): HW Dover +0300;
at (b): HW D +0500;
at (c): –0545 HW D.
These times are approximate.
There is a strong eddy down tide of Bardsey Island and overfalls throughout the area.

The tide turns to the SW or SE (ebb) as follows:
at (a): HW Dover –0300;
at (b): HW D –0100 ;
at (c): at HW D –0030.
These times are approximate.
There is a strong eddy down tide of Bardsey Island and overfalls throughout the area.

(c) 2.5k   (a)   (b)

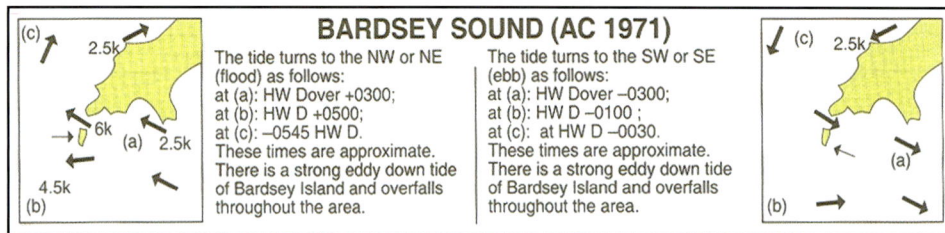

Jalina came through Bardsey Sound with 5 knots of tide, (tidal gate extract from Reeds PBO Almanac).

I cast off at 1145 and soon cleared the fairway. The day was bright and sunny with little wind, so I decided to motorsail for a while to clear Bardsey Sound by 1600, at which point I bore away, put out full main and No 2 genoa, and set course for Holyhead.

As *Jalina* cleared Bardsey Island I decided to put up the cruising chute to give a little more speed, adding a bright yellow and red splash of colour to the Welsh mountains. We were then making 5.6–6.0 knots of hull speed through the water. By 2000, the sun was slowly going down in the west, casting its bright orange rays on the sail and giving the white tops of the sea swell an orange glow. The mountains were also glowing red; all we needed was the 'Welsh Dragon', to complete this great picture.

The wind was still north-westerly force 3; a fair tide started to pick up, pushing *Jalina* up to 8 knots over the ground.

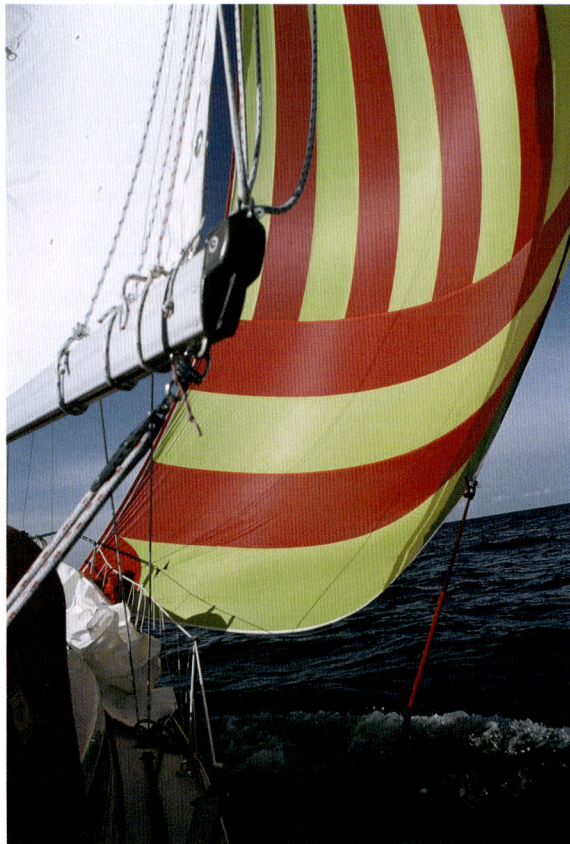

Jalina on a beam reach with cruising chute doing over 5 knots.

Our ETA with Holyhead Coastguard was 2300; we were well set to achieve this. I could now feel the chill of the evening as the warmth of the sun on my waterproofs faded; there was now a dampness in the air.

I needed some inner warmth, so on went the kettle for a fresh hot cuppa. The wind started to rise so I decided to hoist the No 2 genoa to cover the cruising chute (making it easier to drop the chute) which I repacked and stowed in the fore-peak.

Dropping the chute single-handed

The genoa is hoisted to take the power out of the chute; the bag is hanked onto the guard wire on the foredeck; the clew and tack sheets are eased. At this point you may get the odd dollop of water in the foot of the chute. The halyard is then led from the cockpit, through a block on the stern, forward to the bow, from where I can then hand the chute under control into the bag.

On this occasion all went well, but not without plenty of spray at her bow as *Jalina* pitched into the swell. *Jalina* was doing what she does best: pressing on with the wind building – now force 4.

We were now closing on Penrhos Bay south-west of Holy Island. By 2230 we had reached WP Amber. South Stack light was flashing every ten seconds, clear and bright. WP Stack would help to clear South Stack and the overfalls. At the same time I wanted to take advantage of the strong flood tide close to these overfalls in Penrhos Bay to push *Jalina* on; we reached 10 knots over the ground. To be safe I gave South Stack an offing of just over a mile.

A north-westerly wind and a fair north-going tide would produce an uncomfortable swell off South Stack and the approach to Holyhead harbour entrance; it would also put me on a lee shore; WP Stack would keep me well clear of North Stack.

It was dark on the final approach to the harbour. The

Holyhead harbour makes a good refuge as it is sheltered from all winds.

wind was rising and the sea was likely to be turbulent. I decided to change the foresail from the lowcut genoa No 2, to the high cut jib; this would allow me a clearer view ahead under the sail to identify the navigation lights.

The final approach was a little to the north of the entrance. Being a busy port, you need to keep a good lookout for approaching ferries from Ireland. There was a little mist coming and going; the final WP Holy would assist me until the harbour lights could be picked out. The first light was the Fl G (30) 10s on the North breakwater.

Care is needed as there is a patch of shoal water and a small boat channel running along the inside of the breakwater.

Although we sailed into the harbour, *Jalina*'s engine was ticking over and I used it as necessary. Once I was inside and clear of ferries, I handed and lashed the sails. Using my searchlight, I soon found a vacant visitor's mooring at the Holyhead Sailing Club.

I called Holyhead Coastguard and signed off at 2320; this done, I ate the second half of a casserole and was in bed by midnight.

Facilities

Marina and Holyhead SC can be called on ChM; for ferry traffic monitor Ch14 or 16. Facilities include a mooring-to-shore ferry service provided by the Holyhead Sailing Club, available from 0900–2100; Fri/Sat 2330; there is also water, diesel, AC power (marina). The town has a laundrette, banks, supermarkets and good air and rail links.

The Holyhead Coastguard overlook the harbour, and so I paid a visit to their modern facility to thank them for their support and to put faces to the kind voices I heard over the VHF even though the five-day weather reports they had provided were not good reading, with winds forecast of up to force 7 for some time.

Holyhead to Peel (Isle of Man)
Distance: 67nm
Passage time: 12.5hr

The weather forecast was NW winds backing SW force 3–4; showers, visibility good, sea state moderate. The following 24 hours gave SSE force 4–5; locally force 6 veering SW, rain, showers, visibility moderate to good.

This forecast would give me a fair-wind passage the following day from Peel to Ireland.

Going via the Skerries off Carmel Head was ruled out, when ever possible I prefer to avoid TSS (Traffic Separation Scheme) lanes, I would also avoid the overfalls off the Skerries.

I planned to slip at 0620 HW Dover + 4, clear the harbour, head west, and lee-bow the last two hours of ebb tide to cancel out any leeway with the south-west wind. Once clear of the TSS I would bear away for the Isle of Man as the tide turns, giving over 10 knots of fair tide. I made up a tidal vector; once clear of the TSS there would be 9 knots of tide for 5 hours, half a knot of foul tide off Calf of Man, then two more knots of fair tide to take me along the coast into Peel.

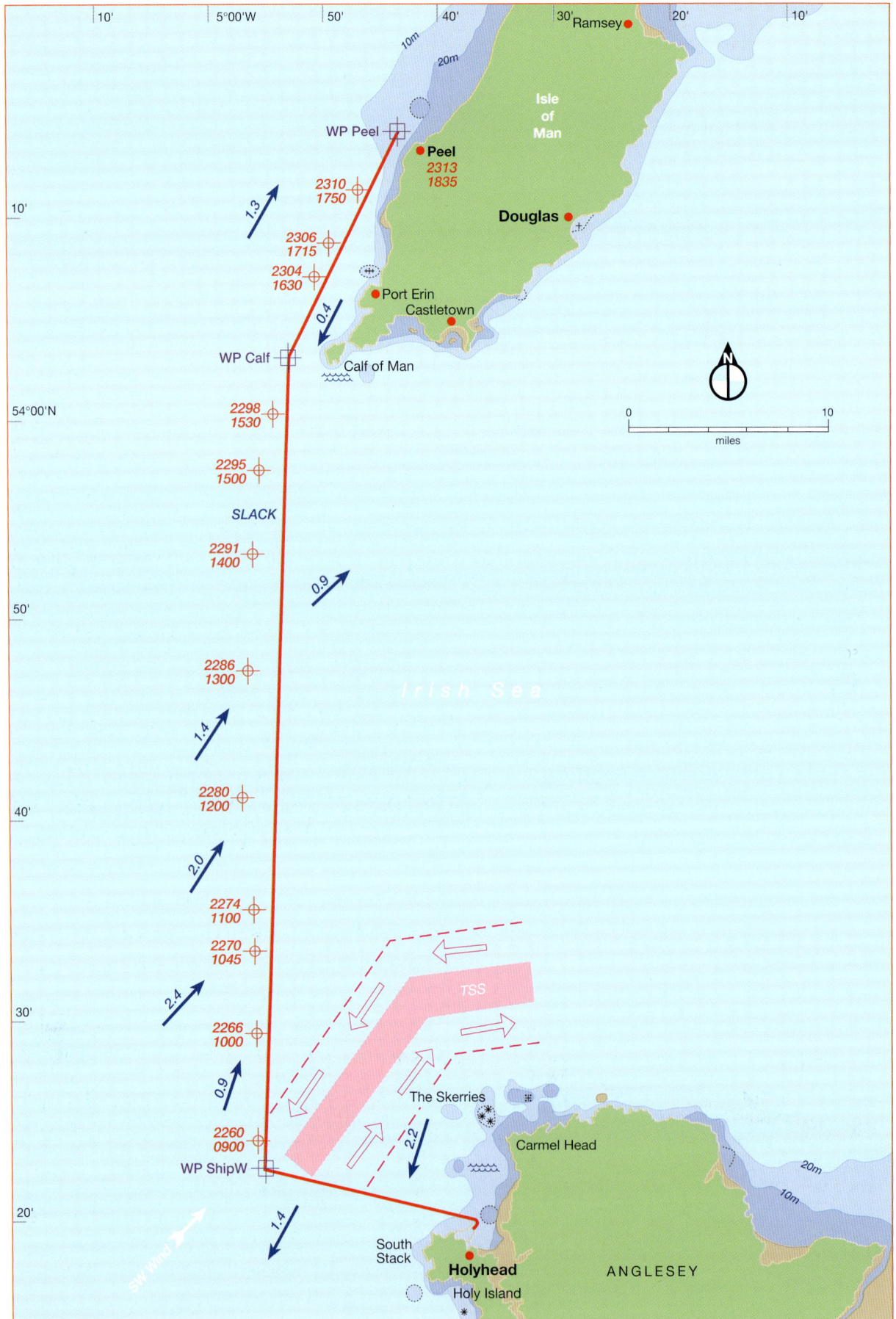

The weather had settled, and under full main and No 2 genoa, we approached Calf of Man.

Should the weather deteriorate, making it uncomfortable in Peel harbour, I had made up WPs and clearing bearings to go on to Douglas on the east coast of the Isle of Man.

I rose early to check the weather on Navtex and call the Coastguard for a weather report. All was fine and I made a good breakfast: cereal mixed with dried fruit, a boiled egg, toast and hot tea. I prepared sandwiches and flasks of tea and soup. I had prepared charts, made up both GPS sets with WPs, and marked clearing lines on the charts; I also added these to my pocket note book. Once I had donned my waterproofs, I was ready.

It was blowing a force 4 in the harbour so I knew it would be a blowing a good deal more, possibly force 5–6 at sea, so I put two reefs into the main, and a slab in the working jib.

Once clear of the breakwater, the swell was impressive. The passage went well; the weather proved to be changeable with showers, with the occasional squall, and a thunderstorm. The wind increased from force 4 to force 6–7; I had to reef as the squalls approached, and headed up, then when they hit I bore away.

By 1830 I had picked up one of the three yellow moorings in Peel harbour; these are too big for small boats so in future I will probably anchor.

I then signed off with Liverpool Coastguard, this gave me a sense of *Jalina*'s progress north, and with Ireland in prospect tomorrow, I had the excitement of going foreign.

It had been a good sail with *Jalina* averaging over 5 knots; we were tied up in good time to enjoy the evening with a good hot meal, watching the sun go down.

Facilities

Facilities at Peel include: water on the quays, a slip, provisions in the town. Early closing is Thursday. There is a Calor Gas Manx gas service centre. Showers are available at the Peel Sailing and Cruising Club with the key available from the harbour master.

Peel IOM to Strangford Lough, Ireland

Distance: 35nm
Passage time: 7hr 40min

During the last passage the weather forecast for the period was: WSW force 4–5, veering S to SE force 4–5, locally force 6, fair, rain or showers, visibility moderate to poor in rain, sea state smooth to moderate, rough in open waters.

Peel harbour, Isle of Man. The three yellow moorings provided here are 'at your own risk'!

I prepared a tidal vector as I would have cross-tides for this passage. I worked out the course, loaded WPs into both GPS (these had been worked out during the stay in Holyhead),

My main concern was the timing of my arrival at Strangford Lough. Tides through here can be up to 8 knots at springs; I was three days before neaps. The main WP is Bally close to the Fairway Buoy; from here I would use

pilotage and local navigation transits taken from the *Irish Sailing Directions*, and *BA chart 2156* to guide *Jalina* into Portaferry Marina.

It was an early start, rising at 0400. All my passage details had been sorted the day before, giving me more time to linger over a good breakfast, with *Jalina* rocking gently from the swell coming into the harbour.

With the possibility of force 5 to 6 winds for this

50'　　　　　40'　　　　30'

0　　　　　　　　　10
miles

20m

10m

2322
0800

2318
0700

Isle
of
Man

2313
0600
● Peel

Contrary Head

6'0

1.1

● Port Erin

Calf
of Man

On the approach to Agnus Rock (right), I was careful to keep to my track as there are strong cross tides.

Keep to the east side leaving Agnus Rock light to port.

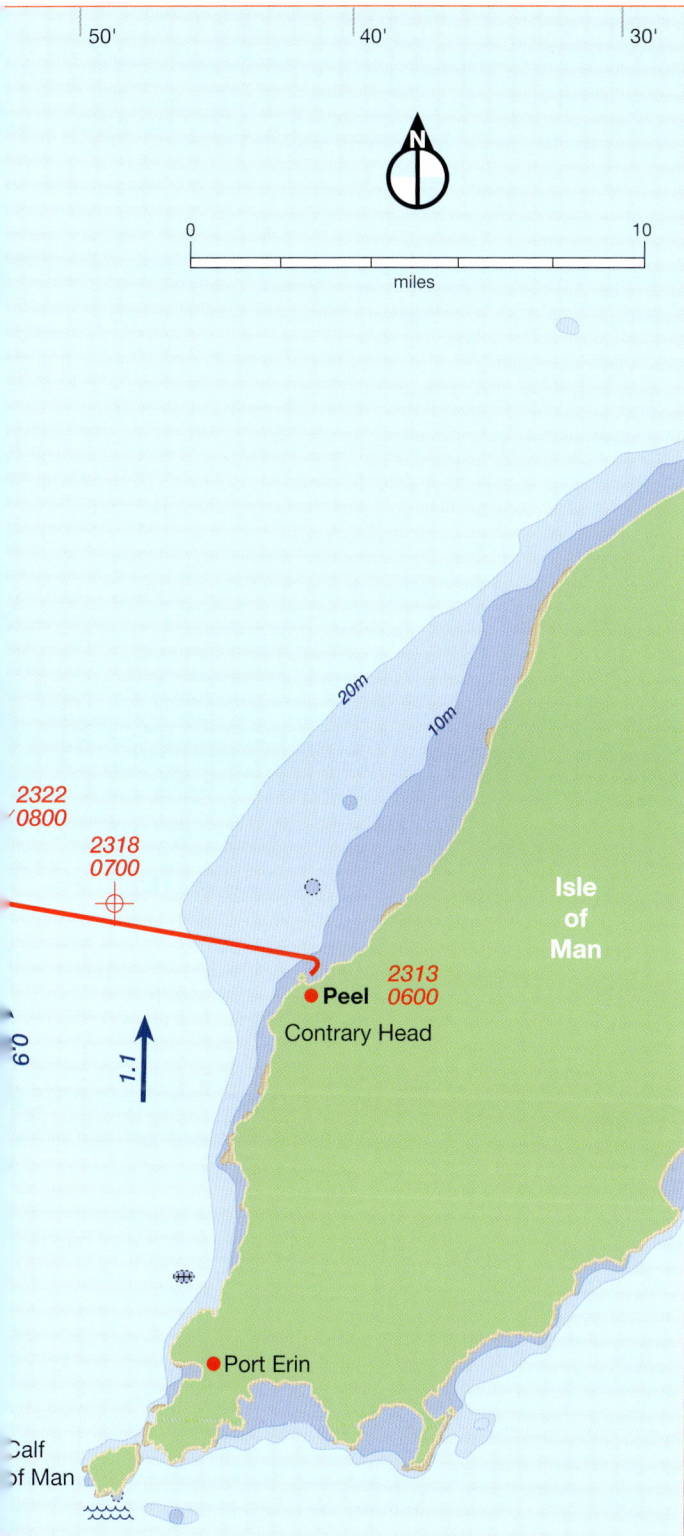

passage, I prepared the No 2 jib and put one reef in the main. I called Liverpool Coastguard to give them my, passage plan and received in return a very detailed weather forecast. I was told that the wind would back south-west to the south.

With my waterproofs on and lifejacket fitted, I slipped *Jalina*'s lines at 0600, clearing the harbour in a moderate swell from the south-west. Progress was good, the wind picked up from the south-west to force 2 to 3. Once we had settled down I then changed *Jalina*'s jib for the No 2 genoa, which increased her speed by an extra knot.

I maintained the same bearing for the passage and at 1230 spotted the Fairway buoy. *Jalina* was on time, arriving at the entrance at 1300 HW Dover −2hr 24min. With a fair tide under us, we soon cleared Agnus Rock light to our port; by 1340 I had tied up in the Portaferry Marina.

Take care not to stray from your track on entering Strangford Lough, as there are many shallows.

Once tied up, I called Belfast Coastguard to sign off from the passage. I was pleased with the passage, it was short, but timing was important for the final part.

If you are a wildlife lover you will not be disappointed; the Lough is full of many species of birds − a bird watchers paradise.

Facilities

Facilities are good with, showers, mains electricity supply, water, gas and Gaz, petrol, diesel and supermarkets.

I gave *Jalina* a good wash down and soaked my Gore-Tex waterproofs to remove salt from the fine pores in the fabric. After I had shopped, checked the engine, filled the water tank, topped up the fuel, paid dues and showered I was ready for dinner. After a good meal of fresh cold meat, salad, and boiled new potatoes, I decided to take a long walk along the lovely Strangford Lough.

Strangford Lough to Bangor (NI) via the Donaghadee Sound
Distance: 35nm
Passage time: 6hr 45min

For this passage I needed to leave the marina on an ebb tide, or just before, then arrive at Donaghadee Sound on a fair tide or slack water; being close to neap tides I did have some slack to go through the Sound.

The 0500 weather forecast from Belfast Coastguard gave no gale or strong wind warnings; winds were forecasted W to SW force 4–5 becoming variable force 2–4, backing S to SE force 4–5 locally force 6; fair, showers then rain, visibility moderate to good, poor later, sea state smooth to moderate in open waters. The W to SW wind would be ideal, giving me a weather shore, but if it went into the SE on reaching Donaghadee Sound, any foul tide would give *Jalina* some swell with wind against tide. Because of the large volume of water moving in and out of this Lough, the ferries have very powerful engines to cope with the tides.

There was no need to prepare food for this short passage; I made up a flask of tea to save me going down below; I needed my full concentration to navigate safely along this rocky shore.

I had a good sleep, rising at 0400 to a full moon. I checked what the tide was doing and I shone the searchlight beam across to a navigation buoy out in the channel and saw that there was still some flood tide. I quickly prepared *Jalina*'s sails, I shone the searchlight again, and

the tide was slack. All was prepared; there was a chill in the air, so I donned first layer thermals and waterproofs.

It was 0445 (HW Dover + 56min). The tide was now on the ebb; the full moon lit up the shores. Before slipping, I hoisted the jib as there was a light head wind. As I slipped, I pulled the stern in to bring her head around and with a touch of throttle, we were out into the Lough. I rounded up *Jalina* (head to wind) and hoisted the main; this done we bore away and were soon doing 6 knots over the ground.

By 0535 I had cleared WP Bally, the next WP was S Rock east of South Rock lightship, which was shrouded by a light mist.

I could just make out the South Rock lightship to my port side.

The half-knot fair tide was with me until I approached the port and starboard buoys of the Donaghadee Sound; the wind had now backed to south-easterly force 4–5. I put a reef in the mainsail; there was now a half-knot of foul tide, and I was on a broad reach. *Jalina* was making 5 knots; the foul tide made very little difference to our progress except we now had a swell building due to wind against tide.

The swell through the Sound was very rough but even so, we made good progress. It is important, on your approach to the Sound, to identify the navigation port and starboard buoys as these mark the safe channel through outlying rocks.

Once clear of the Sound, the wind rose to force 6, so I put a third reef into *Jalina*'s main for the final short leg to Bangor Marina. The first landmark I spotted was the fine red brick building of the Royal Ulster Yacht Club.

Once round the first breakwater, the marina offers plenty of room to round up and hand your sails; with my fenders and lines prepared, I was tied up by 1215.

45'   40'   35'   Lighthouse Is   05° 30'W   25'   20'

Belfast Lough

WP Groon   WP Orlock   Mew Is

2376
1050

WP Ban

Orlock Pt   Copeland Island

Groonsport

Bangor
2389
1215

Donaghadee

WP Dona
2373
1000

0.5

10m

20m

N

0   5
miles

2368
0900   0.4

Ballywalter

2366
0840

54° 30'N   WP S. Rock

Burial Is
Burr Point
Wk

2366
0840

*Strangford
Lough*

**Northern
Ireland**   Portavogie

North
Rocks

25'   0.5

2348
0445
Portaferry   Wk   South
Rock
Lightship   WP S. Rock
South
Rock   2358
0700

Strangford Narrows   10m

20'   20m   2354
0600

Ballyquintin
Point

WP Bally
2352
0535

Bangor (NI) to Red Bay then Glenarm (NI)

Distance: 38nm

Passage time: 7hr 40min

Ireland is a country with beautiful scenery, a magnificent coastline, and wildlife for any country to envy, I will be coming back in the future to enjoy more walking, and visit the many small harbours along these coasts.

During the evening in Bangor I took down the weather forecast from Bangor Coastguard for sea area Mull of Galloway to the Mull of Kintyre: WSW force 4, occasional force 5; showers with some rain, visibility moderate to good, sea state smooth.

I was concerned that the weather would hold for the crossing over to Scotland from Red Bay, or Glenarm; there was a fair early morning tide; and I was two days away from neaps.

Red Bay or Glenarm are good points for crossing and rounding the Mull of Kintyre for passage into Scotland. I felt confident but cautious; my navigation was proving accurate, and *Jalina* was performing well in the heavy Irish seas; her fine prow gave her good pointing.

I prepared WPs to clear a number of headlands and dangers such as, Black Head, The Gobbins, Isle of Muck, Hunter Rock (to the south), Ballygalley Head, Park Head, and Garron Point. I also made up an east WP close to the fish farm in Red Bay; in a swell these fish farms can be difficult to spot.

The weather looked settled with the wind dying down at night. I decided to anchor in Red Bay north of Glenarm marina; alternatively we could go into Glenarm marina for a safer shelter.

The fair tide for the passage would vary from 0.6 to 1.5 knots; the main danger point were the shallows of Hunter

Rock east of Larne, guarded by north and south cardinal markers.

I rose at 0330, prepared a hearty breakfast of mixed fruit cereal, scrambled eggs on hot toast, washed down with tea. After a quick shave and a hot shower, with my thermals and waterproofs donned plus a warm hat, I was feeling comfortable and good with the world. You could hear a pin drop in the dark marina; I was the only soul on the move. My sails were prepared: one reef in the main as a precaution, No 2 genoa hanked on with No 1 jib lashed to the deck.

It was dark and the air was damp as *Jalina* slowly slipped from her mooring. It was 0440 (Dover HW), by the time we cleared the outer breakwater and there was a loom of sunlight to the east. Once clear of the harbour and the shore, *Jalina* picked up a light westerly breeze. I shook out the remainder of the reefs; we were making four knots as I headed north, crossing Belfast Lough; I had a little foul cross-tide coming into the Lough.

I signed on with the Belfast Coastguard; at the same time I was given the latest inshore weather forecast, SW force 3–4, occasional force 5; showers, moderate to good, mist patches, with much the same forecasted for the following 24 hours.

There was a light mist covering the headland of Black Head lighthouse, but I could see her light flashing every three seconds. There was a cold chill in the air, what little wind there was fell away to nothing, so the trusty Yanmar came to life, spoiling the peace. As I cleared Black Head, a little wind started to come in from the south-west, bringing with it the odd white top on the swell.

By 0900 the Mull of Kintyre could be seen to the north-east through the mist. My initial plan was to anchor in Red Bay; it would give *Jalina* a five-mile start to cross over to Scotland and round the Mull of Kintyre.

As I approached Garron Point under full sail with a force 2 breeze, the mist had cleared. On rounding the Point, I could see white tops with a large swell even in the shelter of the headland. I pushed the tiller over, backing the jib to hove-to and put two reefs into the main. I quickly changed down the foresail to a working jib, then continued my passage into Red Bay. The first thing which impressed me were the steep mountains rising to 396m and 350m respectively on each side of the bay, with a deep valley running through the centre. The wind was now force 5 and

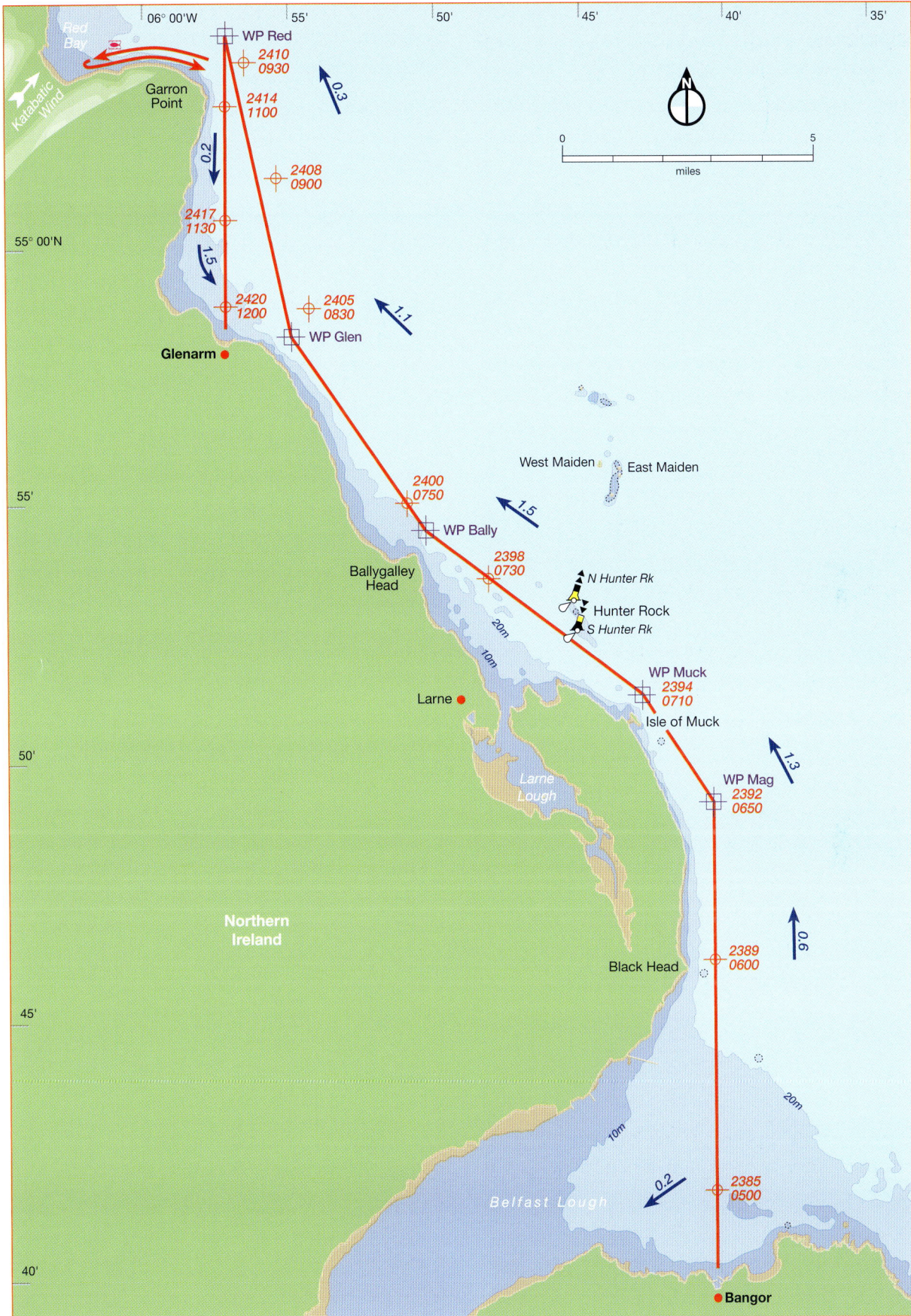

06° 00'W

55'

50'

45'

40'

35'

Red Bay

Katabatic Wind

Garron Point

WP Red

2410 0930

0.3

2414 1100

0.2

2408 0900

2417 1130

55° 00'N

1.5

2420 1200

2405 0830

1.1

WP Glen

Glenarm

West Maiden

East Maiden

55'

2400 0750

1.5

WP Bally

Ballygalley Head

2398 0730

N Hunter Rk

Hunter Rock

S Hunter Rk

20m

10m

WP Muck

2394 0710

Isle of Muck

Larne

Larne Lough

WP Mag

2392 0650

1.3

50'

Northern Ireland

Black Head

2389 0600

0.6

45'

20m

10m

0.2

2385 0500

Belfast Lough

40'

Bangor

N

0

5

miles

as I cleared the fish farm, it rose to force 6. I decided that a katabatic wind such as this would make an anchorage very uncomfortable, so carried out my second plan which was to head back around the headland of Garron Point, where the wind had dropped to force 2. Taking an inshore eddy, we soon entered the calm of Glenarm Marina, arriving at 1210.

The harbour master took *Jalina*'s lines and guided me to the shore facilities; I was made very welcome.

In retrospect, knowing the wind direction, I should have looked a little closer at the chart and realised that those high hills at Red Bay would produce such strong winds; the experience was well worthwhile.

Facilities

There are showers, water, diesel and small local shops in Glenarm village.

After I had showered, I enjoyed a good meal. The hills were still shrouded in mist; it was very pleasant to sit out on deck, with the backdrop of misty hills, to plan the next passage. This would take me from Ireland around the Mull of Kintyre to the Island of Gigha in Scotland.

The weather was settled so I needed to press on with the next day's passage. If the forecast was for strong winds, I would wait for the weather to settle; my tidal window still had several days of good timing and strength. I had sailed continually for several days so I was feeling a deep-seated tiredness and needed to rest for a couple of days. Once moored in Gigha, I would rest up and enjoy one of the most beautiful islands in Scotland.

Glenarm made a good stepping off point for Scotland.

Glenarm to Ardminish Bay, Gigha, Scotland

Distance: 44nm

Passage time: 8hr 35min

The weather forecast for Mull of Galloway to the Mull of Kintyre given out by the Clyde Coastguard was SW force 5 or 6 going force 3–4 cyclonic later; rain showers, visibility moderate to good, sea state smooth, locally moderate. For Mull of Kintyre to Ardnamurchan the forecast was S force 5–7, going force 3–4, backing N variable SE later; showers, visibility good, sea state rough to moderate.

The forecast looked fine with light winds later, but I would prepare for a south-west force 6, on rounding the Mull of Kintyre as it would give me a weather shore. I would then lose the wind and once I had rounded the Mull I would have to step out a little from the land to get the south-west wind.

This was a good exercise in preparing a vector to work out the tidal effect to compensate my heading so that I

The tides for the crossing to the Mull of Kintyre.

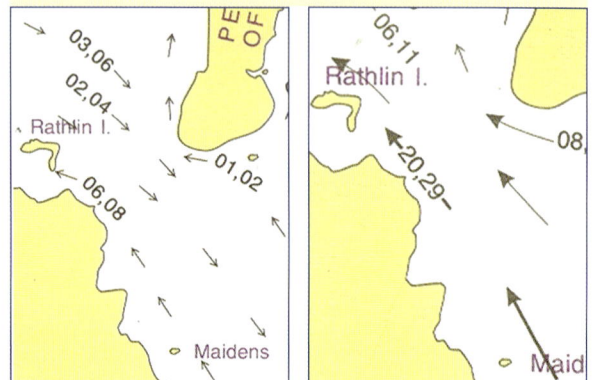

HW Dover   HW Dover + 1

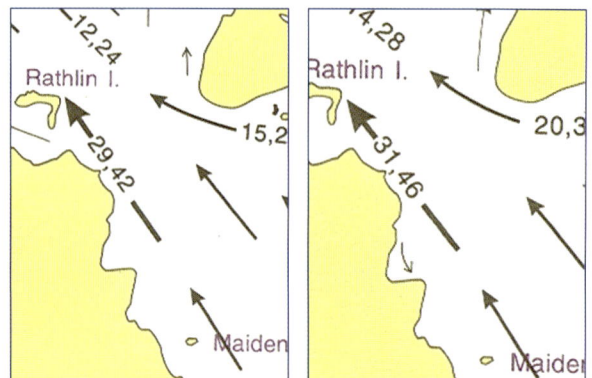

HW Dover + 2   HW Dover + 3

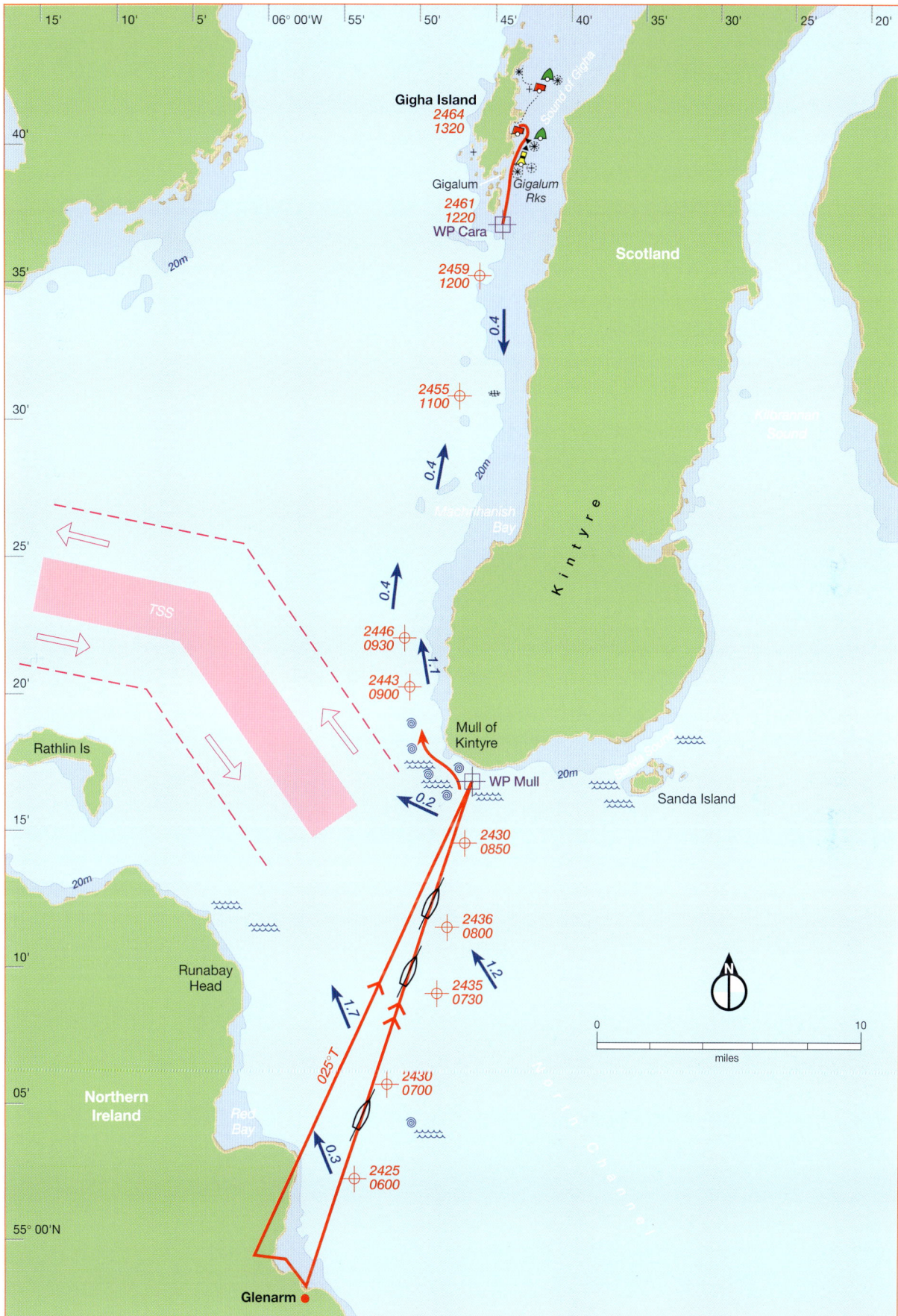

15' 10' 5' 06° 00'W 55' 50' 45' 40' 35' 30' 25' 20'

40'

Gigha Island
2464
1320

Gigalum
2461
1220
WP Cara

Gigalum Rks

Scotland

35'

2459
1200

0.4

30'

2455
1100

20m

0.4

Machrihanish Bay

25'

0.4

K i n t y r e

TSS

2446
0930

1.1

20'

2443
0900

Mull of
Kintyre

WP Mull

20m

Sanda Island

0.2

15'

Rathlin Is

2430
0850

20m

2436
0800

1.2

10'

Runabay
Head

2435
0730

025°T

1.7

0 miles 10

05'

**Northern
Ireland**

Red Bay

2430
0700

0.3

2425
0600

55° 00'N

Glenarm

arrived close to the headland and round inshore of the Mull of Kintyre. I always use British Admiralty Tidal Atlases as they relate to Dover HW times.

I was still chasing the tide: planning to use a fair tide early in the day so as to be in harbour after a 30 to 40 mile passage by midday. I could then use the remainder of the day to plan the next passage, and do all the necessary chores needed to keep the boat and myself in good order. I have lost the tidal gate before on my adventures; I then have to depart late in the day, arriving at my destination an hour or two after midnight, after negotiating the hazards of crab pot lines which threaten to entangle my propeller.

My main concern for this passage was the Traffic Separation Scheme (TSS); I would be passing approximately four miles south of the TSS. During the first part of my passage, ships would be coming towards *Jalina*'s port side as they leave the TSS, then towards our starboard side as we close on the Mull of Kintyre.

I prepared two WPs; the first was 'Mull'. This was plotted close to the shore in a good depth of water; from this I could check the cross-tide as I closed the shore, and would avoid drifting into the overfalls off the Mull, as I intended to clear the Mull by the inner passage. The second WP, 'Cara', was plotted to assist me to clear Gigalum Rocks for my final approach into Ardminish Bay, where I would either pick up a mooring or anchor.

As the sun went down I prepared WPs, marked up charts with clearing lines. I took the sail covers off and hanked on sails in preparation for an early start. I made sandwiches; with no fridge I put these against the hull to keep cool. I checked the engine oil level, the raw seawater filter, and topped up the fuel tank. All was now ready and it was time for bed as I was due for an early start.

As I prepared for bed I could hear a party in full swing on several yachts so it was time to dig out my ear plugs. I set my alarm for 0330 and rose early at 0300; it was a misty morning and the air was still. As I opened the hatch, the damp mist drifted into the saloon. Once I put the kettle on, the heat from the stove soon took the chill off the air. The main domestic problem I had during my first UK circumnavigation was a damp saloon – with no heater it was difficult to dry it out properly. For the second circum-navigation, I had fitted a Taylor's paraffin heater which solved all the damp problems.

By the time all lines were prepared, waterproofs donned and I had signed on with the Clyde Coastguard with passage plan details, it was 0450 (Dover HW −52min), time to depart. A good breeze started to pick up; once clear of the breakwater, the wind was force 4 – a reach – it could not have been better.

We were soon south of the TSS, and the Mull of Kintyre could just be seen through the early morning mist. Several ships passed by, well clear of *Jalina*. I rounded the Mull by

I avoided the overfalls by going through the inner passage to the Mull of Kintyre.

Ardminish Bay, Gigha – it was good to have sunshine after so much mist and fog.

0900 (Dover HW +3hr 18min), the tidal atlas gave 2.0 knots near the Mull, close into the headland, *Jalina* had 4.0 knots of tide (one day before neaps).

The white tops of the overfalls could be seen in the distance to our port side, *Jalina* pressed on, and I set a new course for WP 'Cara'. The sun was now well up, its warmth prompting me to shed the top of my oilies, and put on sun block and sun glasses. I was under full sail now with No 2 genoa and *Jalina* was romping along at 5 knots.

It was stunningly beautiful, with some of the most breath-taking scenery I have ever seen. The water was so clear, that I could see every detail on the seabed.

I poured a glass of orange juice and toasted my arrival in Scotland.

APPENDIX
THE EAST COAST OF IRELAND TO THE OUTER HEBRIDES

Since writing the first edition of this book, I decided to take another three months out to sail a different route north taking in the east coast of Ireland, visit Rathlin Island and make my way through the Sound of Islay to Oban where I was joined by my wife Liz. From here we continued to Tobermory then onto the Outer Hebrides, enjoying four weeks of the wonderful wildlife, mountain walking and making new friends. This account could assist in parts in planning an alternative route when circumnavigating the UK.

Preparing for the passage

The preparation for this trip, as with my full circumnavigation, had to be thorough. I replaced *Jalina*'s engine, all the rigging and guard wires, cleaned out the fuel tank and replaced the fuel filter.

AIS Radar worked well when identifying shipping on my night passage to Ireland.

For the electrics I fitted an AIS Radar receiver and NAVTEX Clipper, serviced the Avon liferaft and fitted a McMurdo EPIRB. I went through all my skipper's checklists for spares, stores, and made up lists of where all the kit was stored.

For this trip I also took the fisherman's anchor including chain and rhode for any weedy anchorage. And I checked the equipment stored in my emergency grab bag; such preparation is particularly important when single-handing.

As with all my extended cruising I started from Gosport making short passages to settle into a routine, check

This EPIRB gave me peace of mind when sailing in more remote areas.

out *Jalina*, ensure all the kit works, and to give me time to correct things if any problems arose. On these passages, when going west and north around the Longships I always call in to see my friends at Newlyn Lifeboat Station. I was sure one of my batteries was faulty during my passage west, and a check confirmed it. I ordered a new replacement to be delivered at Padstow so that I could fit it before my passage to Milford Haven; fortunately I always carry a spare battery so this was fitted in the meantime. I also had a fault with my Simrad Autopilot TP22 so a replacement was ordered, and again in the meantime I used a spare.

Milford Haven to Arklow Harbour
Distance: 87nm
Passage time: 16hr

This being my first full night passage of the season, I allowed myself an extra day in harbour to make thorough preparations for my passage to Ireland. I had planned this passage on a full spring tide so that for some days it would give me an early morning fair tide north.

I'm always concerned about becoming complacent in preparing for such a passage so I make up lists as a reminder. I checked all the navigation lights including the searchlight hand torches, not forgetting my small pocket torch which I find ideal for the chart table. The fuel tank (9 gallons) and spare fuel cans (7 gallons) were all topped up. The battery to my hand-held Simrad VHF went down and would not charge, so I ordered a new one, receiving it the next day. This is one item I keep in the grab bag should I have to abandon *Jalina*.

For some days I had been watching the track of the fronts and studying the synoptic charts to build up a picture of the approaching weather. I was hoping for a weather shore for some days but it seemed more likely the wind could be from the east.

The evening before the passage to Milford Haven, the Coastguard 24-hour inshore forecast was for winds of ENE force 3–4 occasionally force 5, fair, visibility good, sea state slight to moderate with much the same for the following 24 hours. My main concern here was the depth of water on entering Arklow; with an easterly, a deep swell would reduce the depth of water in the troughs when entering the harbour. I had prepared an alternative passage plan as

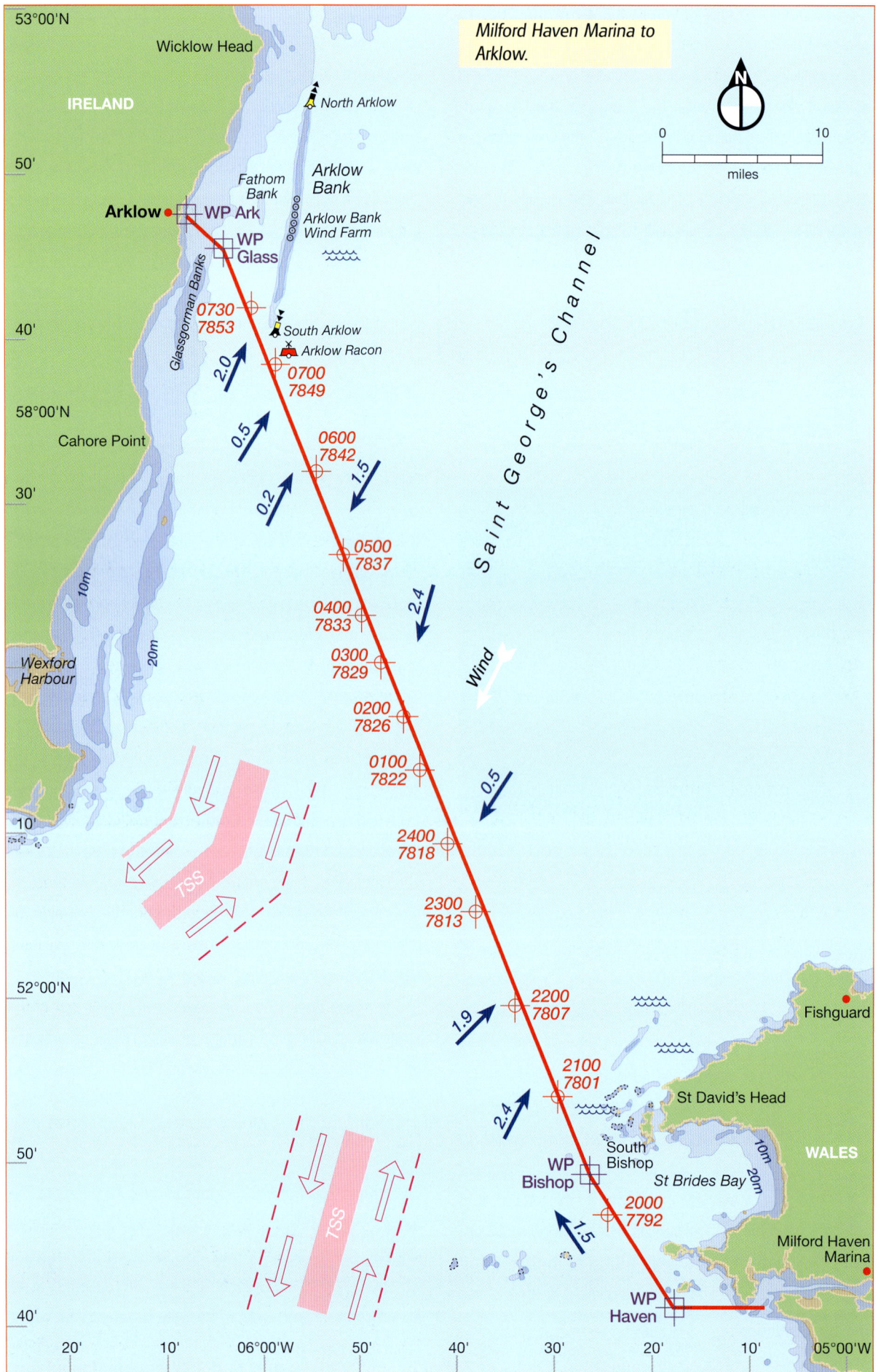

53°00'N

Wicklow Head

IRELAND

North Arklow

Milford Haven Marina to Arklow.

N

0   10
miles

50'

Fathom
Bank

Arklow
Bank

Arklow Bank
Wind Farm

Arklow ● □ **WP Ark**

□ **WP
Glass**

40'

Glassgorman Banks

0730
7853

2.0

South Arklow

Arklow Racon

58°00'N

0.5

0700
7849

Cahore Point

0600
7842

1.5

30'

0.2

Saint George's Channel

0500
7837

0400
7833

2.4

0300
7829

Wind

10m

0200
7826

20m

*Wexford
Harbour*

0100
7822

0.5

10'

2400
7818

TSS

2300
7813

52°00'N

2200
7807

1.9

Fishguard

2100
7801

2.4

St David's Head

South
Bishop

WALES

50'

**WP
Bishop**

St Brides Bay

10m

TSS

2000
7792

20m

1.5

Milford Haven
Marina

**WP
Haven**

40'

20'   10'   06°00'W   50'   40'   30'   20'   05°00'W

a second option whereby I would change course and sail north for Howth, a passage of 41nm.

The extra day in harbour would allow me to rest in preparation for the passage. I had prepared a good wholesome casserole which would give me two hot meals during the passage.

As part of my passage planning I marked off in pencil any danger points on the chart to focus my attention during the passage. On this occasion I marked off Arklow Bank with its many new wind turbines.

I slipped *Jalina* at 1715 and cleared the lock at 1730. It was a beautiful sunny clear evening, and by 1830 we had cleared St Ann's Head (HW Dover −5.5 hours). Once clear of St Ann's Head I had a fair tide until midnight.

I had considered sailing first to Wexford – a shorter passage – but the forecast for easterlies and the shallow water and shifting banks on the approach could make it a dangerous approach.

I have sailed these waters many times, and usually by this time the easterlys had gone round to SW, thus giving me a comfortable and safer weather shore.

As we cleared Bishop Rock there was a cool chill to the air. The NE breeze now setting in was cold, and with the sun going down it was time to dress for the night. At 1930 I heated up the second half of the casserole; it was piping hot and a good start to the long night passage.

I signed on with Milford Haven Coastguard ch 16-67 I was asked to sign off with Dublin Coastguard ch 16-02. Before settling down my mobile was still in range so I put in a call to Liz to let her know all was well. By now the wind was NNE force 2–3, visibility was good, and we had full main up and orange jib.

With two lots of TSS to clear it would be a good opportunity to see how effectively the AIS radar performed. It picked up the first north-going shipping and from its

heading and speed I could see it was going to pass astern of me. With the ship's name shown on the AIS I decided to call it upon the VHF. The officer I spoke to said he had me on his radar and would pass astern; very reassuring.

By midnight I could see the loom of Tusker light to the west and within the next two hours we would meet the north-going TSS shipping lane. As the night went on the wind freshened to force 3, and with it came a lumpy sea. By 0600 I could see the coast of Ireland and the wind generators on Arklow Bank, with the Lanby standing guard on the southern part of the Bank. It was now getting light, but I was put on my guard when I heard a hard knock on *Jalina*'s hull. It was a poorly marked crab pot, and then I noticed dozens of them, most with only black cans to mark them.

Checking the Irish pilot I spotted the light coloured-building and chimney; coming in from the east the southern end of the harbour wall and its lights stand out quite well.

The entrance is dredged to 3.5m. The NE wind had eased, but had it not, a heavy swell would have made the entrance hazardous. As I approached the entrance the tide was on the make. With 1m low water depth plus 3.5m plus the tide on the make that I calculated as 1m, that would give me a total of 5.5m; the swell was about 2m.

During the night passage I had pondered the approach to Arklow – too early and the tide would not be on the make and later the swell could build.

The final approach went well. There was a swell close to the entrance then very little as I entered the breakwater. The depth was 5.5m confirming the 3.5m dredged depth.

Jalina was tied up by 0900 on the pontoon outside the marina. It had been a long night; it was my first night passage of the season, and I was quite tired. I prepared a good breakfast and put my head down for a few hours. The weather forecast was correct; the passage had gone well and I was now feeling a little more confident.

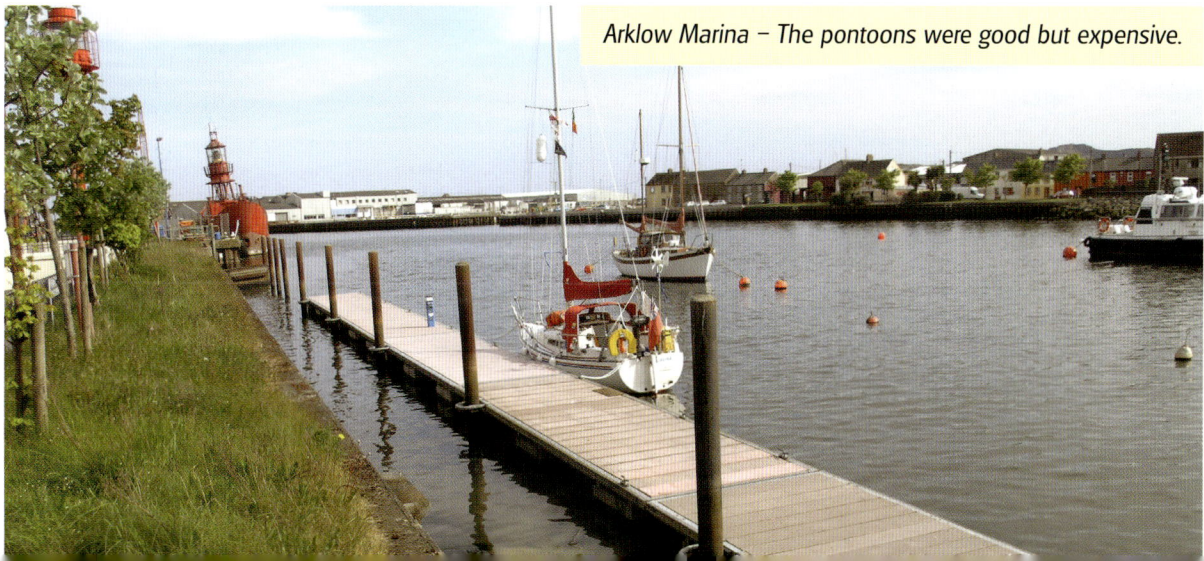

Arklow Marina – The pontoons were good but expensive.

Arklow to Howth

Distance: 41nm

Passage time: 6hr

For the next few days there would be a fair spring tide window early in the morning to take me north. With short passages I would then have time each day to explore ashore.

The weather forecast for the St George's Channel was SE force 3–4 increasing force 5–6 at times, rain, visibility moderate to good, sea state slight or moderate. This weather would put me on a lee shore, I would prepare for a force 6 and a lumpy sea. The one good point here was that the spring tide would be running with me north so I would have wind with tide.

For this short passage I only prepared a flask of tea; it would be an early start after a good night's sleep. I slipped *Jalina*'s lines at 0445 HW Dover +4 hrs.

As we cleared the harbour it was overcast, and an easterly force 3. With two reefs in the main and her orange working jib we were cutting well to windward. For the first hour or so we had a foul tide but once we reached Wicklow Head the tide was with us, and we were making 7.2 knots over the ground.

By 0900 the sea was building with the wind force 6 gusting force 7. By now *Jalina* had three reefs in the main as we made 10 knots over the ground. As we approached Ben of Howth I handed the main, and sailed the final approach under foresail and engine.

Howth Marina – you will be given a very warm welcome.

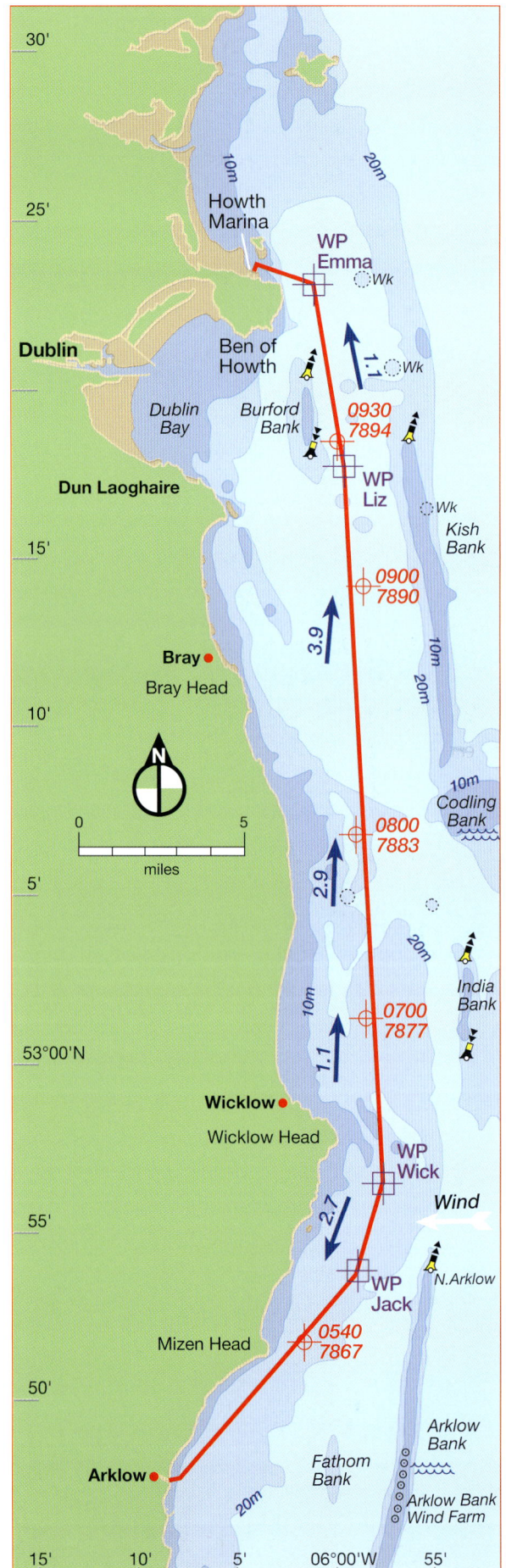

Arklow to Howth Marina.

Howth Marina to Ardglass

Distance: 50nm

Passage time: 9hr

I enjoyed my stay at Howth marina. It has all the facilities needed, and it is clean and well maintained.

The weather forecast for my passage to Ardglass was SE force 3–4 increasing to force 5–6 at times, with rain, visibility moderate to good, and sea state moderate. The following 24 hours were much the same.

With the weather tending to be strong easterly winds I abandoned my plans to anchor in the small coves along the coast. Normally the winds would have been in the SW for this time of year, and we would have had the safety of a weather shore.

Because of the unusual pattern of the tides for this passage we would start with a fair tide, then experience over two hours of slack, then a fair tide again (see chartlet over page).

After preparing sandwiches for the next day's passage, an early night's sleep was needed. I rose at 0630. I had prepared the sails the night before: two reefs in the main and the orange heavyweight foresail.

After a good breakfast, two boiled eggs and toast, I was ready to cast off. I called Dublin Coastguard and informed them of my passage plan. They also gave me a weather update of force 5–7 easing later.

As we cleared the harbour breakwater there was a heavy swell running, with the white tops standing out against the grey sky. I could just make out Lambay Island through the mist. Jalina was cutting through the swell with some swagger the dark sky adding to the drama of sailing.

By 1400 the wind started to ease a little, although the swell was still breaking along her decks, swilling occasionally over the coamings into the cockpit.

St John's lighthouse with its distinctive black and yellow bands.

Mountains of Mourne.

As we approached St John's Point I could make out the lighthouse with its distinctive black and yellow bands. We arrived at Ardglass Marina at 1610, the passage having gone well. The weather forecast for the next few days was not good, however SE force 5–7.

Bad weather pinned Jalina and I in harbour for the next six days, during which time I made many good friends, taking me into their homes meeting their family and visiting many beautiful areas such as the Mountains of Mourne, Carlingford Lough, and Strangford Lough.

Ardglass to Glenarm

Distance: 57nm

Passage time: 12hr

As I had written about my passage to Strangford Lough and passing through the Donaghadee Sound in a previous chapter, for this passage I decided to go direct to Glenarm. The weather forecast was not good for the passage: NE force 4–5, force 6 at first, visibility poor, sea state slight to moderate, and rain. I decided to go but would check with the Coastguard before departing, and at the same time would give my passage plan.

The passage plan was complete: danger points marked on the chart, WPs made up, and as the passage would put me on a lee shore I ensured the passage would stand me well clear of any danger points.

I rose at 0330 and there was a damp wet chill to the air, with the wind NE force 2. After a good breakfast of porridge, hot tea, and flasks made up with hot soup, I put a reef in the main and signed on with the Coastguard and then slipped Jalina's lines. It was a beat clearing the harbour and to clear Strangford Lough fairway buoy.

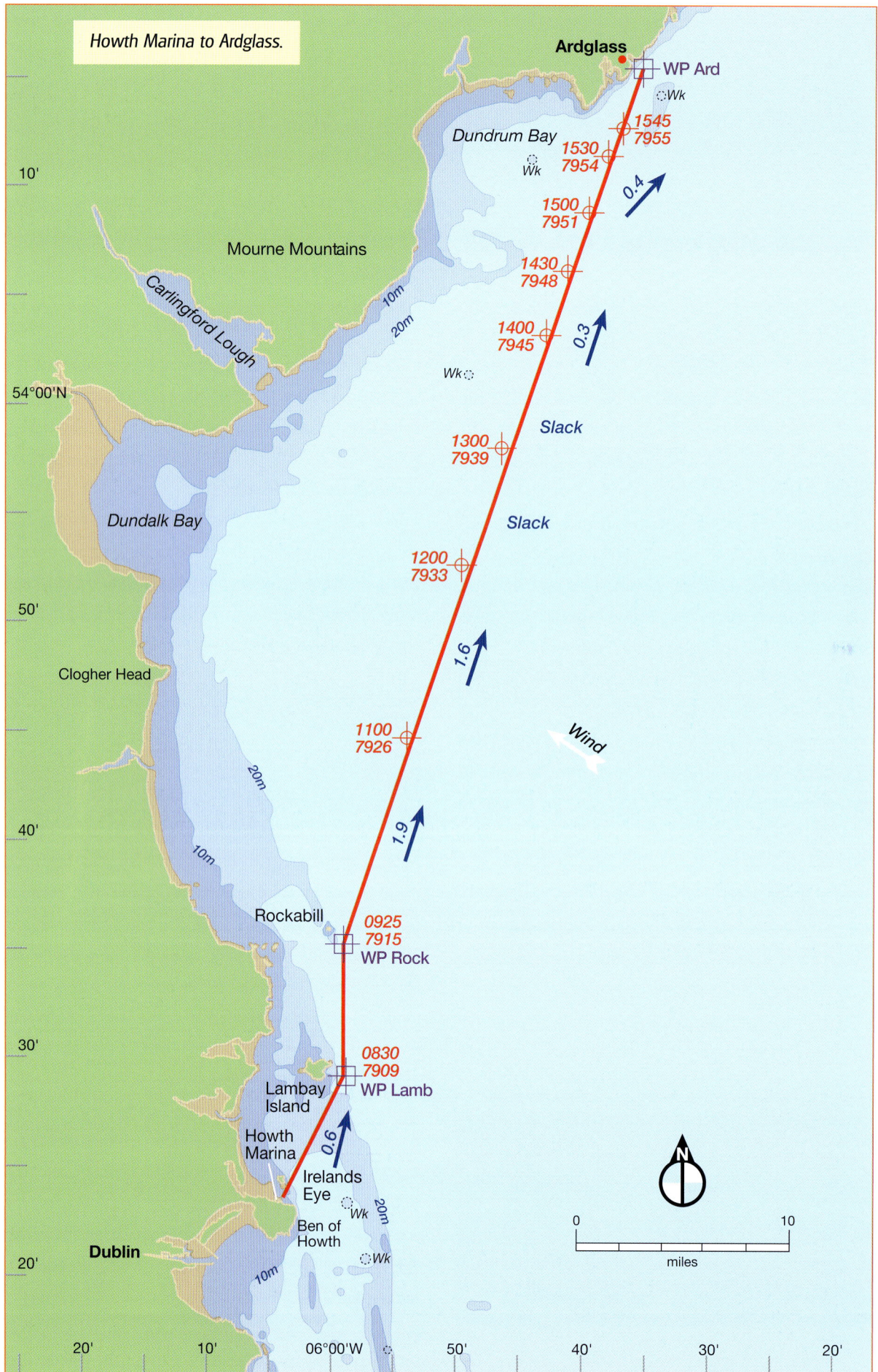

Howth Marina to Ardglass.

Ardglass

WP Ard

Wk

Dundrum Bay

1545
7955

1530
7954

Wk

1500
7951

0.4

1430
7948

Mourne Mountains

Carlingford Lough

10m

20m

1400
7945

0.3

Wk

54°00'N

Slack

1300
7939

Dundalk Bay

Slack

50'

1200
7933

Clogher Head

1.6

40'

20m

10m

1100
7926

1.9

Wind

Rockabill

0925
7915
WP Rock

30'

0830
7909
WP Lamb

Lambay
Island

0.6

Howth
Marina

Irelands
Eye

Wk

20m

Ben of
Howth

Dublin

Wk

20'

10m

N

0   10

miles

20'   **10'**   **06°00'W**   **50'**   **40'**   **30'**   **20'**

Ardglass Marina – a safe and well sheltered harbour.

Fair Head – not a breath of wind.

It was a wet passage with wind against tide for part of the way. At times the visibility was poor, and it was very wet. I paid particular attention to keep well clear of marked up danger points.

I have already given details on Glenarm Marina earlier in this book. On this visit I took time out to visit the nearby walled garden at Glenarm Castle; a real treat. The old mushroom sheds had been converted into tea rooms. For the ladies a visit to Steensons jewellery makers in the village would be interesting.

Glenarm to Ballycastle
Distance: 22nm
Passage time: 5hr

The weather forecast was E veering W to SW, force 3–4, occasionally force 5, showers, visibility occasionally poor, and sea state moderate.

This passage would take me between Fair Head and Rue Point on Rathlin Island. Here I needed to plan a fair tide through the narrows to Ballycastle.

Ballycastle Marina.

This would be a short passage. Slipping *Jalina*'s lines at 0730 HW Dover +1hr, and clearing the marina in blue skies, the sea was still like a mill pond; was this a good omen? *Jalina*'s engine purred away for the whole passage, and we cleared Fair Head with nearly three knots of fair tide.

The approach to the marina is well protected, as the entrance faces east. Had there been strong NE winds down the bay I would have rounded Rue Point and gone into Rathlin Marina on a weather shore.

Facilities
The facilities at Ballycastle are excellent: clothes washing and drying, diesel, showers, electricity, water, good nearby shopping.

Ballycastle to Rathlin Island
Distance: 6nm
Passage time: 1.5hr

It was neaps +2 days, and although this passage is short, I wanted settled weather particularly from the SW for entering the marina and to avoid spring tides if possible.

The weather forecast gave an anticyclone sitting over much of Northern Ireland and southern Scotland. I entered one WP for the passage and one on the Rathlin breakwater as a check.

Ballycastle Harbour entrance.

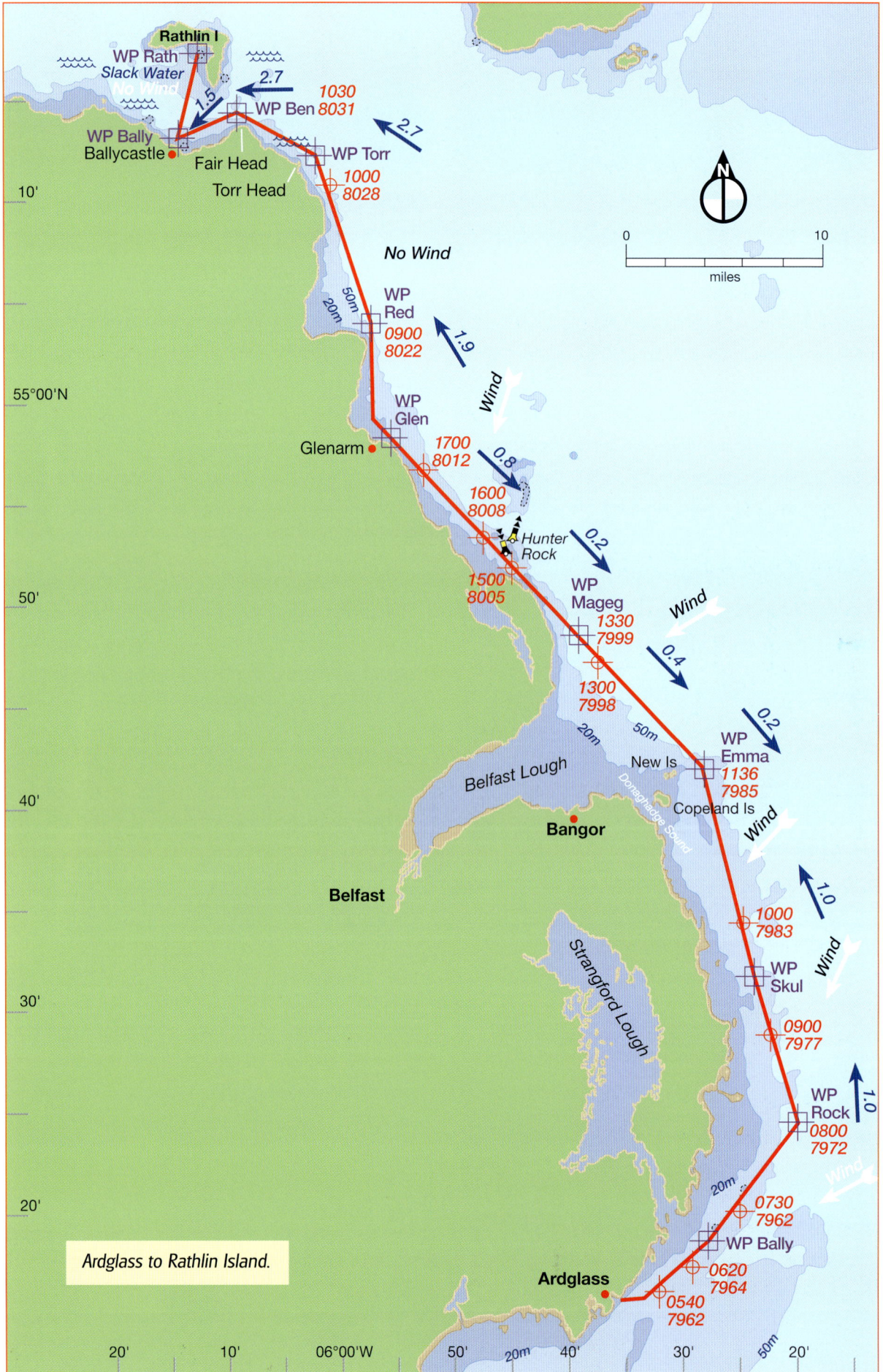

Rathlin I

WP Rath
Slack Water
No Wind

2.7

1.5

WP Ben   1030   8031

WP Bally
Ballycastle

Fair Head

Torr Head

2.7

WP Torr   1000   8028

No Wind

50m
20m

WP Red   0900   8022

1.9

Wind

55°00'N

WP Glen

Glenarm   1700   8012

0.8

1600   8008

Hunter Rock

0.2

1500   8005

50'

WP Mageg   1330   7999

Wind

1300   7998

0.4

0.2

WP Emma   1136   7985

Belfast Lough

New Is

Copeland Is

Wind

40'

Bangor

Donaghadee Sound

Belfast

1000   7983

1.0

Wind

Strangford Lough

WP Skul

30'

0900   7977

1.0

WP Rock   0800   7972

Wind

20m

0730   7962

20'

WP Bally

0620   7964

Ardglass

0540   7962

Ardglass to Rathlin Island.

N

0   10
miles

20m   50m

20'   10'   **06°00'W**   50'   20m   40'   30'   50m   20'

I slipped *Jalina*'s lines and cleared the marina at 1240 HW Dover +5hrs. The air was hot and still, with blue sky, and the sea was like a mirror with thousands of sea birds and the odd seal popping its head up in curiosity. The short passage went well, and the tide was mainly slack.

The entrance to the breakwaters face SE as you enter, and the pontoons are to your starboard. I held back to let the small Ballycastle ferry enter. The HM here has several other duties so you may have to search for him.

Rathlin Island is a hidden treasure, with its many birds and seals. To visit some of the best bird colonies the minibuses gather to meet the ferry. They will take you to the west of the Island to see the thousands of sea birds and meet the RSPB staff who work there, or you can hire bicycles. I would very much like to return here and hire one of the cottages to indulge in one of my other hobbies – watercolour painting.

Facilities

The facilities are limited; there is water and electricity on the pontoons, and there is a store that stocks basic items, as well as several places to eat and drink.

Rathlin to Port Ellen
Distance: 24nm
Passage time: 5hr

After several days on Rathlin I decided, as the weather was holding good, it was time to move on; my next stop would take me into Scotland to Port Ellen. I made two WPs, one to assist me to keep clear of the TSS, the other to enter Port Ellen.

The weather forecast was variable NE force 3–4 sea state slight, fog patches, visibility moderate occasionally very poor – the same forecast as for the past few days, yet there has been no wind and a little mist which has burnt off as soon as the sun came up.

I woke at 0530 to find dense fog in the harbour, I prepared scrambled eggs on toast, some hot tea, and as the sun rose the fog started to clear. There was no wind and not a cloud in the sky – it would be another motoring passage.

After several checks to the engine, I topped up the main

Top: Rathlin Harbour.
Middle: Jalina in Rathlin Harbour.
Bottom: Rathlin Inner Harbour. Good shelter should a gale come from the SW.

fuel tank, and checked access to the main anchor.

We slipped at 0830 and once clear of the harbour I set *Jalina* on a westerly course to clear Rathlin. It was now quite hot; time to put on the sun block and dig out my sun bleached big hat.

Once clear of Bull Point I set a course for Port Ellen. A tidal vector made up earlier gave me approximately five knots of west-going tide. After making the adjustments to the bearing I set WP 'Guard' to ensure we cleared the TSS.

During the passage I checked the latest weather forecast – it was much the same, little or no wind, with some early morning mist.

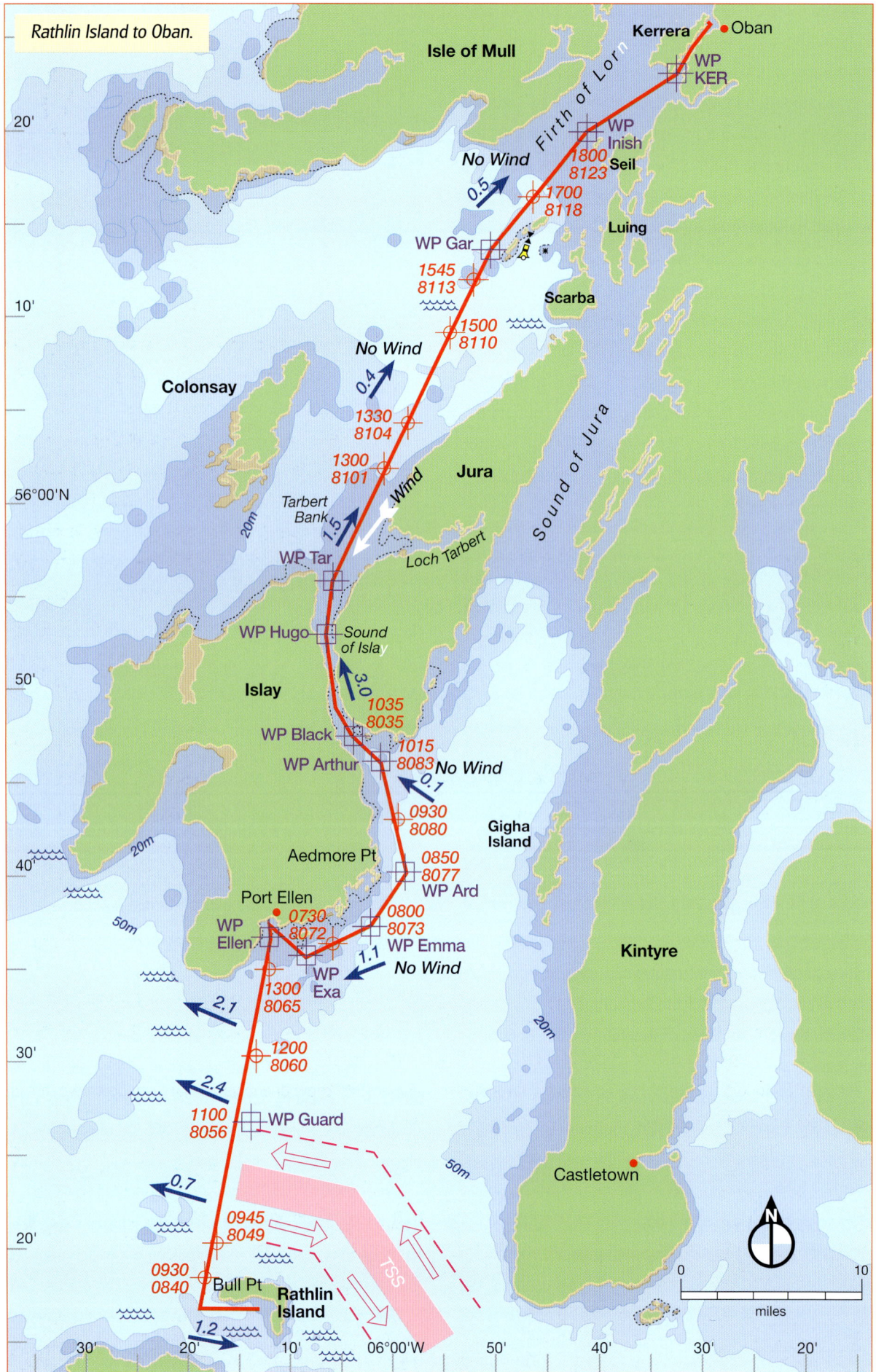

Rathlin Island to Oban.

Isle of Mull

Kerrera

Oban

WP KER

Firth of Lorn

WP Inish

1800
8123

Seil

1700
8118

Luing

No Wind

0.5

WP Gar

1545
8113

Scarba

1500
8110

Colonsay

No Wind

0.4

1330
8104

Jura

1300
8101

Sound of Jura

56°00'N

Wind

1.5

Tarbert Bank

20m

WP Tar

Loch Tarbert

WP Hugo

Sound of Isla

3.0

50'

Islay

1035
8035

WP Black

1015
8083

No Wind

WP Arthur

0.1

0930
8080

Gigha Island

Aedmore Pt

0850
8077

WP Ard

20m

40'

Port Ellen

0730
8072

0800
8073

WP Emma

WP Ellen

WP Exa

1.1

No Wind

Kintyre

1300
8065

2.1

1200
8060

30'

2.4

1100
8056

WP Guard

0.7

50m

TSS

0945
8049

20'

0930
0840

Bull Pt

Rathlin Island

1.2

Castletown

N

0   10

miles

30'   20'   10'   06°00'W   50'   40'   30'   20'

Rounding Bull Point – Rathlin.

I had heard that the ferry stays the night in Port Ellen, running its generators all night, so with a calm night forecast I decided to take up one of the HIE moorings out in the quiet bay. I prepared a supper of boiled potatoes, a tin of wild salmon plus mixed salad and a soft drink; I never drink any alcohol when at anchor or on a mooring. And I also had the sea birds to keep me company and a good night's sleep.

Port Ellen to Oban via the Sound of Islay

Distance: 62nm

Passage time: 13hr

The timing for this passage was perfect, I had a window of five days to complete it so as to arrive in daylight in Oban. I knew I could always anchor in many of the lochs, but I needed to press north as I had already lost many days through bad weather.

The weather forecast was for winds of force 7 in 36 hours' time. For this passage it was to be winds variable force 3–4, rain later, visibility good, sea state slight; for the following 24 hours the forecasts gave winds of force 7. However, as they were not sure of the wind direction, I abandoned my plan to call in at Colonsay and Loch Tarbert.

I rose at 0530, did my usual engine checks, put a reef in the main and hanked on my orange safety easy-to-see

Looking towards Kerrera and Isle of Mull from Oban.

foresail. As I slipped the mooring there was some protest from the many sea birds. We cleared the bay at 0700 HW Dover −3.5hrs; the ferry departed at the same time.

As we cleared Ardmore Point the mist cleared, the tide was setting *Jalina* nicely into the Sound of Islay and we soon had 3 knots of tide pushing us through, making 9 knots over the ground. The approach into the Sound was breathtaking, exposing as we went those beautiful mountains full of colour. As we cleared the Sound the wind got up from the NE force 1–2 but lasted only a short while.

I was interested to look out for a recent chart correction – a west cardinal buoy NW of Scaba; it stood out all newly painted.

The passage down the Forth of Lorne is particularly beautiful with the many mountains reaching so high, covered in greens and browns and with the glitter of water cascading down as it filled the streams.

The passage went well and we carried a fair tide for the whole passage, finally tying up at Kerrera Marina by 1930. There are several HIE moorings close to and west of the town.

Care has to be taken when entering Kerrera Sound as there is a rock in the centre. When entering, there is a red can on the east side and a green can to the west to navigate you around. I do know of one yacht that went down when it hit the rock.

Looking towards Oban from Kerrera.

Oban to Tobermory

Castle Stalker, Sound of Shuna.

I sailed this passage on my second circumnavigation, and it has been explained in some detail in the book.

If you wish to stay longer around the Oban area possibly due to the weather, I have visited Dallens Cove (Sound of Shuna) 11nm west of Oban; a jewel that lets you step back in time. There are moorings here and it has all a skipper needs. (The shower is a must to try.)

Loch Aline, 14nm from Oban in the Sound of Mull, is a good anchorage with good holding; I sheltered here from a gale for several days. The best place to anchor and land ashore is NW of the Loch.

From here there are many walks, including estate gardens north of the Loch.

Loch Aline in the Sound of Mull.

Tobermory has a new marina and facilities recently opened by Princess Anne.

Tobermory to Castle Bay, Outer Hebrides
Distance: 54nm
Passage time: 10hr

I had been planning this passage to the Outer Hebrides for a long while and it was not without misgivings as my wife Liz joined me at Oban for a holiday for several weeks. I had several days awaiting her arrival, so *Jalina* was well stocked with stores. I gave the engine a full service, took a spare diesel (35 litres), paraffin for the Taylors heater, and petrol for the outboard – all checked and stored.

My passage planning for this trip involved changing over and checking again all the charts, looking up the Notices to Mariners for chart corrections on the internet via my laptop, plus a check of all the pilot books; we were prepared.

We had been stormbound in Tobermory for several days. Finally the weather forecast looked hopeful, one given for the area – Minch to Ardnamurchan to Cape Wrath including the Outer Hebrides W force 4–5 occasionally force 6 at first

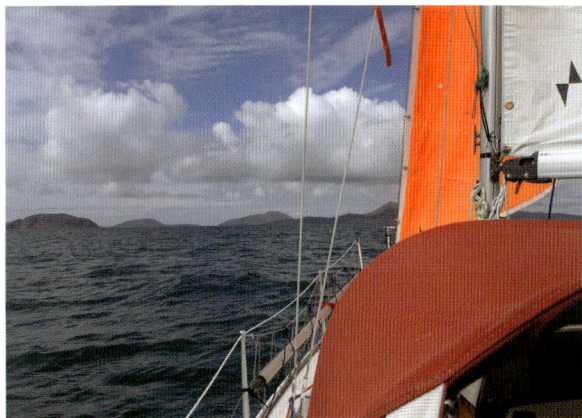

Jalina approaching Barra – Outer Hebrides.

in the north becoming variable force 3–4 later, sea state rough, showers, visibility good. The following 24 hours was variable E force 3–4 backing NE force 5–6 sea state rough, showers, visibility good. This forecast looked fine and because the rough sea state was due to the subsiding gales, this would die down during our passage.

With such exposed sailing in the Hebrides good reliable weather reports are a must. As a back up my NAVTEX is always switched on, I connect the NASA SSB receiver to my laptop to receive synoptic charts, and I use 198kHz for shipping forecasts.

We slipped *Jalina*'s lines at 0500 (HW Dover +3.5hr); it was good to be underway, and we soon cleared Ardmore Point. The light wind was SE. I hoisted full main with number two genoa and set a course to clear Coll, and then settled down with a good breakfast and hot tea.

When I signed on with the Coastguard they warned me that there could be strong winds coming from the north later in the day, but during the passage the wind remained a constant SE force 2–3.

Throughout the passage we were accompanied by dozens of dolphins weaving and leaping around *Jalina*. As we approached Barra the southern mountains shone in the sunlight, and coastal birds by the thousand were feeding from the sea as we closed the coast; it was all of this wildlife that Liz wanted to see and enjoy.

The approach from the sea to Castle Bay is well buoyed but even so great care is needed in planning your approach.

By 1500 we had picked up one of the 12 HIE moorings in the north part of Castle Bay, and for the coming strong wind warning I fitted *Jalina*'s chain to warp mooring system.

Facilities

Facilities available are: a very good Co-op store close to shore (also open 1200 to 1600 on Sunday), a hardware store, water, diesel, showers for £3 at the hostel close to the shore, laundrette close to the hospital, gas arranged at the Post Office and an RBS cashpoint.

Castle Bay is a beautiful natural harbour with Kisimul Castle nestling in its NE corner. Today it is leased to Historic Scotland for a thousand years for an annual rent of £1 and a bottle of whisky. The golden beaches of Vatersay are well worth a visit.

Moorings to the west of the bay are offered a little more protection from SW winds by a nib of rock running out from the shore, its extent marked by a post.

During our seven-day stay we experienced several gales and were unable to go ashore for two days; fortunately we always keep *Jalina* well stocked with stores.

Castle Bay: Jalina is on the right with the protective nib of rock ahead.

Castle Bay Barra – Jalina is the second yacht from the left.

Barra
Castlebay

Vatersay

55'

WP Muld

Muldoanich

1300
8246

1230
8242

Wind

No Wind

1200
8239

1.2

0.8

56°50'N

0.2

1100
8234

Hebrides

1000
8228

45'

Sea of the

0.2

Wind

0.5

40'

N

0   10

miles

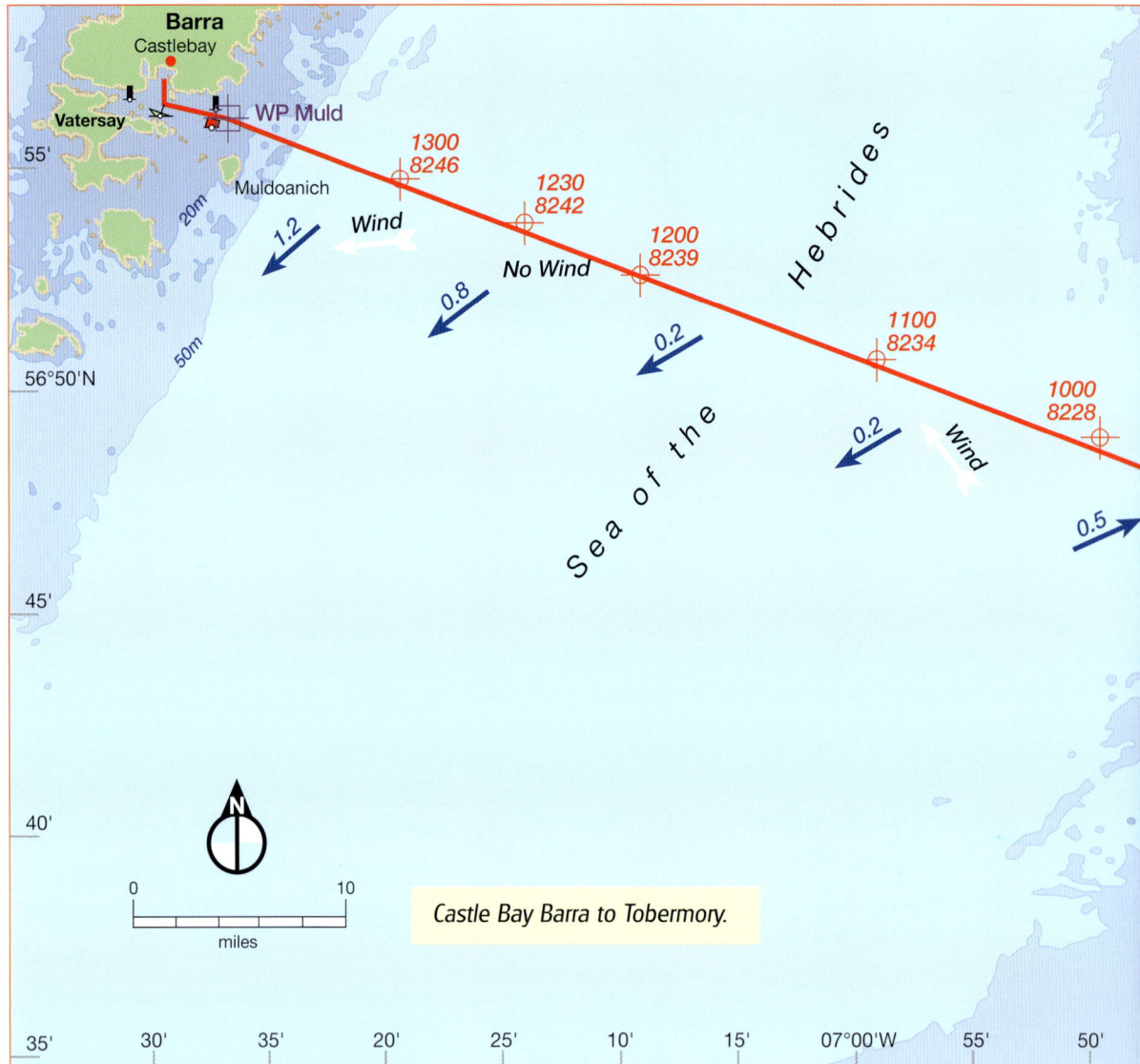

Castle Bay Barra to Tobermory.

35'   30'   35'   20'   25'   10'   15'   07°00'W   55'   50'

Castle Bay to Loch Boisdale

Distance: 20nm

Passage time: 5hr

The weather had not been good with gale after gale passing through. The Coastguard had also been on strike and was not providing regular weather reports, so the shipping forecasts, Navtex and the SSB synoptic charts had been really necessary. In the Coastguard's defence they did provide me with that day's wind direction and strength before I sailed. I was well pleased with *Jalina*'s independent means of receiving weather information.

The weather forecast gathered from *Jalina* was winds SW force 6–8, backing then veering NE force 3–4 later, sea state moderate or rough, but very rough in the west, showers, good visibility. The latter part of the forecast would be midday, so we decided to wait for the wind shift.

The wind eased as it veered to the NE, and as we slipped our mooring and cleared Castle Bay it was overcast. As we entered the open sea the swell was very rough – it would take a little while for it to die down but I decided to press on as it was a close beat and it was slack water. On reaching WP Dale we were able to ease the sails and bear away for WP Loch; this was to clear McKenzie Rock red can buoy, for the approach into Loch Boisdale. Although well buoyed, care has to be taken.

Loch Boisdale.

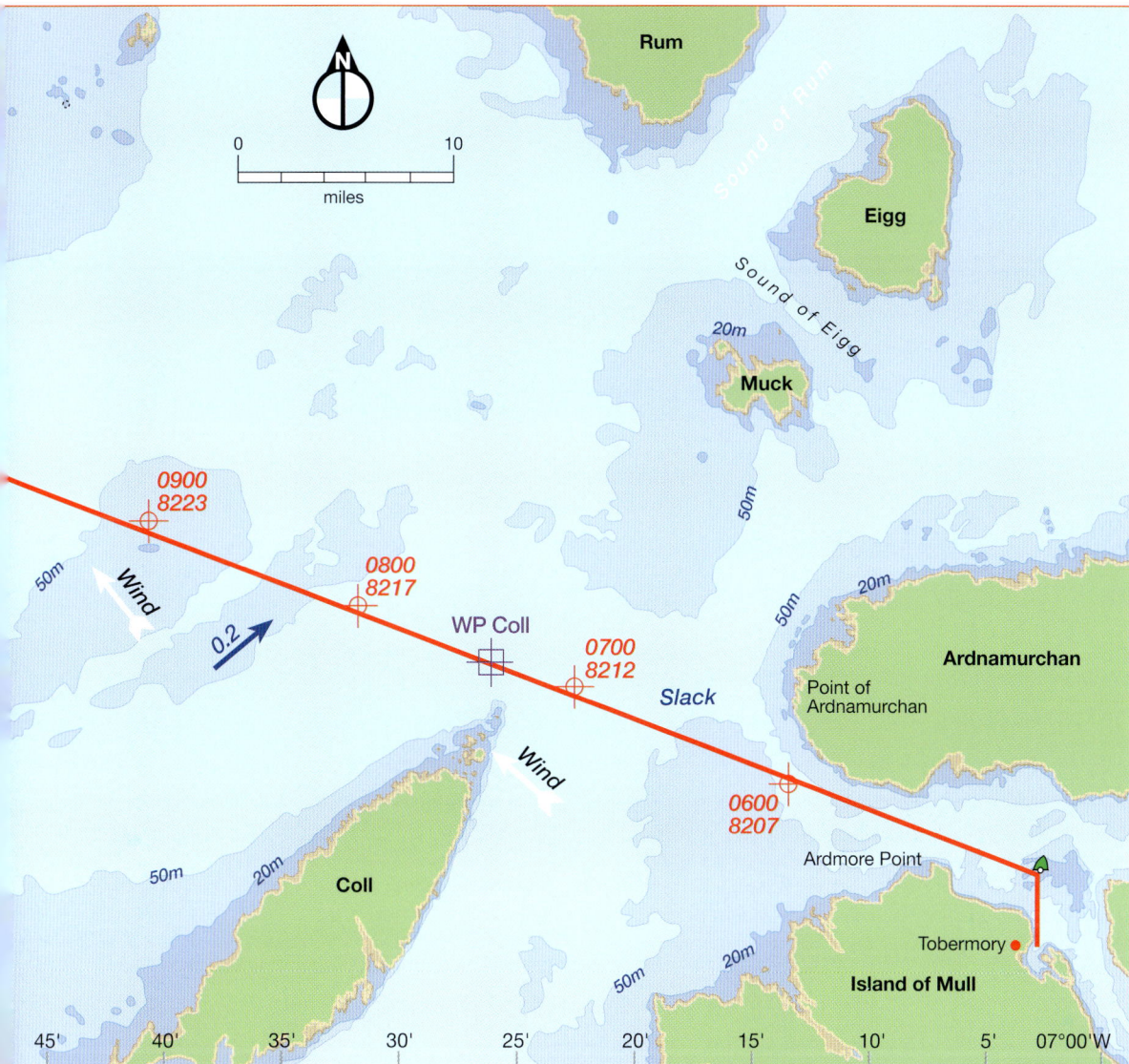

There are four HIE moorings (which take up to 15 tonnes) NW of Gasay Island close to the ferry terminal. There are landing steps on the ferry terminal but we found it safer to go to the opposite side to land on the boat slip.

Bird watchers could visit nearby Loch Druidibeg to see Greylag Geese – the only place they breed in the UK.

Facilities

Facilities are limited here – there are showers next to the Information Centre, a small store, water and a hotel.

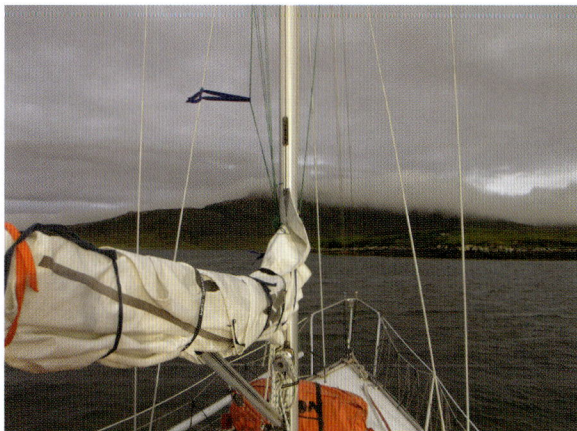

Jalina *on HIE mooring Loch Maddy.*

Loch Boisdale to Loch Maddy

Distance: 31nm

Passage time: 6hr

During our two day stay a SW force 8 gale passed through. We planned to slip the following day as the weather via NAVTEX gave SWW force 5–6, occasionally force 7 in the north at first backing SE force 4–5 later, sea state moderate to rough. The SWW would give *Jalina* a weather shore. I decided to call the Coastguard for a weather report. They

Above: Sponish Harbour Loch Maddy.
Left: Loch Maddy with Oronsay in the background.

gave SWW force 4–5 occasionally force 6 in the N at first, backing SE force 5–7, gale 8 later. It was 0400 so we decided there was a window to slip and reach Loch Maddy in good time and prepare for the coming gale.

We motored out of the Loch under light rain and as we entered the open sea there was a heavy swell running from the passing SE gale. The wind was now W giving *Jalina* a weather shore, and the swell would soon die down.

We entered Loch Maddy at 1000, reaching towards the RoRo under a darkening sky with a freshening southerly breeze; the gale was coming in. We picked up one of the HIE moorings adjacent to the RoRo terminal, and I immediately fitted *Jalina*'s bow chain to warp in readiness for the approaching wind.

The gale that night and the following day made it impossible to row ashore. I removed *Jalina*'s sail cover to avoid chafe to the mainsail.

If able to go ashore, there is a museum nearby exhibiting model boats illustrating local maritime history. The local Adventure Centre also organise trips by RIB to St Kilda – weather permitting.

Facilities

Showers, bar and food at Maddy Hotel, a small store nearby, Co-op store at Sollas, gas, water, diesel and petrol. The Harbour Information Centre will provide you with a weather printout, bus timetables and lots of other information, as they do in all the other harbours of the Outer Hebrides.

Loch Maddy to Scalpay (North Harbour)

Distance: 27nm

Passage time: 5hr

This passage would be a short hop again with very little tide. With the many gales passing through I needed an anchorage with good holding and as sheltered as possible. I met many skippers who recommended North Harbour on Scalpay.

The weather forecast was NNE force 4–5, occasional force 6 later, sea state moderate to rough later in N.

As usual, when sailing the Hebrides great care is needed when planning these passages. Accurate detailed charts are a must. Likewise, for this passage entering Loch Tarbert and the approach to North Harbour would need great care.

Approaching Harris.

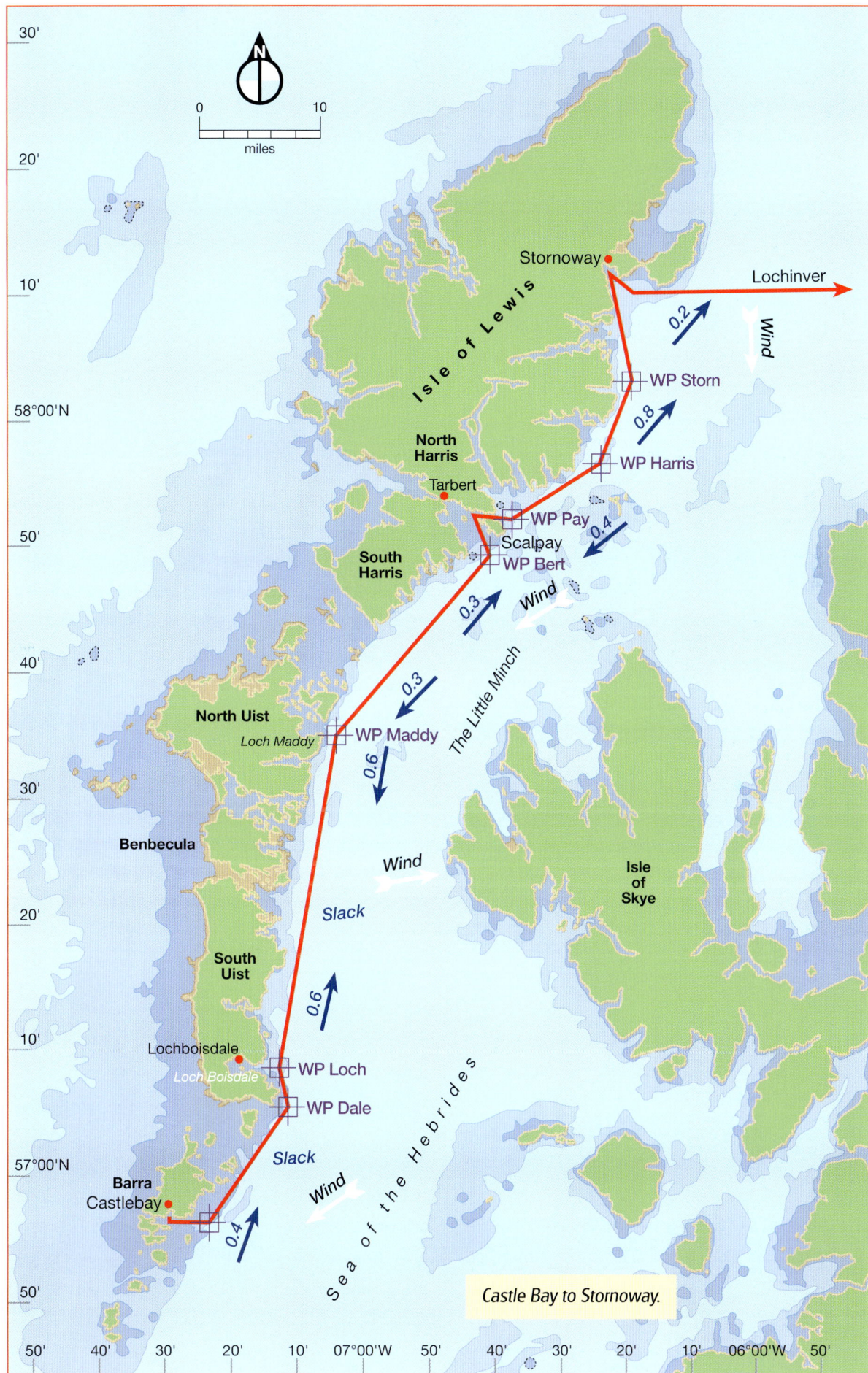

N

0 ——— 10
miles

Lochinver

Stornoway

0.2

Wind

WP Storn

0.8

WP Harris

Isle of Lewis

North
Harris

Tarbert

WP Pay

0.4

Scalpay

WP Bert

South
Harris

0.3

Wind

The Little Minch

0.3

North Uist

Loch Maddy

WP Maddy

0.6

Benbecula

Isle
of
Skye

Wind

Slack

South
Uist

0.6

Lochboisdale

Loch Boisdale

WP Loch

WP Dale

Slack

Barra
Castlebay

Wind

0.4

Sea of the Hebrides

58°00'N

57°00'N

Castle Bay to Stornoway.

We slipped our mooring at 0800. It was good to be underway, and we slowly cleared Loch Maddy, taking care to check clearing lines to avoid several obstacles. Once clear I raised the main and sprayhood then foresail (I drop the sprayhood when entering and departing for easier access and visibility forward). The wind was NE force 2. We were fine on the wind with very little swell, the sun was coming up, and I could feel its warmth through my water-proofs. Liz took the helm with a smile – sunshine at last!

It was one of our best passages, entering North Harbour in full sun and light winds. Sails were stowed, and with the anchor we'd prepared earlier we were soon nodding gently to our anchor. Here we found the holding very good; later when departing we had some difficulty in clearing the CQR from the thick dense mud.

From Tarbert we took a bus ride to visit a cottage industry Harris Tweed weaver demonstrating her skills.

Harris Tweed weaver – Plockrapool.

Facilities

Facilities on Scalpay are limited – showers and one small shop with limited goods – most stores can be purchased in Tarbert. There is a minibus service from Scalpay.

Scalpay to Stornoway

Distance: 26nm
Passage time: 6hr

With so much bad weather coming through during the past weeks particular attention had to be made to accurate weather planning.

With a strong wind warning of N force 6 at first easing to force 4–5 later, it would be on the nose on the final approach into Stornoway.

We decided to wait but prepare to slip our mooring. By 1100 with anchor stowed we cleared Scalpay Road Bridge joining the island to mainland Lewis.

We had considered visiting the Shianti Islands but the heavy swell would make it dangerous so we pressed on for Stornoway.

As we sailed the wind eased making it a very pleasant sail. On arriving we were met and assisted by the Harbour Master who took and secured our lines against the harbour wall. The following day we moved onto the more sheltered pontoon at the marina – a luxury after weathering gales on moorings at anchor. The Coastguard here provided detailed five-day weather reports.

After a short stay Liz reluctantly had to depart for home. With poor weather preventing *Jalina* and I sailing, I was invited to take part in the Sail Hebrides Regatta. If you sail this way try to time your sail so you can take part; you may get the chance to crew on one of the dipping lugs – a traditional work boat of yesteryear – or participate in the many other activities finishing with a sail to a barbeque.

Facilities

Showers, gas next to Tesco store, laundry at the Hebridean Hostel, chandlery, diesel, petrol, and free Internet use at the library.

Having circumnavigated around the UK twice solo, I would certainly recommend including the Outer Hebrides in the adventure. It makes good sailing, with good safe anchorages. From Stornoway I would consider my next stop in the circumnavigation to be Loch Inver, then north to Kinlochbervie before rounding Cape Wrath.

INDEX